MW00908211

Gary Bortolussi MD, MPH
Johns Hopkins
School of Medicine

FROM BROOKLYN
TO KINGSPORT

FROM BROOKLYN
TO KINGSPORT

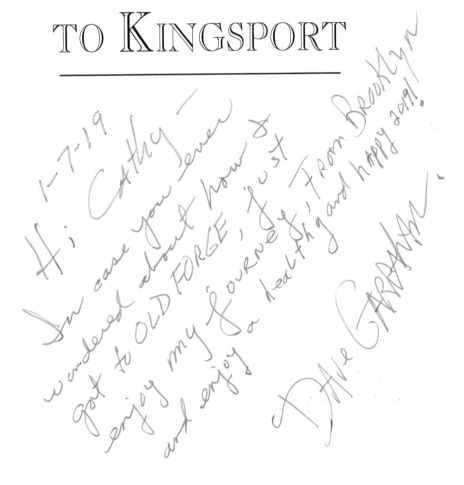

1-7-19

Hi Cathy —

In case you ever
wondered about how I
got to OLD FORGE, just
enjoy my journey from Brooklyn
and enjoy a healthy and happy 2019!

DAVE GARRAHAN

David Garrahan

To order additional copies of this book, contact:
Xlibris
1-888-795-4274
www.Xlibris.com
Orders@Xlibris.com
774055

In memory of my Mother
Ann Buranich Garrahan
(1915 - 2009)

CONTENTS

Introduction ix

Chapter 1 My Life in Brooklyn during the 1940s 1
Chapter 2 From Brooklyn to the Farm 51
Chapter 3 From the Farm to the Larchmont Yacht Club...86
Chapter 4 I'm in College 106
Chapter 5 College Graduate, Married, Mom's Out........118
Chapter 6 Doctoral Study, Building a Home, and
           Columbia University 146
Chapter 7 From Columbia University to Frostburg
           State College 181
Chapter 8 From Frostburg State College to New
           York City 187
Chapter 9 District Superintendent Garrahan 192
Chapter 10 Starting Over..226
Chapter 11 From Prescott to Lincoln Center 233
Chapter 12 The End of the Journey 244

Epilogue 269
Notes 273
Appendix..275

INTRODUCTION

From Brooklyn to Kingsport is an autobiographical memoir. It is the objective history of my life experiences. I have tried to recall events as accurately as possible. I have written about incidents and events that I can recall well—warts and all.

Interestingly, during the past several years, I have noticed that my short-term memory is in serious decline while my long-term memory is becoming sharper. I did my best without sugarcoating or exaggerating. While *I* understand my behavior, some of it is embarrassing.

During the past year, I returned to locations, houses, and institutions so I could better recall my experiences. Significant events in a person's life are never erased from his or her brain.

Herein are the facts, events, and history of my life. The contents, for the most part, are in chronological order starting at age two and ending at age eighty. Although I wrote this book for myself, my children, a few family members, and some individuals with whom I've been associated, other readers may find it interesting. I have documentation in the form of correspondence, published articles, and reports, as well as micro-cassette recordings.

Be forewarned, some content is personal. My brother was dishonest on his deathbed. Wives have been untruthful. These behaviors, to date, have marred my relationship with a few family members. I have set the record straight. The facts are herein stated. Several of my anecdotes are verbose. However, delving into the weeds at these points holds special meaning for me.

Given the publisher's abundance of caution relating to libel/privacy issues, I reluctantly masked the identity of numerous institutions and individuals, including those with national recognition. However, I have left the facts in the book.

My Roots

My maternal grandparents were born in the Carpathian Mountains. They were Lemkos, which is an ethnic Ukrainian subset. My grandmother (Baba), Christina Russin, was born in 1882. Her husband, Cyril Buranich, was born in 1877. He immigrated to America in 1898.

My mother was Carpatho-Rusyn. When we were children, she told us that we were half-Irish and half-Russian. However, when I was studying Russian at Vassar College in 1965, I realized there was a distinct difference between the Russian I spoke and the Russian I was being taught. When I asked my Russian uncle about this, he repeated my question to his mother. She explained that I was being taught high Russian and that we were Ukrainian Russians.

My son, Mark, researched it for me. On October 26, 1918, in Philadelphia's Independence Hall, the members of the Mid-European Union and the United States government officially recognized Carpatho-Rusyn as a distinct nationality. Therefore, I am half-Irish and half-Carpatho-Rusyn. Significantly, I am also a descendant of the Lemko branch of Carpatho-Rusyns. On March 15, 1939, Carpatho-Ukraine declared its independence. The first and only president of the nation was Avgustyn Voloshyn. Within twenty-four hours, Hungarian troops destroyed the nation, but did not destroy the culture or nationality.

My paternal grandmother, Nellie Doonan, was born in Lancaster, New Hampshire, in 1871. Her husband, William Garrahan, was born in Ireland on September 17, 1866. He jumped ship in New York City, and made his way to Berlin, New Hampshire, where he farmed and found work at the Brown Paper Mill. While working at the mill, he wrote a series of articles that were based on his diary, which he had maintained on ships during each of his voyages. His interesting voyages around the world were published in the Brown Bulletin beginning in August of 1920.

In his first article, he wrote,

> "I was brought up in Liverpool, England on the Mersey River . . . . . . at the ripe age of fourteen, I made my first voyage across the Atlantic Ocean . . . we hit foggy weather and ice . . . . .hit an iceberg head-on . . . . .hundreds of tons of ice came down on us. My first voyage came very near being my last . . . . . . I made two voyages to Australia . . . . later voyages to Bombay and Calcutta . . . Ceylon, Mediterranean . . . Red Sea . . . Indian Ocean . . . . Bay of Bengal. Later, I signed on the steamship, Dressong, in which we brought Cleopatra's needle from Alexandria, Egypt to New York City. It stands in Central Park, and is called The Obelisk. I sure had to get home to spend my American money. I stowed-away. Upon arrival in Liverpool, Queen Victoria

had two of her officers escort me to one of her castles . . . . . I lost 29 pounds in 28 days." (See Appendix: The Brown Bulletin)

My father, Francis Lawrence Garrahan, and his siblings left their father as soon as they could. My father's sister, Aunt Eva, told me that their father was a short-tempered man. For example, he would keep a pail of stones on his tractor, so that he could throw them at the boys if they were not working fast enough. They all moved to New York City.

My mother, Anne Buranich, at approximately eleven years old, became a live-in nanny/housekeeper for a Jewish family in Scranton, Pennsylvania. Several years later, they offered her the opportunity of living with, and working for, their relatives in College Point, New York, which was where she met my father. She was sent to buy clothesline at a hardware store. My father, who was working in that store, helped her select the proper line. Apparently after that, they began dating. They were married on July 27, 1933. Mom had just turned eighteen, and Dad was thirty-two. She was a *country girl*, and he was a NYC guy. (See photos: Mom and Dad before they married; Dad dressed up; I did not know this Dad)

I want to note that two of my Garrahan uncles and their sister, my aunt Eva, were all *good drinkers*. At various points in my young life, I lived with each of my six Buranich uncles. They too were good drinkers. However, alcohol was a family plague for the Garrahans. My siblings and I were born into a dysfunctional family.

Frank McCourt described the condition this way,

> Worse than the ordinary miserable childhood
> is the miserable Irish childhood, and worse yet

is the miserable Irish Catholic childhood ... nothing can compare with the Irish version of poverty; the shiftless loquacious alcoholic father, the pious defeated mother moaning by the fire; pompous priests; and bullying schoolmasters.[1]

CHAPTER 1

My Life in Brooklyn during the 1940s

Shake a Leg

I never really knew my father. I don't recall ever having had a conversation with him. In fact, the closest exchange we ever had was the advice he gave me as he walked me to my first day in school.

My earliest childhood memory was of my brother, Artie, and me with our father on a bus full of people somewhere between Brooklyn and Pennsylvania. It was 1940, and I was about two years old.

The bus stopped, and people stood up to leave. Looking at me, my father said, "Let's go. Shake a leg." Artie walked in front of me, and Dad was behind me. We followed the people getting off the bus. When I got to the front, a man in a uniform lifted me up and set me down on the ground.

Dad looked at me and yelled, "What are you doing?" Artie answered, "Dad, he's doing what you told him to do. He's shaking his legs." We probably went inside to a bathroom. I must have wondered where Mom was. Later I would learn that she was in a mental hospital. I woke up in a strange house. It turned out to be

1202–1204 Mine Street, located in the Austin Heights, which was the Russian section of Old Forge, Pennsylvania. (When my maternal grandfather came to America, he hadn't been able to speak English and probably didn't have much money. Within five years, he had built a fourteen-room house for his family. I revisited this home on Russian Christmas, January 6, 2018.)

I didn't recognize any of the people in the house. Artie and I could not understand what they were saying. Dad was gone! In the 1940 photo, Artie and I appear to be well dressed and look like we were fed, though I cannot recall any details of our stay at the house. (See photo: Me and Artie in front of grandfather's house and me and Bulldog in front of the same Fieldstone Wall, seventy-eight years later!)

[Flash forward circa 1956: Uncle John told me about the time my father drove from New York to the house where Artie and I were living in 1940. Dad snatched Artie from the backyard, and drove off. Uncle John told his wife, Stella, to go to the store and call the police. Uncle John drove down the dirt roads, and followed Dad's car into Old Forge where the local police picked up the chase. Dad was caught and arrested. Uncle John brought Artie back to Baba's house. Grandfather Buranich managed to get my father out of jail and then sent him on his way.]

Back to Brooklyn

At about age three, I ended up back at our home at 293 Oakland Street, in the Greenpoint section of Brooklyn, which was almost entirely Polish, Irish, and Italian. The building was five stories tall, with two families living on each level. All the apartments were the same—a kitchen with bathroom which was separated from a bedroom by a curtain. There was a door into a second bedroom, which was separated from the living room by a curtain. Mom came home. In October of 1941, Loretta was born.

Dad worked on the docks. I remember the names of some of the shipyards: Todd Shipyard, Erie Basin, and the Brooklyn Navy Yard. World War II was raging. Dad would often have to work "around the clock," as he told Mom. Sometimes he would be gone for two or three days. That's when Mom and Dad started fighting again.

It was a scary time. There were air raids about once a week. We had to wear dog tags on a chain around our necks all the time. Once, an air raid warden banged on our door, entered, and yelled at my father to never have a light on when the air raid sirens were going off. Mom explained to Artie and me that no one was allowed to have any lights on.

Dad sat at the kitchen table each night, reading the newspaper, smoking his Camel cigarettes, and drinking his Rheingold beer, which he took straight from the icebox. Artie's job was to empty the basin of water from under the icebox. He did not have much work. as we rarely had money for a block of ice.

Mom and Dad Fight

Mom would tell Dad to come home right after work. Often, he didn't, and when he would come home, Mom would tell him that she smelled whiskey on his breath. Sometimes, there would be a fight. He would give her some money from his wallet, and she would yell that it wasn't enough to pay the rent and to buy food. Our rent was seventeen dollars a month. [Flash Forward to 2018: I saw that a two-bedroom apartment rents for $3,400!]

Dad would throw a few more bills at her, grab his jacket and cap, and leave. Once she threw a heavy iron at him as he slammed the door shut, and it broke the glass top on the door. The wire mesh inside the glass held it together. Mom asked the landlord, Mr. Yourga, to fix it, but he never did.

Sometimes the police would come down the hallway yelling, "Police! Police! Trouble." They knew to come to our door at apartment 1-A. I was glad when they arrived to end the fighting, but they never could. They would always say, "No more fighting. If the problem continues, go to family court," and hand Mom a card. She never went to court, and the fights continued.

Once during a fight, Dad broke off the bottom of his beer bottle and went at Mom. I ran behind him and kicked the bottle as hard as I could. Blood came out of the tear in my sneaker, and the fight stopped. Seventy years later, I'm reminded of that fight when I see the scar it left on my foot.

Dad did other things that bothered me. Once I went down the wooden steps into the cellar. When I got to the bottom, I could see Dad kneeling on the floor doing something with our kittens. Artie and I had waited a long time for the mother cat to have her kittens. As I walked closer, I could see that Dad had tied all the kittens around a brick and was lowering them into a pail of water. I could hardly believe my eyes. He yelled at me, "Get the hell out of here!"

At times, he did *good things*. I had a metal box where I kept the food that I never shared with Artie or Loretta when they were hungry. I hid the box in our empty coal bin. One day, I went down there and saw Dad up on a ladder doing something with the electric meter, which was near the ceiling and was attached to the wall. He showed me how to open the glass cover on the meter and to press a penny in a certain spot inside the box. When we went upstairs, we had electricity in our apartment.

Mr. and Mrs. Frayer lived next door to us in apartment 1-B. Sometimes Mrs. Frayer would come over and talk to Mom about the noise and the fighting. She would also ask Mom to pray for her son, Jimmy, who was in the army.

One day I was sitting on the front stoop when two soldiers came up the steps. They walked up the hallway. Then I heard screaming and crying. The Frayers' only child, Jimmy, had been killed in the war. The Frayers put a sticker on their outside window, which showed everyone that they had lost a son in the war.

The death of their son changed the Frayers' lives. Mr. Frayer would get drunk and fall down in the hallway. I had never seen him like that before. He died about a year later. Mrs. Frayer moved out of her apartment and into one on India Street.

Mr. and Mrs. Carney moved into 1-B with their son, Phillip, who was younger than I. Soon, they began complaining to Mr. Yourga about the yelling and fighting in 1-A.

When Dad went to work, Artie and I would walk up to the India Street subway station at the end of the day. We would wait, as the subway trains came in every fifteen minutes, to see if Dad got off the train. When we spotted him in the crowd getting off the train, we were relieved and happy. For some unknown reason, when Dad didn't come home from work, Mom would beat us. Once she hit Artie so hard, blood came out of his ear. Loretta was always spared from these beatings. [Flash forward to 1976: Some thirty years later, Mom explained to me why she had beaten us. She thought that if we screamed loud enough, our father would hear us and come home.]

Ready for School

On my first day at St. Anthony of Padua Catholic School, my brother, Artie, was in fourth grade. I was about six. I never did find out why we had been sent to this Catholic school, which was eight long blocks from our home. Never, in my life, did I see my mother or father in a church—not even once! Dad walked me to school on that first day. (See photos: My dog tag; St. Anthony of Padua Church)

When we got close to the school, Dad said, "Don't take any guff. If you have to fight, go for the nose. When he sees his blood, he'll stop fighting." He told Brother Irenaeaus that I was "as smart as a whip."

The boys at the school were taught by Franciscan Brothers. They were very strict. The girls were taught by the Sisters of St. Joseph. Girls were kept in an entirely separate part of the large building. We were instructed to never set foot in that section. I did, however, and got caught by the principal. I pretended that I got lost in the hallways.

We went to confession every Saturday and received Holy Communion on Sunday, which was obligatory for all students. This meant that I was involved in religion every day of the week.

The Fighting Irish

I got into my first fight in first grade. I fought Patrick Burkrey III. I don't remember why we fought or who started it. Maybe I thought that he was giving me "guff." I remember how it ended. Fat Pat was on top of me, banging my head into the cobblestoned street.

In second grade, I started a fight with Richard Eaton. It didn't last long. He threw me all over the place. Brother Brian pulled us apart and marched us into the building where he gave us a good beating with a wood paddle. In fourth grade, a kid grabbed my white sailor hat off my head and threw it to another kid. There were about five kids. Every time I ran to grab my hat, a boy would throw it to another kid. My hat was getting dirty.

I waited until the smallest kid caught my hat. Then I pounced on him, punching him until he let go of my hat, and I fell on top of him.

Brother Alexis blew his whistle twice, which was the signal for all students to walk to our designated lines. A single whistle meant we were to march into the school. Edmund Orlowski was left lying on the curb. Brother Alexis did not notice him.

Later, the principal, Brother Irenaeus, came into my classroom, walked me into his office, closed the door, and asked, "Were you fighting with Edmund?" I said that he had my hat. He said, "That's not what I asked," as he struck me in the face repeatedly. When my nose started bleeding, he stopped and told me to return to his office at the end of the school day.

Edmund had been taken to the hospital. I was ordered to visit him at his home every day with a gift until he returned to school. Edmund had a broken ankle. It was a long time before he could walk to school again, but I brought him a different comic book every day. He always walked with a limp after that. We became friends. [Flash forward to 2017: I was in NYC and went to Edmund's building in Brooklyn, but his family no longer lived there.]

Franciscan Brothers wore black, hooded habits (robes) that went from the top of their heads down to their black shoes. They fastened white ropes, which hung to their shoes, around their waists. They carried a string of large, black rosary beads in a pocket, which they would touch and say prayers with repeatedly, as they walked up and down the sidewalk in front of the school. I remember wondering if it was normal for Brothers to never marry and have children.

The Brothers were advocates of corporal punishment. At times, it was both abusive and unwarranted. For example, in sixth grade, we were dutifully lined up in the street waiting for Brother Cipriani to blow the whistle which was our signal to begin walking single-file into the building. However, he stepped off the sidewalk, walked straight to me and, without uttering a word, struck me in the face with such a forceful slap that it knocked me backwards into the student behind me. I asked the kid, "Why did he hit me?" He whispered, "You had your hands in your pocket." I didn't even know what that meant.

Once in religion class, I asked, "How long is eternity?" Brother Cipriani began his answer by asking me what the circumference of planet earth was. "Thousands of miles," I replied.

He told me to picture a solid steel ball the size of the earth in my mind. Then he told me to picture a white dove flying down, sweeping its wing on the surface of the steel earth, and flying back into the sky. One year later the dove returned and again swept its wing on the earth's surface. Each year, the bird's wing would rub against it, and a tiny bit of the steel globe was removed by the friction of the bird's wing rubbing against the steel globe. The bird continued returning once a year. When the solid steel ball of the earth wore down to the size of a metal BB, it would be the end of the first day of eternity. I must have been speechless.

Later, I asked Brother Alexis, "What is the quickest way to get into heaven?" He said that if you died in service to the Lord, as soon as your heart stopped beating, your soul would be in heaven. I didn't believe some of this, even though I did think about becoming a missionary and getting killed in Africa. I thought that way I'd get right into heaven and not take the chance of dying with a mortal sin on my soul and going to hell for eternity. I also knew that nothing could burn forever.

I remember one day a Brother asked me if I could run an errand for them after school. I said yes, and after school I walked across the street to the large house that the Brothers lived in. Brother Alexis came to the door, and gave me money and a list of food items to buy. When I returned with the groceries, Brother Alexis gave me a few coins and invited me to come inside for a brief visit. I could see that the Brothers were walking about, but not wearing their robes. They were wearing regular clothes, and some were not fully dressed. Feeling uncomfortable, I declined. I believed that they knew that I lived in a fatherless home.

Mom's Gone, Dad's Gone

One day, Dad told Artie and me that Mom had to go away because she was sick and that until she came home, Aunt Mary and Uncle Walter would take care of Loretta at their apartment. Aunt Mary and Uncle Walter took care of Loretta whenever Mom had to go away. Loretta lived fulltime with them from age eleven until she was twenty-one years old.

Aunt Mary was Mom's sister. Sometimes she would travel by subway to visit us. She and Mom would sit at the kitchen table, smoke cigarettes, and talk about "L," which was what Mom called Dad (short for Lawrence). Sometimes they would whisper.

Once I heard Mom spell "b-a-b-y." I asked Artie what that meant. He said they had been talking about a baby. Later, I would learn that Aunt Mary and Uncle Walter had been unable to have a baby.

One morning, Aunt Mary and Uncle Walter surprised us by showing up at our apartment. Unk explained that he had been drafted. Then off he went carrying a duffel bag. Aunt Mary started crying, so Mom thought it would be a good idea to keep themselves busy with work.

As they were washing the large kitchen window, they broke it. Mom wrapped a towel around Aunt Mary's arm, which was bleeding. Aunt Mary said that it meant bad luck, but Mom said, "No, that was only for mirrors."

Later they sat at the table and smoked. Mom brought out a jug of wine and filled two glasses with it. Aunt Mary said it tasted bitter. Mom told her to drink it, and she would feel better.

Hours later, I was in the bathtub. Mom left the bathroom door open. I guess the reason was to keep an eye on me. They began cooking supper. Then the door was thrown open, and Uncle Walter walked in. He said that the army didn't want him because he had failed an examination. He was completely blind in one eye. He said that he had forgotten about it because it had happened years ago. When he was a child, he had been cracking coal, and a shard had pierced his eyeball. Mom and my aunt were really happy.

Once, Aunt Mary came to our apartment and asked Mom if she could take Artie and me swimming. Mom told her that we didn't have bathing suits. We had never been swimming before. Mom said that I could use my regular short pants as a bathing suit. Aunt Mary said, "Let's make a bathing suit for Artie with some cloth."

I watched as Mom cut a pattern out and Aunt Mary began sewing. Presto! We were ready to go. Mom had to stay home with baby Loretta. We had to take several subway trains to get to the Coney Island Beach station.

Once we were there, we had fun running in the deep sand and into the water. Artie looked funny when he came out of the water in his homemade bathing suit. We both got very sunburned.

Getting Food

One day after Mom had gone away and Dad had taken Loretta to live with Aunt Mary and Uncle Walter, Dad came home with two bags of groceries. Then he didn't come home for several days. When he did come home, he brought more bags of food, but didn't return after that.

Artie and I lived alone in our apartment for several months. We ate all of the food in the apartment. I remember Artie sticking his finger inside of a mustard jar, trying to get the last bit out.

Once, Artie and I bought a can of dog food. We didn't like the taste, but finished the whole can. Then we went to Mr. Rolo's grocery store on the corner of Oakland Street and Java Street. Artie asked him if we could buy some food, "on the cuff." Mr. Rolo told us that our bill was too high already and that Mom or Dad should come and talk to him. Artie and I found food out back in Mr. Rolo's garbage cans. We found better stuff in the cans that were behind coffee shops and restaurants.

At times, I'd look through the baker's window so I would know when he had finished putting a loaf of bread through the cutting machine. When he had, I would dart in and grab the ends of the loaf that he had left in the cutter.

Sometimes I would follow the fruit peddler's wagon. When he was taking care of customers on the sidewalk side of the wagon, I would take fruit and string beans from the street side of the wagon and run. I knew he would not run after me because he wouldn't want to leave his horse, wagon, and customers behind. But he was on the lookout for me after that. I believed that anyone would steal if he or she was really starving. However, Artie would never steal, and I would never share whatever food I had with him.

Artie thought we should start selling newspapers, so we would earn something to buy our food. We asked a newspaper boy where he got his papers. The *Brooklyn Eagle* plant was pretty far away. The newspaper boy told us that you had to have at least a dollar to buy even the smallest amount of newspapers.

I got an idea. The sidewalks near the subway stations had built-in grates. I had seen lots of coins at the bottom of the grates. When people took money out of their pockets, sometimes the coins would accidently fall through the grate and down to the bottom. The grates were about twenty feet long, eight feet wide, and ten feet deep. The grate openings were about two and a half inches long and one inch wide where people walked over them.

Artie searched our apartment for a jar of Vaseline while I went into Mr. Yourga's workshop, where I found a padlock and a ball of string. We had never seen anyone fishing for coins before, so we went to a busy subway station to see if my idea would work. We could see several coins at the bottom as we looked through the grates. We tied some string to the padlock. We put Vaseline on the bottom of the padlock. The padlock fit through the grate and then dropped down. When we pulled it up, it had dirt and junk on it but no coins. So I wouldn't waste Vaseline, I lowered the dry padlock down several openings in the grate before the lock landed on a coin. Then I put Vaseline on the lock and tried it, but the coin fell off before I pulled it all the way up.

I learned that I needed to do a dry drop so I could line up the coin with the grate opening. That way I used less Vaseline. Ready, set, go! I dropped the padlock right on it, slowly pulled the lock up, and eased it through the grate. Wow! I had a quarter in my hand. We *fished* all day at about five different grates. People would stop and watch us. They had never seen kids on their knees fishing for coins. We fished up more than a dollar that day. (see photo: August 2018, I am kneeling on the same subway grate that I did seventy-four years ago)

The next day, we went to the *Brooklyn Eagle's* newspaper place and bought as many newspapers as we could. I sold papers on the corner where the Greenpoint Savings Bank was. The 94th Police Precinct was just around the corner. (photo: the Greenpoint Savings Bank with the 94th police precinct next to it.)

[Flash forward to 1952: When my mom chased us with a knife, Loretta and I ran to the 94th Precinct.]

We were in the newspaper business. I yelled, "Paper, paper, extra, extra, read all about it." Apparently, I had heard newspaper boys yelling this in the newsreel at the movie. I did not understand what it meant, but it helped me sell my papers fast. A couple of men asked me what the big extra was. I faked it and said, "You have to read the paper."

Sometimes in the headlines, I saw, "HST." I did not know how to read, so I asked Artie what HST was, and he told me that it stood for President Harry S. Truman. I started yelling, "President Truman did it."

By the second week, we bought about three times as many newspapers as we had before. We would go to Rolo's and buy a loaf of bread, some baloney, peanut butter, and milk. Artie and I were living alone, and feeding ourselves.

[Flash forward to August 2017: My wife, Erika, and I were in Manhattan, and I took her to Greenpoint. We found the Greenpoint Savings Bank. I got down on my knees and leaned over the subway grate. Sure enough, there were coins down there. I told her that I had started a bank account at Greenpoint Savings Bank, but when things had gone crazy at home, I had never withdrawn my two dollars. She wanted to go into the bank and inquire about my two dollars, but I reminded her that we had just paid $740 for our room the night before at the Plaza Hotel and had enjoyed a $115.00 breakfast.]

Locked Out of Our Home

One day, Artie and I came home after selling all of our newspapers, but there was a padlock on our door. Mr. Yourga had apparently done this. I knew that the only unlocked window was the small one over the bathtub in the back of the building. Being smaller, I climbed up a ladder, opened the window using Mr. Yourga's screwdriver, and was able to get inside. I dropped down into the bathtub. Then I unlocked the kitchen window, and Artie climbed in.

A few days later, Artie and I were on our front stoop when a lady came up the steps and asked us what our names were and if Mom or Dad was home. Artie told her that Mom got sick and had to go away. He told her that Dad worked on ships and sometimes was away all night, but that he thought Dad would be home that night. Then she asked me what I had eaten for breakfast? I told her that I had had cereal, eggs, and toast. She wrote our answers in her folder and left.

Artie asked me, "Why did you tell her that you had all that food for breakfast?" And I asked Artie, "Why did you lie about Dad coming home tonight?" He said that he hadn't lied because Dad might come home. Dad didn't come home.

Soon after that, Mr. Yourga came into our apartment. A man in a suit and a tie was with him. The man asked us questions. Artie said, "Dad's away at work, and Mom is in a hospital." He asked us what we had to eat, as he looked inside the icebox and opened some of the cupboards. He asked us about school. I think Artie said that he went to school. I said that I was in the first grade at St. Anthony's school. Then he told Mr. Yourga that he would take us somewhere else to live because we were too young to be living on our own.

He took us to Mr. and Mrs. Frantangelo's apartment, a couple who lived on our own block. He talked to the woman and gave her some papers. He showed her how to put check marks on the paper for breakfast, lunch, supper, sleep, and school. Mr. Frantangelo worked in the A&P on Manhattan Avenue. They had a young son named Louis.

After a few weeks, Mr. Frantangelo told us that we couldn't live there anymore, but that he would help us find another home. I had stolen something from him, but I don't think that he knew about it. He took us to a house on Java Street. It sounded like he knew the people who lived there. He gave the man the papers and explained how they would be paid by the city.

I cannot recall the family's name, but I recognized the daughter. During the previous summer, I had decided to "play doctor." My "office" had been behind Rolo's store. The space had a solid wood fence with a door. I had started seeing girls who came into my 'office' for examinations. It went well, until one of the girls told her mother about the examinations. Word spread quickly around the block. When the lady realized who I was, she booted Artie and I out.

Sleeping in Church

We tried but couldn't find a place to live. I got the idea that we could live secretly in St. Anthony's large church on Manhattan Avenue. We slept on the pews at night. We couldn't stay there at any other time because people were always coming in to light candles and to pray.

At this time, Artie and I got into a big disagreement. I had gotten into the habit of taking coins out of the poor-box. Artie said it was a mortal sin to do this. He also wanted me to share the food that I had bought, but I always refused. In the 1940s, a kid could feed himself for thirty or forty cents a day. A hot fishcake cost ten cents; a baloney sandwich was a nickel, and I think milk was about fifteen cents.

We agreed to separate. He went looking for a home. I stopped stealing from St. Anthony's and just slept there. There were plenty of other churches in Greenpoint. I visited lots of them to say a prayer, and to dip into their boxes for the poor. I went into the Catholic Charities Store on the avenue and bought a good, warm coat for twenty-five cents.

New Homes

I tried a few other families, but had no luck. I wondered if they had known about my reputation, or maybe it was because I was smelly and had lice in my hair.

Then I remembered that a few times, Mom would visit some Russian people on Lorimer Street, who had two daughters. I found the building. The lady knew my Mom. I told her that Mom had gotten sick, and had gone away. I told her that my Dad had not been home in a long time and that the landlord had locked us out.

She took me in. She made me take a bath and cut my hair. Then she rubbed some kerosene into my hair and washed it out in the kitchen sink. Living there was good. The house was also close to St. Anthony's School. I don't think the father liked me being in their apartment. One day, he gave me my knapsack and said that I should ask the Brothers at the school to find me a home.

I did not go to school. Instead, I went looking for churches. I went to Dupont Street where I saw a woman with a pail and a brush scrubbing steps. I went over and asked her if I could help scrub the steps. She asked me a bunch of questions: "Are you looking for money? Where do you live? Where does your father work? What about your mother? Do you have any brothers or sisters?"

I told her that I usually slept in churches. She took me inside. She said that her husband, Abe, would be home soon and that we would talk. They lived in a dark basement apartment. She told me that her husband worked in a store as a cigar roller and that they did not have any children.

When her husband got home, he asked me more of the same questions. Then they talked in a foreign language. When they finished, he told me, "This will be your home." He also said, "We have rules, and we are Jews."

I did not know what to say, but then I remembered. I said, "My Mom worked for a Jewish family and lived with them when she was about twelve years old." He asked where the Jewish family had lived. I said that they had lived in Pennsylvania. After a few years, they had let my mother go to live and work for their relatives in New York. "Do you have any belongings, clothes, or books?" they asked. I told her that they were locked in our apartment. We ate supper. I slept on the living room floor on a blanket.

The next morning, Mrs. Abe walked me to school. As we got close, she said that she would talk to the principal. I told her that his name was Brother Irenaeus. She pointed to a spot and said that she would meet me there after school.

Later while walking home, she asked me about school. When we passed the Catholic Charities Store, I said that that had been where I had bought my coat. She said, "Let's go in and see what we can find for you." We picked out shirts, pants, underwear, and socks. When her husband came home from work, he set up an army cot in the living room for me to sleep on.

A couple of weeks later, I took Mrs. Abe to our apartment to see if we could find anything that I might need. However, the padlock was still on the door, so we couldn't get in.

One day after eating supper, Mr. Abe took me for a walk to the Dupont Street Park. I told him that my mother used to take us to that park. She had even taken a picture of me there; I pointed to a place in the park. Mr. Abe sat on a bench as I climbed the monkey bars.

(See photo: Me, circa 1942, and coincidently with the same posture, my son Mark in 1972 at Riverdale Park in the Bronx)

Later I met up with Artie at school. I told him that I was living in a good home and that I wasn't stealing anymore.

Dad's Home, Mom's Home

About a month or two later, Artie found me during recess. He told me that Dad had come to the school the day before and had said that he was bringing Mom home in a few days. After school, I returned to where I had been living. When Mr. Abe came home from work, I explained what Artie had told me. It felt like good/bad news to me.

After supper, I packed up my knapsack, and the three of us walked to my real home. They talked to my Dad and asked about my Mom. Then they shook hands. Mr. Abe told my Dad that if it ever became necessary, he should bring me to stay with them.

Dad told us that he had gotten a job at the Brooklyn Navy Yard. A few days later, he brought Mom home. She hugged us and cried. She said that we would go to Aunt Mary's and bring Loretta home on the following day. All of this was happening so fast, it was as if I was having a dream. But sure enough, the next day, we took subway trains to Aunt Mary's, and Loretta came home with us.

Things were okay. Sometimes Mom and Dad would argue, but there was no more fighting or screaming. Mom always had Loretta at her side. They mostly stayed in the living room where Mom would read magazines. Dad would sit at the kitchen table with his newspaper, radio, cigarettes, and beer.

Failing First Grade

I was sitting with my classmates when Brother Irenaeus entered the room. We all stood up. He asked us to be seated. Then he asked me to stand up. I wondered what the heck it was all about. I was not in any trouble.

Then he spoke. He very seriously told the class that I was not being promoted to second grade. As I stood by my desk and listened, he explained that I had not learned how to read…. that I get lost while going home after school, and come back to school crying. I don't remember doing that, but it must have been true.

He told me to be seated. He thanked the class. He told us to have a good summer and to remember mass on Sundays. I was embarrassed. No one said anything to me. I thought, *Am I the dumbest kid in the room?*

I met up with Artie on the walk home. I told him I didn't get promoted to second grade. He said something like "I told you to go to school more." I wondered if the Brothers knew how many different homes I had lived in while I was in first grade.

To this day, seventy years later, I have recurring nightmares. The frustrating and frightening theme is always the same. I am a man, but behave as a child who is lost in a large city. At times, strangers try to be helpful and give me directions, but most turn away from me. I wake up in a sweat. The nightmares are occurring more frequently as I write this memoir.

Brother Irenaeus had known about the last home I had been living in with Mrs. and Mr. Abe. I wondered what they would think of me now? There was nothing I could do about it. I told Mom, and she said everything would be okay. When Dad came home, he got mad and started cursing the Brothers "in their skirts." I think he wanted to go up to my school, but Mom calmed him down.

[Flash forward to 1973: Writing as Professor Garrahan on Teachers College, Columbia University's letterhead to St. Anthony of Padua Catholic School, I asked to review my school records. I was told that there had been a small fire, and unfortunately, my records had been destroyed.]

Summer in the Streets

The war ended when Japan surrendered. Now it was summer vacation. We played in the streets, wandering all over Greenpoint. There was always something going on.

I used to watch a truck deliver beer to the bar on the corner of India Street. The driver would open the metal cellar door, which was located in the sidewalk, while his helper would enter the cellar through the bar and place a thick, roped cushion on the floor directly below the open door on the sidewalk. The driver would carefully drop the kegs of beer through the door and onto the cushion.

When all the kegs were in the cellar, the driver would sit behind the steering wheel while his helper would crank something, which looked like a tire iron, on the front of the truck. Sometimes he would have to crank it five or six times before the motor would turn over and start running. Other peddlers still rode along cobblestoned Oakland Street in wagons pulled by their horses.

My friend and I would sneak up behind the scrap peddler and pull metal from the back of his wagon. When we had a good pile of metal, we would take it to a scrap-metal dealer who would separate the copper from the iron, weigh each pile, and pay us. Artie never stole anything.

Stealing from the ragman was fun. My friend and I would grab rags off the back of his wagon, stuff them into the sacks that we carried, and sell his own rags back to him the following week.

Some days, we stole big potatoes off a wagon. We would then dig a hole in an empty lot, load it with sticks, light a fire, add the potatoes, and then eat roasted potatoes in the dark. It was fun.

For adventure, we would go to the Newtown Creek. Sometimes we would hold onto a thick rope, which hung from something that was high above us, and swing off the dock and out over the polluted creek in a half circle. When we swung back, we would let go of the rope and land back on the dock. It never happened to me, but sometimes a kid would lose his grip on the rope and fall into the filthy, oily water.

[Flash forward to 2017: I read an article in *The Wall Street Journal* that stated that Newtown Creek was the worst and most expensive superfund site in the country. Seventy years later, the government is still trying to get the oily sludge out of our creek!]

Nearby on Provost Street, there was a very large navy storage place of some sort. It had a high fence around it with barbed wire on top. The only things visible were thousands of gray rafts stacked about twenty to thirty feet high.

We were curious. One of our guys came up with a pair of wire cutters. We picked a place along the fence where we thought nobody would notice us. The kid with the cutter climbed up the fence first, cut the lowest barbed wire, and bent it out of the way, so there was just enough room for us to get under it. Then three of us climbed up and over the fence. The hard part was climbing up the rafts and then squeezing in between them.

It was worth it. Inside, we found large metal containers filled with chocolate bars, rations in tiny cans, and a bad tasting drink. Mostly, we took the chocolate bars. In one raft, I found a gadget, and took it. I did not know what it was.

The next day as I was fiddling with it in our backyard, I pulled on a metal ring, and it blew up. Clouds of orange smoke went up the back of our building all the way to the rooftop. What was worse, it left an orange-colored stain on the back of our building and on the concrete in the backyard. This caused a big commotion. I ran down into the cellar and took my outer clothing off. Then I went upstairs and put clean clothes on. Everyone suspected me. Mr. Yourga questioned me so forcefully, I thought his eyeballs might pop out. Dad was home. He said it looked like someone had found an emergency signal bomb. That scared me pretty good.

It was time for me to go back to school, and I was not looking forward to it. Some things in school were different now. During the previous year, our morning prayers had consisted of asking for the safe return of our soldiers. Now we only said our regular prayers. I knew most of what was being taught and was receiving good grades.

Several years later, I applied to be an altar boy, but was not accepted. Disappointed, I went to Brother Irenaeus's office and asked him why they would not let me be an altar boy. He said that it had to do with the way I looked—shoes with holes and soles flapping. You can't kneel on the altar like that. Some students would tease me about my *flappers*. So I put rubber bands around both shoes, but they broke before I got to Kent Street. Then I waited and put the rubber bands on when I got inside the school. That worked pretty well. Aunt Eva gave me a box of rubber bands from her office so I would have a good supply.

One day, one of the Brothers told me to go to the principal's office. Brother Irenaeus asked me if I had taken Andrew's lunch. I said, "no", and suggested that Andrew always leaves his lunch bag on the curb, and runs off playing ringolevio. "Maybe the street dogs ate his lunch." Brother Irenaeus looked at me as if I was the street dog, and sent me back to class.

Sometimes Mom would receive a booklet of raffle tickets in the mail. We called them "chances." She showed me how to write the buyer's name and address on the stub. I would go down into a subway station, and sell the "chances". The bad thing was that there was never a winning ticket. Mom would throw the booklet of stubs out and buy food with the money. I knew it was wrong.

Dad had been laid off from his job. Every morning he would go down to the docks for the shape-up. (Recently, I saw *On the Waterfront* with Marlon Brando in a shaping-up scene at the docks just like Dad. Before this, I had never really understood what the expression *shape-up* meant). Sometimes, the boss would pick Dad, and my dad would work for a few days.

Then he got a job with the Circle Line—boats that would take people for a ride around Manhattan Island. His job was to catch the rope, and to tie the boat up when it returned to the dock. I don't think he made much money.

He quit that job when he got a better one unloading cargo from ships. Once when he came home from work, he pulled out a large salami from under his shirt.

Then he got a better job. I noticed that Dad took his toolbox to work. I could tell he liked this kind of work. He treated that box of tools like jewelry. Often, I watched him cover the kitchen table with a large rag. Then he cleaned and wiped each tool down with oil. Several times when he could find no work, he would put his toolbox on his shoulder and go to the hockshop. The man there would give him money for his tools. It probably bothered him when he had to do this.

Dad would send me to a store over on Kent Street where a man would sell me loose cigarettes and beer. Mr. Rolo wouldn't let us buy cigarettes or beer. Artie wouldn't go because of the Kent Street gang. These guys would chase us, and then Dad would get mad if we came home without the beer and cigarettes.

I had found a BB gun in a garbage can. It didn't have the wood stock, but it worked anyway. I tried it out in our backyard. One day, Dad gave me a cloth bag and sent me to buy some beer and a pouch of Bugler tobacco so he could roll cheap cigarettes. I put the BB gun inside the bag and went over to Kent Street.

Sure enough, the guys crossed the street and came at me. I took the gun out, aimed over their heads, and started pulling the lever. They turned and ran. I kept shooting. "Pop! Pop!" I aimed at their backs. I am not sure if I hit any of them. After that, when I went to the store with the bag, they just watched me from their stoop.

Every neighborhood had a gang, and there was an unwritten code that you didn't violate someone else's territory. For example, you could walk through the neighborhood on your way to school or to the subway. Anyone could use Manhattan Avenue and Greenpoint Avenue, but you could not play on any streets or go into stores which were not in your neighborhood.

The same was true of our territory which was relatively small, and we had good protection. Our area was from Java Street along Oakland Street to India Street, with both sides of Java and India being ours up to Manhattan Avenue. The men in the Italian social club watched the Java/Oakland corner, and the six or seven Sullivan brothers took care of India Street. There were always a couple of them sitting on the stoop, hanging around on the corner, or playing stickball in the street.

We immediately knew when someone didn't belong in the neighborhood and kept our eyes on that person until he passed through. I saw several fights, but most happened at night. One guy from the social club always fought and got cut up. Both of his hands were usually wrapped in bandages the following day.

We All Pitched In

One day, Dad left with his toolbox and didn't come home. By this time, I had figured out that when Dad left with his toolbox, we probably would not see him for a very long time. This time he was gone for about two years.

Mom began making beautiful flowers out of crepe paper. She bought packets of different colored crepe paper. I watched her as she cut petals out of crepe paper, curled each petal with one blade of the scissors, and attached them to a wire stem. Then she wrapped green crepe paper around the stems.

She would give both Artie and me a bunch of flowers. We would sell them on the avenue. We sold a lot of them. They were very pretty. But I don't think Mom was making enough money.

Mom did her best to keep us nourished. At times she would send me or Artie to the butcher shop to buy a bag of bones from which she would make us a stew for supper. But potatoes was our most frequent meal. She would make us potato cereal for breakfast, and then maybe add some spices to it and we had potato soup for supper. We were 'on our own' for lunches. I remember the day that Mom took me, Loretta, and Artie on a four mile walk to visit her sister, Aunt Mary to borrow some money for food. Mom stopped at Calvary Cemetery where she knew there were some "fruit trees". Mom picked several 'choke cherries', ate them, and asked us to do the same. They were tiny bitter berries. But we were all hungry. Later we saw a man with his hot dog wagon. Mom bought one hot dog, and asked the man to put lots of everything on it. Loretta was given the first bite, then me followed by Artie. Then Mom ate what little was left. When we got to Aunt Mary's apartment, she gave Mom about $5.00. We returned to Brooklyn by subway where we all ducked under the turnstile, but Mom put her nickel in the turnstile.

It is interesting to note that many years later, before Christmas Artie would rent a trailer and dress up in a Santa Claus outfit. He filled the trailer with boxes of food. I recall that each contained a smoked ham. He would drive to Brooklyn, ring his bell, as he handed the food to residents in our neighborhood.

It was getting close to Christmas. Mom sent us up to the avenue where men were selling Christmas trees. The men let us gather up the twigs and limbs they had cut from the trees. We took them home, and Mom fastened them with wire to a broomstick. It made a pretty good tree.

The day before Christmas, two policemen knocked on our door. It was my father's brother, Uncle Louis! We had never met him before, but Aunt Eva had told us that her brother was a NYC policeman. The two policemen sort of looked around our apartment. Uncle Louis said they were going up the avenue and would be back. When they returned, they had a real Christmas tree and two boxes of all sorts of food. We had a good Christmas, without Dad. Years later, I came to the realization that Dad must have asked his brother to see how we were doing at Christmas time.

[Flash forward to 1971: The next time I saw Uncle Louis, I was thirty-three years old. Aunt Eva had mentioned to me that he had been driving to Massachusetts to visit his son. He had pulled off the road in a snowstorm to sleep. When he awakened, his feet and fingers were frozen. He was taken to a hospital where both his feet and the tips of his fingers were amputated.

Artie and I drove out to a Long Island nursing home where my uncle was. Uncle Louis was in bed, trying to light a cigarette. He appreciated the two tiny bottles of whiskey we brought and hid in a plant for him. It was a sad visit. Uncle Louis died in 1973.]

Aunt Eva had given me a photograph of Uncle Louis in his NYPD uniform. I kept it in my wallet. I think it saved my bacon several times. The NYC cops took good care of me ...especially on St. Patrick's Day.

[Flash forward to March 1970: After watching the St. Patrick's Day Parade, I stopped at a pub with two of my children, Mark and Susan, who were two and three years old. Upon leaving the pub and clearing my head, I thought, *I've got to find a crosstown subway station so we can get over to the west side of Manhattan. Then we can find an uptown subway and go to the 242nd Street station.*

Somewhere in this adventure, I became trapped inside a revolving door with Mark and Susan in the stroller. Two maintenance men were able to get us out, and two policemen arrived on the scene. They asked me questions and suggested that it would be better if they took us to our apartment in the Bronx.

When we got within a block of our building, I asked if they would let us out on the corner because I didn't want the neighbors to see the NYPD bringing us up the front steps. The two Irish cops watched from the corner of Tibbett Ave to be certain that we made it inside safely.]

A few times, Mom tried to get us Home Relief (welfare). She was told that her husband was employed, and therefore we were not eligible. She would have to take Dad to court, but she never did. In retrospect, it appears likely that Dad was working somewhere on the docks in Greenpoint.

We're in the Shoeshine Business

Artie got the idea that we should become shoeshine boys. We went to the fruit store on the avenue. The man let us have two wooden fruit crates. I do not remember where we got the saw, hammer, and nails (probably from Mr. Yourga's workshop). We built two solid shoeboxes. We did not know where to buy a shoe last, the metal piece that the men could place their foot on when receiving a shine. So we just made simple ones from wood. We bought polish, shoe brushes, and cleaning liquid. Mom cut some rags up for us to buff the shoes with.

I took the corner of Greenpoint Avenue and Manhattan Avenue. This corner was a major subway stop. There was a bar and a newspaper stand on that corner. I said, "Shine, mister? Shine?" I did get a few customers that day, but mostly, I learned.

I had never shined leather shoes before. I had to be very careful not to get any polish on the men's socks or the cuffs of their pants. Some men would read the newspaper while I shined; others would talk to me. Sometimes if it was near the end of the day, I would follow a "shine," staying on the opposite side of the street. I was curious about where these men who wore suits and neckties lived. I noticed that some of these men went into bars.

So one day, I asked one of my regular shines, if he had ever seen a boy shining in a pub. He said that he never had. I talked to Artie about my idea of shining in pubs. He said, "Don't do it." But I decided to try it out.

I probably got into ten or fifteen pubs that day. Mostly, I heard, "No shining in here. Get out!" A few days later, I tried walking in quietly and whispering, "Shine, mister? Shine?" But I still was not getting enough shines.

I learned more. In beer gardens, working men wore work shoes, but in fancy places (called saloons or pubs), men wore suits and dress shoes. So on my black shoebox, I painted, "Pub Shine" in white lettering. Then I planned a route from Manhattan Avenue, up Greenpoint Avenue, and on to Queens Boulevard, where there was an elevated subway. The busiest subway station for people coming from Manhattan was the Queens Plaza station. Whenever I went shining, I carried my shoeshine box in the cloth bag that I used to carry with me when I bought Dad's beer.

In one pub, a customer said something like, "Give the kid a chance. I could use a good shine." In one fancy saloon, a guy handed me a dollar bill, and as I reached into my pocket for change, he said, "Keep it, kid." When I got outside, I went right around the corner and out of sight, thinking that he might change his mind and come after me.

I knew, right then, that I was on to something good. When a bartender would start to wave me out, I would hold up my box so he could see that I was a "Pub Shine" kid. Maybe the bartender would think that a lot of other pubs were letting me in to shine.

Over the weeks, I refined my route and just did select pubs where I began shining regulars. Drinkers were good tippers in these fancier bars. Most places were regular bars and were a waste of time. So I depended on my Queens Plaza post. (See photo: I shined across the street, catching the men coming down from the elevated subway.

A couple of times I had to defend my spot from other shoeshine kids, and it was far away from my own neighborhood.

There was no way I'd even let a kid shine down the block from me. I always carried a knife in my box.

The men in suits came down the steps from midtown Manhattan. There was a White Castle restaurant one block away. Sometimes Mom would walk up to my post, and I'd empty out my pockets for her. We would have a square hamburger and coke at White Castle. I think the hamburgers were twelve cents. They were good. Mom would walk home, and I would keep shining shoes.

I had explained to Brother Irenaeus that I wouldn't be coming to school on Fridays. Friday and Saturday were the best days, and I would shine until it got dark. Now I had to work so that we could buy food.

At times I felt like the Brothers treated me unfairly, and were too severe in their physical abuse. This behavior may have been the norm, as Frank Mc Cord indicated in Angela's Ashes. The Brothers knew that Mom never came to the school in eleven years. She never contributed any money to the parish. Artie, Loretta, and I did receive a good free education.

[Flash forward to August 2017: My wife and I decided to retrace my pub-shine only shoeshine route. As we were approaching Queens Boulevard, I commented to her that in the 1940s, directly around the corner and on the left, there used to be a White Castle! We made the turn, and there stood a White Castle! The same steps were there, coming down from the subway. It was the exact spot where I had shined shoes seventy years earlier. The odometer indicated that the distance was 2.1 miles from my house!(see photos: the White Castle in the exact location where it was in the 1940s.]

After a long time, Dad came home again to live with us. Soon my parents started to fight again. Mom would yell at Dad, "Go back to your siffed up whores, don't bring gonorrhea back here." We must have heard Mom say that a dozen times. I didn't know what it meant. I asked Artie why Mom was telling Dad to not come back home, but he didn't know any more than I did.

A lot of fights ended when Mom would hit Dad with the heel of her shoe—right in the middle of his forehead. He would grab a wet towel and hold it on his forehead to stop the bleeding. He would chase Mom, whipping her with the wet towel as she locked the door and retreated to the living room. Once he was so angry, he pulled the knob off the door. These were scary fights. Then Dad packed and left for a long time.

One day, I was hanging out on India Street. Dad had been gone for a couple of years. Then I happened to glance up the street, and to my shock, I saw Dad walking down it, but he was coming down on the wrong side of India Street. I quickly stepped into the alley to watch. I was pretty sure that he had not noticed me. I was suspicious because I had noticed a pretty woman in high heels walking down that side of the street several times before. It looked like she had gone into Mrs. Frayer's building. This woman was not from our neighborhood.

Dad walked past me, crossed Oakland Street, and went into Mrs. Frayer's building. I went to Mrs. Frayer's building. I peeked through her keyhole, and in a mirror on the wall, I saw Dad in bed with the pretty woman. I was beginning to understand why Mom told had him to go back to his whores. I wondered if Dad might have been living somewhere in Greenpoint, all this time, while we did not have enough money to pay the bills at home?

I noticed that Mom had started going out for several hours each day. When she came home, she didn't bring food or anything else with her. So one day, I watched as she walked to Kent Street, crossed Oakland Street, and then headed in the direction of Newtown Creek. That was odd because there were no stores there or any people who we knew.

I ran to the corner of Kent Street and peeked around the corner. Mom had just gone into a house. I walked by it a couple of times, and Mom finally spotted me. She said it was okay for me to come in. She introduced me to her friend John. He was short, and one of his arms was missing. I felt uncomfortable but was not completely surprised. Once when I had been about to enter our apartment, I had seen shadows through the broken glass top of the door. When I had peeked through the broken hole, I had been shocked to find Mom sitting on a man's lap in the kitchen, and they seemed to be kissing. I had recognized the man. He had been from the Italian social club. I had backed out, but never told Artie or Loretta what I had seen. I was embarrassed. This scene affected me much more than seeing Dad in bed with the woman.

Mr. John asked me if I knew where the potato chip guy was around the corner. I said that I knew it and that I had bought potato chips there twice. He gave me twenty-five cents and told me to go buy potato chips for Loretta, Artie, and myself. I did. The guy made really good potato chips. The bags were not sealed at the top, so he filled the bags right to the very top. They cost five cents for each bag. It wasn't a store but a little business that he ran from his house.

As it got close to the end of the school year, Mom said that Artie and I were going to go to Pennsylvania for the summer. I thought something strange was going on, but didn't know what.

After a few weeks, Mom took us to Aunt Mary's, where she said that her brother was going to meet us and take Artie and me to his home. Uncle Pete came to Aunt Mary's apartment and picked up Artie and me. He was driving a large food truck. The three of us sat up front. I think I must have been ten or eleven years old.

He drove us to his brother Adam's home in Pittston, Pennsylvania. We had fun there. Bobby and Eddie were teenagers, but they took us wherever they went. Bobby had his own junk car. He took us swimming in a river. I liked it best when he took us to the stock car races. The cars would speed around a dirt track, kick up dust and smoke, and bang into each other. We had never seen anything like it before.

After about three weeks, Uncle Adam drove us to Uncle Harry's home in Dunmore, Pennsylvania. He had two kids, Butch and Joanie, who were both younger than I was. It wasn't as much fun there.

Next, Uncle Pete and Uncle Huggy picked us up and took us to live with them in Old Forge. This was different. It was more like a small farm. I don't remember when or how Artie and I got back to Brooklyn. Also, I do not recall that Artie or I recognized that we had lived in this house about nine years earlier. It seemed like we were moved around for a long time in these different houses.

Once we were back home, Artie and I continued shining shoes. Loretta was now old enough to sell Mom's flowers up and down the local streets. Dad was still gone somewhere. But one day, out of nowhere he stopped me on my way home from school. He asked me to secretly take a photograph album from a particular drawer and take it to Mrs. Frayer. I did as he asked. The photos of Dad in this book came from this album!

The apartment was smelly and dirty. When I got home at night and turned on the light, the kitchen table would be covered with cockroaches, which would run off the top of the table and underneath it. My bed was full of bugs, including cockroaches, and many times, I woke up in the morning with a cockroach in my ear. To this day, I am repulsed by cockroaches.

Mom had started beating Artie and me again. We were afraid to tell anyone because Mom might get in trouble and have to go to the hospital again.

One day, I was up on Manhattan Avenue. I was standing with my back to the stores just looking across the avenue. A trolley was going by. I could hardly believe my eyes when I saw Dad looking out the window of the trolley. When he saw me, he turned his head forward and away from me. Running with my shoebox, I ran after the trolley, yelling for Dad. I couldn't catch up with the trolley. I think I cried. That was the last time I ever saw my father.

I knew he had seen me. I knew that the trolleys did not cross the water into Manhattan, so Dad must have been living and working right in Greenpoint for all these years. I had seen him drowning the kittens, in bed with a whore at Mrs. Frayer's apartment on India Street, and other bad things. I didn't like him. (See photos: Dad all dressed up and sitting on car)

It has been said that one of the greatest gifts parents can bestow on their children are moments of their own happiness. My siblings and I never received this gift.

The End

At this point, it is important that you know the conditions I have described—the physical abuse, the fighting, the hunger, the beatings, and the stealing occurred during a seven-year period (1945–1952). Dad never returned. Somehow, Artie had gotten a job, and he was also living where he worked. Loretta and I were home with Mom.

Mr. Yourga had given Mom a paper that said we had to move out of our apartment in thirty days. We didn't have any place to move to, so Mr. Yourga evicted us, and our furniture and belongings were carried out onto the sidewalk. Mom had not been paying the rent or any of our bills. Gas to our apartment had been turned off. Without electricity, I would light a candle when I got home from shining shoes and watch the cockroaches run for darkness. Things were really bad. Mom always seemed nervous and mad.

There was an Italian-American social club across the street at the corner of Java and Oakland. Our neighbor, Mrs. Carney told me that the men from the club had taken up a collection in the neighborhood and had raised enough money to give Mr. Yourga our back rent. The men from the club carried all of our furniture back into our apartment. Now, all of our neighbors knew that we were very poor. It was getting scary.

Then one day, Mom called Loretta and me into the kitchen and sat us down at the table. Mom looked at us and said, "I love you, but I have to kill you. Don't be afraid. You are good children and God will take care of you. You will go straight to heaven." I did not have any time to think. Mom stood up and went to the kitchen counter. She took a large knife from the drawer, turned, and faced us.

I screamed to Loretta to run to the police station as Mom came at me with the knife. I somehow managed to get behind her and tried to hold her arms, but she threw me off. My back slammed into the icebox. The knife fell to the floor, and I ran out of the apartment.

I caught up with Loretta near the top of Java Street. As we turned onto Manhattan Avenue, I looked back and saw Mom running after us with the knife in her hand. We ran into a drugstore and asked the man behind the counter to help us. He chased us out.

We kept running, block after block, nine long city blocks. Finally, we reached Greenpoint Savings Bank. We turned the corner and ran into the police station. (See photo: the red line traces our long run)

A policeman was sitting at his desk on top of a platform. "You have to help us. My mother is chasing us with a knife to kill us!" He looked up and said, "What's your name? Where do you live?" I answered, and he wrote and asked more questions. I didn't answer the questions but screamed, "She's going to kill us!"

I heard a noise and turned around. Mom had entered the police station. She still had the knife in her hand. Loretta and I jumped down and headed for a door. I looked back and saw Mom leap over the desk, swinging the knife at the policeman's face. He must have pressed a button because alarms began to blare and lights flashed on and off.

We ran up the steps, as policemen came running down the steps. We entered a big room. A policeman took us into his office and closed the door. He tried to talk to us. Loretta was shaking and crying (Loretta never saw Mom or Dad again for the rest of her life.).

The alarms finally stopped ringing. Other police came in. They took us to sit at a long table. A woman sat next to Loretta. There was a policeman next to me and one across the table. I answered their questions. Someone brought in a tray and gave us blueberry pie and milk. We didn't touch it.

Then I heard a different siren. I stood up and walked over to a window. There was an ambulance parked across the street, and the back doors were open. By now, there were two policemen standing at my side. I saw Mom being rolled across the street on a gurney to the ambulance. She was tied up in a jacket and strapped down. They lifted her into the back of the ambulance, which then drove away with red lights flashing and its siren on.

I learned that Mom had been taken to Bellevue Hospital where she had spent a month. She had then been transferred to

Brooklyn State Hospital where she would spend the next nine years of her life.

I walked back to the long table. Loretta was talking to a woman. I answered all of their questions: "Was anyone else in the apartment when your mother sat you down? Do you know where your father is? Do you have any relatives in Brooklyn?" Another policeman came in and said that they had been to our apartment several times over the years when there had been problems.

It is interesting to note that I completely forgot to tell the police that my Uncle Louis was a policeman. I had only met him once when he had come to our apartment before Christmas several years earlier. Apparently, he had not been assigned to the 94th Precinct, but he was NYPD. If I had said something, they certainly would have brought him to that police station. Obviously, there is no way of knowing how his involvement might have affected the decisions that were being made.

Upon reflection, I realize I never wrote a letter to Mom during her years of confinement. Actually, I don't recall ever thinking about her. Was the experience with her repressed? For one aspect of our doctoral training, we were required to participate in sensitivity training sessions. This would have been an opportunity for my repressed thoughts and feelings to surface in a supportive environment. However, I was very mistrustful and didn't want anyone to know about my childhood. The other students revealed aspects from their hidden pasts along with their full emotional consequences.

When I visited Mom once in the hospital, we were separated by a thick glass wall. I don't remember but assume that we were probably able to talk through some kind of opening. We put our hands on the glass as if we were trying to touch. Mom kissed the glass at the end of the visit. (Later, I took care of Mom for the last forty-seven years of her life.)

After a long time, two policemen came in with Aunt Mary. We told her what had happened. About an hour later, Aunt Mary told us that the police were going to take us to her home. Aunt Mary and Uncle Walter lived in an upstairs apartment of a private home in Elmhurst, Queens. Their bedroom was at one end. There was also a bathroom, a tiny kitchen, and a small living room. Uncle Walter worked on the docks. They slept in the bedroom. Loretta and I slept in the living room—she was on the couch, and I was on the floor.

After a few days, Aunt Mary took Loretta and me on the subway to Greenpoint so that we could gather up our belongings. When we got into our old apartment, it was obvious that others had already gathered up our stuff. The apartment had been trashed. I did find some of my report cards.

The scene did not surprise me. We knew that the government had taken control of our side of Oakland Street from one end to the other. We had heard they were going to tear down all the houses to build a big highway across Greenpoint and into Manhattan. Today it is McGuinness Boulevard.

Actually, my guys and I had already begun cutting the copper pipes out of the empty buildings. If there had been anything of value in our apartment, I'm sure my guys would have been the first ones inside. I wondered who had gotten my BB gun. Aunt Mary seemed to be upset as we walked through our apartment. It didn't bother me; I understood.

Aunt Mary and Uncle Walter treated us well. Every day when Aunt Mary would hear the door downstairs open, she would pour whiskey into a small glass. As Unk got to the top of the steps, they would kiss, and she would hand him the glass of whiskey. I remember thinking, *That's neat. Unk doesn't have to stop at a bar on the way home.*

At the end of the summer, Aunt Mary and Uncle Walt explained that I would not be able to live with them any longer. The owners had complained about the noise from their apartment and that we were using too much water. Their apartment was really too small for four people. Aunt Mary had written a letter to her brother, John, in Pennsylvania. She had told him of our situation and asked if he could take me in. I guess he had written back because Uncle Walter said that I could go there. Otherwise, I would have to live in some kind of institution. I said that I'd go to Pennsylvania. When Uncle John came, he told me that I could live with them until I graduated from high school, and he literally kept his word!

My "die had been cast" in the crucible of Brooklyn's streets in the 1940s—my survival instincts, my mistrust, and my bad habits. I had learned to live by my wits. I had been damaged.

My Last Visits with Aunt Mary and Aunt Eva

Whenever Mom had been hospitalized, Aunt Mary had taken Loretta in to live with her and Uncle Walter. They squeezed me into their apartment for three months after Mom was taken away at the end.

At some point in the 1980s, my second wife, Eileen, and I visited Artie and his family in Washingtonville, New York. After my first wife, Janet, and I sold our home in Washingtonville, Artie built a home directly across the road from the home that I had built.

Aunt Mary and Uncle Walter drove up from their retirement home in New Port Richie, Florida, and stopped in to visit Artie. It was a brief but good visit. Aunt Mary and Unk had bought their first home and their first car and were enjoying retirement. Unk died at the age of ninety-six.

[Flash forward to 2012: I drove to Port Richie, Florida, and found my Aunt Mary living in a nursing home. Unfortunately, she did not know who I was. I showed her photographs of four of her brothers, but she was unresponsive. Then I went back to my car and found a slightly larger photo of her mother, my *baba*. When I placed the photo in her hand, she held it up to her eyes and with emotion, she said, "My momma. My momma."

While holding the photo of her mother, Aunt Mary looked up at my face. It was obvious to me that she was trying to figure out who I was and who would bring this photograph to her. However, she was unable to go beyond that singular recognition from her past; her momma.]

The following year, I enlarged photographs of her brothers and my mother. However, when I phoned the nursing home to let them know of my visit in advance, I learned that Aunt Mary had passed away. She had had a good marriage and had enjoyed her life.

Aunt Eva was very different than Aunt Mary. She was an office worker at Con Edison in Manhattan. During our childhood, Aunt Eva would take the subway to Greenpoint Avenue and then walk to St. Anthony of Padua Church. She never came to our apartment. For some reason, Mom didn't like her. Aunt Eva did this about three or four times a year. Every Sunday after mass, we would scan the crowd as we descended the steps, looking to see if Aunt Eva was there. We knew that she would walk us to the bakery and treat us to breakfast. I remember that she always shook our hands, gave us some spirited words, and then disappeared into the subway.(See photo: Loretta and I dressed up on Easter Sunday. Aunt Eva took this picture)

When Loretta and I were living with Aunt Mary and Uncle Walter, Aunt Eva came to visit us several times. We all gathered in the living room. Loretta and I were on the floor playing checkers as our aunts and uncle talked. Unk would give Aunt Eva a glass of whiskey with ice cubes. Aunt Mary would have a beer, and Unk would drink a whiskey with beer.

They all smoked. Aunt Mary was the only one who could blow rings with her smoke. I remember she asked Aunt Eva about her stockings. Aunt Eva stood up and sort of showed off her new seamless nylon stockings. Aunt Mary said something about being careful of the men. Aunt Eva replied that they were always hanging around her desk and asking her to go for a drink with them. Aunt Eva always appeared to be outgoing and cheerful, but inside, I think she was very unhappy.

I remember a lot. I was about ten years old when Artie and I had to go live with Aunt Eva because Mom had gone away and things were bad for us. Loretta always went with Aunt Mary and Unk during these times.

Aunt Eva lived with her mother, Nellie, who was completely blind. They lived in a two-room apartment in Jackson Heights, Queens. Aunt Eva slept in the tiny bedroom with her *hope chest*. Artie and I slept on the living room floor. Nellie, whom Aunt Eva sometimes referred to as the "blind bitch," slept on the couch. In a corner, there was a sink, a gas stove, and a table with two chairs where we ate our meals. The bathroom was out in the hallway, and we shared it with two other families who were renting upstairs apartments. The owners of the house lived below on the ground floor.

Aunt Eva worked in an office at the Con Edison building on Union Square in Manhattan. She had been a typist but had likely advanced to a higher position before she retired at the age of sixty-five. Once she gave Artie and me lead pencils, small boxes of lead refills, and a box of rubber bands. My thought then was that she had taken them from work.

From her tiny bedroom, I would look out the window around the time I expected her to come home. Several times, I saw that she exited a side door of the tavern located on the opposite corner. Sometimes, Nellie, who apparently smelled whiskey, would say something like, "You would do better to drink at home." Once, Aunt Eva yelled, "Mind your own business. The boys all ran off to make babies, and I got stuck with you."

One day, I was in the street throwing stones. I accidently broke a window in the owner's living room. He was really mad, and when Aunt Eva came home, he told her that I couldn't stay there anymore. She took me to Aunt Mary's apartment.

Nellie lived to be ninety one years old. Artie and I visited her in the hospital. When she felt my hand, she told me it was dirty and that I should "go wash them now." I thought that was an odd thing for a blind grandmother at her age to say, but I washed them. She and Aunt Eva must have had some tough times living all those years in that two-room apartment. (See photo: Aunt Eva in front of the house where I broke the window)

After Nellie had passed and whenever I was in the city, I'd stop to visit Aunt Eva. Artie did this also. She and I would sit at her small kitchen table, smoke, drink her scotch, and talk.

Once, she became overly involved in asking questions about sexual relationships and where babies came from. It was a bit strange, and I didn't visit her for about a year. When I did visit again, I brought my wife, Eileen, with me. Aunt Eva opened the door, looked at us, and said, "You must be the Jew that he married!" We turned around and left. Artie must have told her that I married a Jew. I never saw Aunt Eva again.

Artie continued his obligatory visits. One day, he received a phone call from the owner of Aunt Eva's apartment. He said that there was something wrong with our aunt. Artie later described to me what he had seen when he entered her apartment: "She was sitting slumped over the table with a half empty bottle of scotch and a cigarette, which had burned to the end, in her fingers. A broken glass was on the floor." Artie gave her a Catholic burial; I didn't attend. Sadly, Aunt Eva never used the items in her hope chest. Aunt Eva was a good woman who lived an unfulfilled life.

45

GREENPOINT SAVINGS BANK

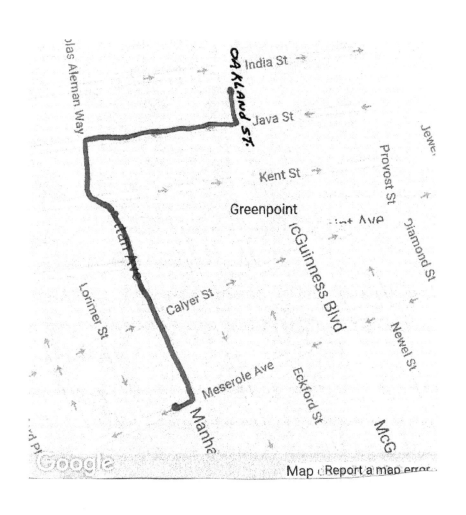

India St

OAKLAND ST.

Java St

Kent St

Greenpoint

Provost St

Jewe

Diamond St

...int Ave

McGuinness Blvd

las Aleman Way

...ttan Ave

Calyer St

Lorimer St

Meserole Ave

Eckford St

Newel St

Manh...

McG

d Pl

Google

Map · Report a map error

CHAPTER 2

From Brooklyn to the Farm

Getting to Know My Russian Relatives

Going from the streets of Brooklyn to the countryside in Pennsylvania was a huge change for me. On Mine Street, Aunt Stella and Uncle John lived in the 1204 side of the house. Their son, Junior, lived with them. Junior was about twenty years old.

On the 1202 side of the house, my maternal grandmother, Baba, lived with two of her six sons, Uncle Pete and Uncle Mike (Huggy). Verna also lived there with her teenage daughters, Martha and Theresa. Their father, my Uncle Joe, was in prison. Later, I would learn that the sisters had a brother, Tony, who had been living with them up until a year before I had arrived. I also learned that Aunt Stella's brother, Tony Krupski, had fathered a boy with Verna while Uncle Joe had been doing time.

[Flash forward to 2005: While visiting with my stepchildren in Seattle, I looked for the Buranich's name in the phone book and found a Harry Buranich. I phoned him and we met. He introduced himself as Tony. "Everybody calls me Tony since I was a kid at Baba's."

Now whenever I visit him, we go to his favorite casino. He always asks me to tell him about his father (my Uncle Joe), and to find a photograph of his mother, Verna. I have never been able to find a photo, but I tell him many things about my Uncle Joe. Once, I told him about castrating a pig that escaped and ran bleeding up Bennett Street, and watching him try to stuff a slippery duck, which also got away. It slid off the table onto the dirty kitchen floor.

We usually enjoy a few drinks. Then I tell him a story. I told him how Uncle Joe sprung my mother from Brooklyn State Hospital. But I never mention Aunt Stella's brother, Tony.]

Uncle Pete was a terrific person. He was a truck driver for a food company in Wilkes-Barre. Six nights a week, he would walk over to Andy Butch's house to play cards and drink in the basement. He finally married Deborah Finnerty. They named their only child David.

Aunt Debbie had difficulty accepting David's struggle with learning to talk and later, to write. She began drinking too much and died too soon.

At her funeral, Uncle Pete sat next to me. He had whiskey on his breath. I talked to him about it. I had previously visited him in the hospital when he had almost died from pancreatitis. He said that he had been drinking since he had gone into the navy and couldn't stop. I reminded him that Artie had been in the navy for four years and had continued drinking but then had stopped (I lied. Artie had died from liver cancer). It didn't matter, a few years later Uncle Pete died from the affliction.

Over the years, I'd send my namesake, David, money at Christmas. Artie and I visited him once when he was living over a grocery store. Then I lost track of him. In 2002, I phoned the Wilkes-Barre Police Department and was readily told that he was living in Lincoln Plaza. I replied, "That sounds fancy." The cop said, "Trust me. It's not."

[Fast forward to 2017: Erika and I visited David. He lived with his lady friend in Section 8 housing in Wilkes-Barre. In January of 2018, we returned with my son Mark to take David's family out for a Russian Christmas dinner. David had two wonderful children. On Russian Christmas Day, Mark led us on a search through cemeteries to find his great grandparents' tombstones. He found both of them in different cemeteries. The temperature was -2°F! The date on Cyril's headstone was incorrect. He had been born in 1877 and not in 1880.]

(See photos: Russian cemetery and headstones, I'm wearing my Goodwill Industries jacket)

Baba wore Uncle John's worn-out shoes for everyday use. On Sundays, she wore her own black shoes and walked downtown to the Russian Orthodox church.

She fed the chickens and planted the garden. I found it interesting that she received a Russian language newspaper in the mail. She would read articles about Khrushchev and laugh, talking in Russian.

Uncle John was a carpenter. Uncle Huggy worked about three months each year on the bean farms in the Poconos. Later, I would learn that during the War, he had shipped out to Africa. When he returned, he was not the same, and never wanted to get a "real job". He was a little odd, but I liked him.

He received a veteran's disability check every month. One day, I watched him scrubbing his arms with a block of Baba's homemade brown soap. He had not used any water. I did not say anything. That night I asked Uncle John, and he explained, "Yeah, he has to rough up his arms before he goes to the VA for his examination."

I understood. They had done that kind of stuff in Old Forge. Three of my uncles had received black lung disability checks. Even Uncle Walter in New York, who had never worked in a coal mine, had gotten into the program. He had come out to Old Forge and had paid some money. Then a doctor had diagnosed him with black lung! He received checks until he died at the age of ninety-six.

(See photo: In front: Me, Uncle John, Baba, Aunt Stella, and Loretta. In back: Uncle Walter and Uncle Pete. Aunt Mary took this photo and mailed it to Mom at Brooklyn State Hospital. From its tattered condition, I can imagine Mom looking at the picture frequently during her nine years of confinement.)

Aunt Stella was tough and always had a cigarette in her mouth. She seemed to be the boss on both sides of the house. No one messed with Stella. She took me upstairs and said, "You sleep in the bed with Junior." Then she told me the rules and gave me my chores: Scrub the outhouse every Saturday, feed the animals, gather eggs in the morning, and crack coal.

This sure was different from Brooklyn. There was no bathroom in the house. I scrubbed the outhouse every Saturday morning. Aunt Stella would give me a roll of toilet paper only when we were expecting company. I didn't like this job because I had heard that little Charlie fell down the hole and died.

I did not particularly like Junior. He probably did not like having to sleep with me.

I asked questions. "Aunt Stell, where does all the stuff go once it drops through the holes in the outhouse?" Junior answered, "He's goofy, Ma." I asked, "Why is this egg different from the others?" Junior replied, "He's goofy." It was a fake egg that was used to urge a chicken to start laying some eggs 'or else'. One day, I learned what 'or else' meant. Baba carried a chicken who had stopped laying eggs out to a tree stump and cut its head off. This chicken got away from her and ran around the yard bleeding until it fell down. That was strange to me, but so was Baba's reaction. She laughed in Russian.

On Saturdays and Sundays, Aunt Stell would fill a small bottle (about 5 oz.) with whiskey in the morning and give it to Uncle John. Usually when handing him the bottle, she would say, "Cork your ass when you finish this." That was an odd expression. All of my Russian relatives would often use the expression, "There are more days then Kil-ba." I figured out what it meant by the circumstances. This was all new to me. But no one could tell me who or what Kil-ba was? I remember thinking, there people don't think very much. To this day, I still use the expression.

Country Life

I know why our dirt road was called Mine Street. Junior and I would take his truck to the mines, which were located up the road. We would walk along the railroad tracks filling our burlap bags with big chunks of coal that had fallen off the trains. The bags felt heavy as we carried them to the truck.

Once we got home and unloaded all the bags, Junior told me it was my job to crack the coal. It took me about a week to crack it all while trying to screen the coal dust out. I had to shovel it all into the fieldstone coal bin. The only part I did not like was when the shards of coal hit me in the face. I had no goggles.

Junior got drafted and shipped out to Korea. *Oh shucks*, I thought. *Now I'll have to sleep alone in Junior's bed.*

I heard Aunt Stell ask Uncle John, "J, where's Korea?" He answered that it was near China and Japan. Aunt Stell had never learned to read or write. The only thing she could write was her name. She baked trays of cookies and rolls with prunes inside, and then packed them in a box. Yep, Uncle John would take these boxes down to the post office and mail them to Junior in Korea. Junior had learned how to type in high school, so he was pretty safe. He was typing papers in an office in Korea.

Uncle John worked at Lockett Lumber in Old Forge. Mr. Lockett also owned a thirty-acre farm close by on the Lackawanna River. He let Uncle John keep two cows and six pigs there.

My first summer, I worked on his farm. I didn't like some of the work, like dusting the potato and tomato plants. The white powder would get into my mouth and up my nose. He also made me run through the cornfield to chase the blackbirds out so he could shoot scatter shots at them. Then I'd gather up these small birds for Mr. Lockett's stew. On those days, I'd go home with red scratches all over my arms and chest from the tough corn leaves.

At the end of the summer, Mr. Lockett gave Uncle John fifty dollars to buy me some clothes. I could have made a lot more shining shoes! I did steal a great cabbage knife from him. But I was learning a lot about farming—how to plant vegetables, ride a tractor, dig up potatoes, pull carrots, and save every scrap of food in a swill pail to feed to the pigs. I also learned about cow magnets and salt blocks.

Baba and Aunt Stell did a lot of canning. Down in the cellar, there were long shelves full of all kinds of canned foods: tomatoes, string beans, cherries, plums, and chowchow. Uncle John had built large wooden boxes. One was for potatoes, one was for cabbage, and one was for onions. There was enough food in that cellar to feed everyone all winter long. By spring, the onions and potatoes had tails growing out of them.

[Flash forward to 2012: My son Mark and I went to my sixtieth Old Forge High School class reunion. We visited the house my grandfather had built more than a hundred years ago. The cellar still had an earth floor. The original tree trunks still supported this large house. Baba had given birth to eight children in this house without a doctor!] (See photo: Grandfather's house still had the same brick tex that was on it in 1952.)

The owner let us look around, inside and outside. He was renovating the house for his son and his son's family to live in. He had torn down the garage, the outhouse, and the barn. He asked me about a rumor. He had heard that a kid had drowned in the outhouse. I told him it was true. Cousin Theresa had been in charge of watching little Charlie, but Charlie wandered off into the outhouse, climbed up onto the wood seat, and fell down the hole. A few months ago, I found a newspaper article on the internet about this accident.

Back to School

When September came, Aunt Stell walked me over the hill to Sibley School. I had brought my last report card with me. She handed it to the principal, Mr. Morgan. He had been teaching a class and had come out to talk to us. He told Aunt Stell that they did things differently in New York but that it looked as if I could come to his school or go downtown to the high school. Aunt Stell said, "I don't think he's too smart, so he better go here." Aunt Stell could neither read or write. She had learned to sign her name. Mr. Morgan took me into his eighth-grade classroom.

It did not take me long to realize what great teachers the Franciscan brothers had been compared to Mr. Morgan. We stayed in Mr. Morgan's classroom all day. He taught us all subjects except health. I started raising my hand in class and asking questions. It seemed that sometimes, Mr. Morgan was not too sure of his answers. I'm not certain, but I might have thought that if I answered all the questions, maybe Mr. Morgan would tell Aunt Stell to send me to the high school.

One day when I raised my hand to answer a question, he snapped at me, "Put your hand down. We know you're from Brooklyn and know everything." Wow, I never raised my hand again. I did make some friends in eighth grade. To this day, I exchange emails with my eighth-grade buddies, Bulldog and Decker. (See photo: Bulldog, me and Decker sity-six years later!)

One night, Aunt Stell woke me up when she yelled up the stairs to me. It was 1953, and I was fifteen years old. It was two or three in the morning. Snow had been falling all night. "Davey, come down. Your father is here to see you." We hadn't seen each other in years. I yelled back down, "I have no father. My father is dead."! I never saw him, nor did he see me.

I heard Uncle John tell Dad that he could sleep in the barn until morning. I did not see my father or hear his voice. He did not sleep in the barn. I have no idea how he had gotten to our house. Austin Heights was a mile from Old Forge, there was no bus service, and it was a cold, snowy night.

In retrospect, I made a bad decision. It has bothered me ever since. I should have talked to him. Later that year, we got word that he had died. Artie got an emergency leave from the navy. I took a bus from Scranton to New York City and met Artie and Loretta at Aunt Mary's apartment. At the funeral, I remember Aunt Mary saying, "Somebody better go find a camera and take a picture of L because when Ann gets out, she will never believe that he's dead."

Dad was fifty-three when he died in August, 1954.

Back at Aunt Mary's apartment, we spread Dad's possessions out on the floor. Artie, Loretta, and I took turns choosing items. I chose several interesting photographs of Dad and a ring with a large G on it. Years later, I gave the ring to my daughter. Several of his photos are included in this book. These were very likely the photos that Dad had me sneak out of our apartment and leave with Mrs. Frayer. Photos of Dad dressed in fancy clothes. I had only seen him this way in the photos. Dad was living two different lives.

Smoking Kielbasas Brooklyn Style

I had watched with interest when they slaughtered the hogs. Mistakis, who sometimes worked on Mr. Lockett's farm, hit the pig on the forehead with a heavy hammer. The pig fell over dead. The pig was butchered right there. The various parts were thrown into separate pails.

Later, Aunt Stell would fasten a meat grinder to the edge of the kitchen table. She would attach a casing to the snout of the grinder. She had already cut up pork into small pieces. She had added some special pieces of veal and had mixed it all up with a few added spices. She shoved this mixture into the grinder, pressing it all down with a wooden plunger. As she turned the handle on the grinder, the meat was forced down into the long casing. When the casing was full, she removed it from the grinder, formed a ring, and tied the two ends together.

The day before, Uncle John had shown me how to smoke the kielbasas. There was a trench in the yard about twelve feet long and maybe ten inches deep. At each end of this trench, a round hole had been dug. At one end, the hole was the size of the bottom of an oak barrel. We placed a ten-foot sheet of corrugated metal over the trench from one hole to the other. We placed the oak barrel in the shallower hole.

The oak barrel had two small holes bored out of each side near the top of the barrel. A steel rod was put through the holes so that about an inch stuck out of each side of the barrel. We then placed a burlap bag over the top of the barrel.

Uncle John explained how it worked and what my job would be on the next day. "Davey, you put some sticks in the bottom of the big hole. Then you get three or four of those logs over there—from the apple and cherry trees.

"Next, you put as many rings of kielbasa on the steel rod as you can so they hang from end to end inside the barrel." The ends of the rod should stick out of the barrel. Next, you cover the barrel top with the burlap bag. Have a pail of water next to the barrel.

"When it's set up that way, you light the fire at the other end. As the logs burn, the smoke goes through the tunnel and up into the barrel. Keep the smoke trapped in the barrel by sprinkling water with your hands on top of the burlap. Every once in a while, go down to the other end and sprinkle some water on the logs so that more smoke goes into the tunnel. "Aunt Stell will come out and tell you when they are smoked enough." It seemed like a very interesting process. I really liked to eat kielbasa with horseradish on it.

The next day, Aunt Stella gave me a bunch of the raw kielbasa to take out to the barrel. I put them on the steel rod and covered the barrel with the burlap. Then I lit the fire—so far, so good. I sat on the stump and sprinkled a little water on it every so often.

Then I heard the sound of a basketball bouncing off a metal backboard just over the hill at Sibley School. I really liked playing basketball. I had already hung a wire ring on the garage so that I could shoot baskets by myself. I could hear the guys yelling. I wanted to run over the hill and get into the game. I could hardly contain myself.

I remembered that Junior had thrown a couple of worn-out tires from his truck behind the barn. Without thinking, I grabbed a tire and put it on top of the fire knowing that it would produce lots of smoke very quickly, and then I could go play basketball. We used to burn tires in Brooklyn at night for fun. The tire started smoking quickly. The clouds of black smoke went up into the air. Smoke went through the tunnel and up into the barrel. I became a little scared that this might not have been a good idea.

I think Baba saw the black smoke first and must have told Aunt Stell. She came running down the porch steps screaming at me. She grabbed the pail of water and threw it on the fire. She pulled the burlap off the barrel. She said, "Look, just look at what you did!" I looked into the barrel. All the kielbasa rings were black. The casings had burst open. It was a mess. I was speechless.

Aunt Stell was not. She cursed at me in Russian. Then she said that all the kielbasa rings were ruined. "All my time ... the pigs ... the meat," she went on and on. When she stopped, she marched me up to the porch and told me to take off my pants. Then she poured a pail of ashes and rice onto the concrete. "Kneel down in it and don't get up until Uncle John gets home," she said.

When Uncle John got home, Baba came out and spoke to him in Russian. Uncle John just sat on the steps. Uncle Huggy came out and gave him a bottle of beer and a shot of whiskey. He downed the shot and lit a cigarette. "All right, Davey, get up," he said. I got up and picked the ashes and rice from my knees. "Was that the first batch of kielbasa?" I answered, "Yeah, it was the first." I felt so much better when I remembered that I still had a bunch of raw kielbasa in a bucket and even more in the house. What a relief!

No More Religion

About this time, I broke from religion. It had been building in me for some time. In Brooklyn, I had prayed frequently, asking God to help with our difficult conditions. As far as I could see, he never answered my prayers.

I had always doubted the definition of eternity that Brother Cipriani had given me years earlier. In Austin Heights, going to confession became a very bad experience. The Brothers had taught us that even having impure thoughts in our heads was a sin that had to be confessed. Now that I was a teenager, whenever I saw a pretty girl, I would have impure thoughts and had to confess them to the priest.

Father Stanislaw usually made it more uncomfortable by asking me questions about what I was thinking. The questions did not feel right to me. His questions became so embarrassing that I started lying to him. Walking home from confession, I thought, *This is very bad. I'm lying in the confessional booth. My regular sins can't even be forgiven, and I'm committing more sins by lying.*

I stopped going to church. When Aunt Stell asked me why I wasn't going to church, I told her I didn't believe in God anymore. She sent me with Baba to the Russian Orthodox church, but I found that experience to be very strange.

[Flash forward to 1961: Janet, my wife, came from a very religious family. We joined the Belvidere Methodist Church, and I took an active part by becoming an usher. The following year, on World Order Sunday, I spoke from the pulpit for fifteen minutes (It felt like an hour). My father-in-law was among the congregants. I saved a newspaper clipping, showing that the title of my sermon was "The Importance of World Law." At age twenty-two, it is likely that I knew very little about what I was preaching.]

Over the years, depending on my wives' preferences, I've participated in the Hebrew religion, the Unitarian Universalist church, and the Ethical Culture Society. I have always taken things very literally. As such, I eschew unprovable hypotheses, be they supernatural beings or eternal life. For me, these commonly accepted beliefs hold no resonance. I am more comfortable with the thought of my ashes becoming part of nature. Actually, I've already told my wife that when I die, I want my ashes to be scattered around the ground of our wonderful property.

Unrelated to religion, something great happened. My four top teeth had been pulled out at a dental clinic. I had never been to a dentist or brushed my teeth in my life. I tried not to smile. I think Aunt Mary may have mailed some money to Uncle John. I know that Artie sent some. Uncle John took me to a dentist in Pittston. The dentist made four teeth that hooked on to my remaining real teeth. Wow, what a difference they made. I felt so much better.

Breaking Bad

Aunt Stell had lots of names for me. I was a hooligan, a Brooklyn bum, but mostly a *tsyganskiy* (Russian for gypsy). I probably deserved them all. She would say, "He's like horse shit—all over the place." I did wander all over the place, just as I had done in Brooklyn. Yes, I had developed bad habits in Greenpoint: fighting, stealing, cursing, and smoking opbs (other peoples' butts) from off the street.

Even in eighth grade, I managed to cause trouble. My buddy, Delford, lived alone with his mother. Kids called his mother, "Crazy Escha." I can't recall how Del and I got into trouble, but Escha came up to 1204 Mine Street, yelling at Aunt Stell in Russian. Uncle John told me that she had said I was a bad influence on Delford.

Then I got involved with some tough guys who lived in the Austin Heights. At night we would go up to the mines and steal anything that we could sell, including a lot of copper wire. One night I could not go up with them, and they got caught. The mine had started using a night watchman. They got in serious trouble, but they never mentioned my name. That was pure luck.

I should not have been this way because I had a good life now. I just had to get used to their different ways, such as taking a bath once a week in the summer (once a month in the winter). Aunt Stell would heat up several large pots of water on the kitchen stove and then pour them into a round galvanized tub in the kitchen. She would take her bath while we sat out on the porch. Then she would call Uncle John in for his bath. When he was finished, he would call Junior in for his. I was the last person in the tub. By then the water had cooled and really wasn't clean, but I knew my position. When I finished, Junior and I would carry the tub out to the dirt road where we dumped the water into a ditch. That was another reason why I wouldn't miss Junior going into the army. My bath water would be a little cleaner and a little warmer.

My first week in high school, I decided it was stupid to carry all the books back and forth to school every day, so I stole a second set of books from my classmates. Very quickly, I had a set of books at home to do my homework, and another set in my homeroom desk. It was a great idea, which I used all through high school.

Once, I got in trouble for starting a fire in a field behind the school building. Another time, I got into a school bus, turned the key on, and somehow banged it into a wall. Sometime later, I had my eye on Jackie Terruso, and when she asked for a knife, I gave her mine. Then she took it out to scare someone. I got called to the principal's office for that.

Mr. Fabbo was the principal. We called him Tuffy Fabbo because he wasn't tough at all. I spent two periods a day in his office: my study hall period and my algebra period. Mostly, he would roll back in his chair and spit tobacco juice out the window. Sometimes he would give me a dollar, send me up to Belladonna's for coffee and a donut, and tell me to get something for myself. I think that he liked me.

I played hooky from school a lot, especially once Escha let Delford drive her car to school. The car really expanded our territory. One day, we played hooky and drove to Scranton. I have no idea why we went into Westside High School. We got into a tussle with guys we didn't even know. I guess we thought of ourselves as big shots because in those days, to have a car was a big thing.

On the way back to Old Forge, we stopped at a small shop to play the pinball machine. We got into a fight with two guys who were waiting to play the machine. We managed to break a glass door. The owner kept us there until a policeman came. He asked us where we were from and then started writing our names on a pad: Delford Gatz, Tommy Zupko, and William Connelly. I don't know why I gave him a phony name, I never even knew a William Connelly?

The next day at school, I was sitting on the bleachers in gym class because I did not own a pair of sneakers, and we had to wear them to play. The gym door opened, and in walked Tuffy Fabbo with a policeman. They walked right over to where I was sitting. The policeman looked up and said, "That's William Connelly." Mr. Fabbo said, "Garrahan, get down here!" He suspended me from school. We had to chip in and pay for the glass door.

Another time, Bulldog and I were getting poor grades in French. I noticed that Mrs. Kowalchick, the French teacher, used a pencil to write our test grades in a black book. She always put the book in her desk drawer. One night, Bulldog and I went down to the high school. Bulldog stood on the ground under the classroom's window and boosted me up. I had unlocked the window during the day, so I was able to get in. I found her record book and pencil. I erased the bad grades and wrote in mostly Bs.

I figured that Mrs. Kowalchick would never tell Mr. Fabbo because everyone in class knew she was afraid of him. When we would get noisy in class, she would put a finger to her lips and point to the speaker box up on the wall, which meant that Mr. Fabbo might be listening. I don't think she even knew the grades had been changed, but it worked. We passed, but did not learn French.

Camp St. Christopher

Whenever we played hooky, I would come up with a bogus excuse for being absent. When we went to Pittston, I spotted an employment office. Bulldog and I went in, thinking we could get a piece of paper with an official agency name on it to use as an excuse for our absence. However, we actually got summer jobs from it working at Camp St. Christopher in Tunkhannock, Pennsylvania. Catholic seminarians, who were in the process of becoming priests, ran Camp St. Christopher. Bulldog and I found that it was easy to fool the seminarians. Our boss was Sam Riccio who brought food to the camp.

We started working there a week before the camp opened. Bulldog's father drove us there in his truck. Mr. Riccio took us to our cabin. He gave us our first assignment, which was to get the kitchen, cafeteria, and canteen ready for opening day.

I laughed when Bulldog stole two white chef's outfits. He thought I was stupid when I filled my pockets with play money. I got unlucky when the campers arrived. The campers were required to exchange their real money from their parents for this play money. They used the play money to buy stuff at the Canteen. I also started buying stuff at the Canteen with my play money, and the seminarians knew that I didn't buy any play money, so I had to confess that I stole the fake money.

Then Bulldog and I got into trouble. We walked out of camp one night with Bob Zamboni, a camp employee. On a country road, we found a bar and went in for a few beers. On the way out, Zamboni kicked the screen door open, knocking it off its hinges. We ran. The next morning, a state trooper showed up at the camp with the owner of the bar. We had to pay for the door and go to confession. We were pissed at Zamboni for involving us.

Some nights, we played poker for money in our cabin. I marked the deck by putting small cuts on the backs of aces, kings, and queens. Zamboni had a lot of money. When he ran out of money, he said his fancy belt was worth five dollars. I took his belt and won the five dollars back. It was a great belt which lasted me for three years.

St. Christopher's was a good experience. To swim in the lake, we had to pass a swimming test. I told the lifeguard that I knew how to swim. When it was my turn, I jumped into the lake and paddled out, around, and back to the dock. Just as I got close to the dock, the lifeguard told me, "Stop swimming", and I struggled to keep my head above water. He knew that I did not know how to swim. I took swimming lessons with the six-year-old kids. "Bend, extend, whip, glide," the instructor repeated as we went through the motions on the dock. I learned to swim, before I got fired.

Every Wednesday night was raid night. The cabins would raid each other, taking items that were then returned the following morning. Bulldog and I did some raiding of our own. We hid flashlights, knives, and dumb stuff under our cabin where we had already stashed a dozen cots and other stolen items.

Zamboni quit his job in midsummer. When he went out of the cabin to greet his parents, I stood watch at the door as Bulldog opened his large black chest and selected choice items from it. Then Bulldog helped Zamboni carry the chest to the car.

Then the seminarians became suspicious, and found all of our stolen stuff under the cabin. I took the rap, and got the boot.

Mr. Riccio was at the camp, and I asked him if he would give me a ride to Scranton where he owned a restaurant. He told me that he wasn't going there, because he had to deliver stuff to the Mt. Airy Lodge. He would take me there which was closer to Old Forge. During the ride, he said that he might be able to get me a job at the lodge. He did, and I became a dishwasher.

One of the waiters started talking to me, as if he was a friend trying to be helpful. He asked me where my room was, and I said that I don't know. He offered to let me stay in his large room. That night he showered and got into bed, as I made myself comfortable in lazy-boy type chair. Then he started talking about his years of wrestling, and coaxed me onto the bed to show me what Greco-Roman wrestling was. As he demonstrated the first position, I jumped off the bed, grabbed my duffel, and headed for the door which was locked, I backed up, and kicked out all of the wood loovers—as he was yelling at me to calm down. I jumped through the opening, and ran out of the building, and down to the highway where I hitched a ride to Old Forge. That was the shortest job I ever had!

I returned home from camp earlier than I had expected. My uncles Pete and Adam were getting ready to drive up to the Poconos to pick beans on the farm where Uncle Huggy was some kind of supervisor. They let me join them. It was good money: twenty cents for a basket of tomatoes and forty-five cents for a bushel of string beans.

We were coming off lunch break. I had stupidly left an almost full bushel of string beans in the row before lunch. I saw another worker picking it up. I yelled, "My beans."

He yelled at me in Spanish. I took my cabbage knife out as I signaled for him to put my bushel down. The other pickers watched. If there was going to be a fight, I knew that I'd have to cut him. I hoped that he would put my beans down. I took a few steps forward, and he put my beans down.

Once or twice a month, I still use that cabbage knife I stole in 1952 from Mr. Lockett's farm. The blade is fastened to the handle with screws and nuts that I have never had to replace or even tighten. (See photo: 66 yrs. later, and I'm still using Lockett's knife.

That night in the bunkhouse, I took my turn as my uncles passed a bottle of whiskey around. I fell asleep on the porch, and woke up in a patch of poison ivy. When we got back home, Aunt Stell was mad at Uncle Pete and Uncle Adam. She had me make some mud and put bopkie leaves all over my poison ivy. We used this remedy for all skin problems. Uncle Pete said,

"Ah, Stell, you should have seen the way Davey fought that spic for his beans."

Russian Drinking and Irish Drinking....Russian Weddings

I have experienced a distinct difference between Irish drinking and Russian drinking. The Irish drinking life that I am familiar with is best described by two gifted writers and drinking colleagues, Jimmy Breslin and Pete Hamill in the book, *A Drinking Life: A Memoir.*[2] My father afforded me a passing glance at this life. When I was three or four years old, I remember him, lifting me up and placing me on a barstool next to him. I also observed snippets of the Irish drinking during my pub-shining days.

Clearly, there is a hereditary component to one's affinity for alcohol, however, the pleasure of bar drinking is largely cultural and environmental. Having lived for various lengths of time with each of my six Russian uncles, I consistently observed that when they described a man, he was either "a good drinker," "not much of a drinker but takes his turn buying rounds," or "not a drinker." It is interesting to note that I never saw any of my Russian relatives take a drink of vodka.

I never had the pleasure of drinking with my Irish uncles, but I doubt that they would describe a new acquaintance as a good drinker. Likewise, none of my Russian uncles would ever perform "The Face on the Barroom Floor" skit. I happened to witness this skit twice at Paddy Murphy's in N.Y.C, which I describe in Chapter 6.

(See photos: I am seen proudly drinking a shot of whiskey at Aunt Stell's kitchen table. The sign around my neck notes the date and my age, which was fifteen. Bulldog and I were at the reservoir. There is a cigarette in my hand. Enjoying a Ukranian meal north of Kiev where whiskey and vodka are on the table with every meal. And 2017, having a few shots at Loggie's on Mine St. where my uncles sat in the 1950s)

At age fifteen, Aunt Stella and Uncle John gave me permission to drink whiskey and smoke in the house. These teenage behaviors, which were reinforced by my uncles and friends, became habits.

[Flash forward to 2003: At a hospital in Manhattan, the chief of surgery looked at my scans and told me that I had pseudocysts and several smaller liver cysts. He added that they were growing slowly, which was somewhat comforting to me. I'm eighty, I still smoke and drink]

Aunt Stell and Uncle John took me on a long ride to Lopez at the top of Red Rock Mountain where we attended our Russian family wedding. We stayed at Baba's younger sister's farm house. I learned that Russian weddings last for three days: beginning with the wedding and reception day. The second day is spent at the bride's parents' home. The final day is spent at the groom's parents' home. Russians do a lot of drinking at weddings. It is as if the father gets 'bragging rights' for the quality and quantity of his whiskey.

At the end of the first night as Uncle John was driving us back to Baba's sister's farm, the door on the car we were following flew open. Someone was thrown out of the car. We stopped and got out. A woman lay on the side of the road. I could see that she had cuts and scrapes all the way up her legs. The next morning, we learned that she hadn't broken anything and that she was okay.

However, the second night's celebration ended badly. Sparky crashed his car and died. I listened to everyone talking about it. Sparky was not a member of our family. They recalled that once he had been drunk while using a chainsaw, had fallen, and had ripped his leg open.

As we were getting ready to go home, Aunt Stell asked me, "Davey, did you take money from anyone's porch"? I lied, "No." But I did wondered why people left money on their porches. It was for the milkman to take, when he delivered fresh milk. Apparently, a neighbor asked Baba's sister if I might have taken the money.

Fired from All Three Jobs

While living with Aunt Stell and Uncle John, I managed to get fired from three jobs. My aunt and uncle never knew why I had come home from Camp St. Christopher's two weeks before Bulldog had.

There were two brothers in Old Forge named Vinni and Bobby Belcastro. Vinni ran the bar that Uncle John would stop at after work for a shot of whiskey and some beer. Next door, Bobby ran a pool hall with a bowling alley in the basement.

Uncle John got me a job as a pin picker in the bowling alley. I was fast. I could pick two lanes at once, jumping back and forth between the lanes. It was a little risky because some bowlers were wild and threw balls so fast and hard that pins would fly back where we sat. I liked the place because Mr. Belcastro would let us use the pool tables for free while we waited for the bowlers to arrive.

On a Sunday evening, a major league tournament was being held, featuring Frankie Clause, an Old Forge resident who was called the "bowling schoolmaster" in the newspapers. He had bowled a record number of 'three-hundred games,' and he was a teacher at Old Forge High School.

I thought I had a good idea: we would form a union and call a strike so we could get a raise in our pay. Just as the teams were getting ready to throw their practice balls, all the pickers walked out holding strike signs that I had made. Mr. Belcastro came out. I started to explain that the pickers in Scranton earned eleven cents a game and that we only got nine cents. He said, "Shut up." Then he asked each picker, "Are you on strike?" Each person answered, "No."

Then he told me to get the hell out of there and that he didn't want to ever see my face in the Rec (Recreation Time) again. Uncle John must have been embarrassed. He had gotten his friend to hire me. My name was mud.

Then Uncle John got me a job at the Maxson plant in town. He was a forgiving soul. I worked from 4–10 p.m., setting up food and coffee on a wagon. I would push the wagon through the factory. Making the urn of coffee and loading up the sandwiches, chips, and cakes was easy work. The men were given fifteen-minute breaks, and I made regular stops where they were.

Then I got another good idea. Without permission, I bought a bag of bagels and a few packs of cigarettes, thinking I could make some money on the side. I was fired. Apparently, I mixed up the money. Uncle John never got mad, but I could tell he was not happy with the trouble I had caused him.

Mr. Fabbo had a habit of standing across the street from the Rec and smoking his stogie. One day, he saw Uncle John coming out of Vinni's bar and called him over. He told Uncle John that I was a troublemaker, that I missed too much school, and that I got into fights. This time, Uncle John gave me a serious talking to and told me that I had better straighten out. I tried to do this, but not hard enough.

Big Trouble

One Sunday afternoon, I saw a few of my guys out near the barn. They asked me if they could borrow my guns to scare some guys up at Haddocks in Avoca. I had stolen two guns from a car and had hid them in a shed. Reluctantly, I loaned them the guns but told them that if they screwed up, they were to say that they found the guns.

Monday morning, I was sitting in math class when I saw Jack Hatala out in the hall signaling for me to come out. I asked Mr. Kuzmich to let me go to the boy's room, and he did. Jack told me that my guys had been arrested with my guns the night before. Oh, crap! That afternoon's issue of the Scranton Times had a news item: "Old Forge Gun Toters Arrested in Avoca."

Several days later, a policeman came to the house and asked me about the guns. Fortunately, Uncle John and Aunt Stell were still at work. But Baba and Uncle Huggy saw the police car. I pretended I was surprised to hear that those guys said they got the guns from me.

A week later, Bobby Malinowski's lawyer came to the house and said, "Bobby has a record, and he will get sent away unless you admit that they were your guns." I gave him the same answer I had given to the policeman. Bobby was sent to Camp Hill, a juvenile reformatory. One of the other guys had to join the military.

There was a lot of talk in Austin Heights. Even Mr. Babrosky, the butcher, asked me about it. He told me, "A lot of people are saying that they were your guns." I held the line.

From then on, I just hung out with Bulldog. We did some small stuff at St. Nick's Hall during events on Saturday nights. Bulldog would stand in the doorway of the coatroom as I took anything people had left in their coat pockets. Then we would hit certain parking lots. We knew people did not lock their cars.

Let's Go to Canada

Our Senior Class was going on the senior class trip to Washington, DC. We could not afford it. We had just paid fifteen dollars for a class ring. So I said to Bulldog, "Let's hitchhike to Canada." I told Aunt Stell we were going to camp and fish on the Susquehanna River for a week.

We hitchhiked to Canada in one day. We left Austin Heights early in the morning, got a couple of long rides, and walked over the Rainbow Bridge on the first day. We saw the sign, "Welcome to Canada," and a man painting a white fence.

Bulldog talked to the painter in Polish. He cleaned up and took us to his home. We ate supper with his wife and two children and then went to sleep on the floor in an empty room. Before we fell asleep, the man came in and said that his wife was afraid of us, and that he would have to search our duffel bags. We had a couple of knives that we let him hold for us. We ate breakfast with them. We told him that we were going to look around Niagara Falls and that we would be back for supper. We never got back.

We walked around Niagara Falls and then hitched a ride. I am not sure why, as we had no destination. We had made it to Canada. The man who gave us a ride said that he owned a racetrack in Toronto. He asked if we would like to go there with him. We agreed. It was a long ride. The guy was being straight with us. We arrived at his horse-racing track. He said hello to people and paid for our food. We had a good time watching the races.

The following day, a Canadian soldier, who was in uniform, gave us a ride. I sat in the front with the driver and could see that Bulldog was searching through the guy's big army bag on the back seat. He paid for our supper and then drove us to Buffalo, New York.

I became suspicious about why he was taking us back to New York without saying anything to us. Then he took us to a lounge where he seemed to know people. We sat on a platform in a large booth with plants on both sides. We ordered shots and beers. Thinking my suspicion that he was a homosexual might be right, I began pouring my whiskey in the planter.

Then he said, "It's getting late. I know a hotel nearby that we can stay at." When we got to the hotel parking lot, I told him that we didn't have money for *our* room. He said he would pay for it. The hotel was a crappy place. I listened as he talked to the man behind the wire mesh. I got the soldier's attention and reminded him that we wanted two rooms. "Not necessary, it's a large room," the soldier said. The man at the desk said, "Talk outside."

We went outside, got into the soldier's car, and began to argue. When I called him a "f***'in blockhead," he got out and went to the back of the car. I got out of his car and ran. Looking back, I saw that he was holding a tire iron and that Bulldog was still in the car. I ran back and hit the soldier in the back. Bulldog got out and finished it. We left the man there in the parking lot, and walked into downtown Buffalo. The night clerk at a fancy hotel let us sleep in the big chairs that were in the lobby. In the morning, we decided to head back home.

The return trip took three days. On the first night, we stayed in someone's cellar. The Bilco door was unlocked. We heard the owners when they came home. We still went to sleep there and hit the road at daylight. We ended that day sleeping in a barn. It was a great vacation.

When I got home, I told Aunt Stell the truth—that I didn't catch any fish. She never found out about our adventures in Canada. Bulldog and I have stayed in touch for sixty-seven years. Once my colleague got a DUI in New York and lost his license. Bulldog got him a Pennsylvania license.

(See photos: Bulldog and me, still friends at 80!)

Graduation Day

Aunt Stell and Uncle John did not come to my graduation. I walked home alone. It was getting dark as I went up the steps with my high school diploma in my hand. Aunt Stell and Uncle John were sitting on the back porch. I noticed there was a suitcase at the top of the steps.

Aunt Stell spoke first, "Davey, we bought you a suitcase for your graduation. I packed all of your belongings inside it." Aunt Stell kissed me on the cheek. Uncle John stood up, shook my hand, and wished me good luck. I thanked them for taking care of me, took my suitcase, and walked out to Mine Street.

They had kept their word. They had taken care of me until I graduated from high school, just as Uncle John told me in 1952. I had probably caused them more problems than I realized. But I wasn't prepared for such a rapid departure. I didn't know what to do. I walked over the hill to Bulldog's house.

As I got close to his house, I could hear music. I saw colored lights hanging around the front porch. His relatives were there for his graduation party. He spotted me. Walking over, he said, "Hey Dave, what's with the suitcase?"

I told him that I was going to New York and that I needed some money. "How much?" he asked. He had received quite a lot of money for his graduation. I think he gave me fifteen dollars.

(Over the years whenever I visited Aunt Stell and Uncle John, I brought them a present. If they were not at home, I left a twenty-dollar bill at Belcastro's bar for Uncle John. After Uncle John retired, he built a small house downtown. Once I brought them a spruce tree and planted it for them. My wife and I saw it in 2017. It was about thirty feet tall.)

I hitched a ride to Scranton and bought a bus ticket to New York City. The bus wasn't leaving for a few hours. I checked inside my suitcase to make sure that Aunt Stell had packed my cabbage knife. She had. However, one thing she did not pack was my composition book. I had written about my life experiences in Brooklyn while I was in high school. It was not an assignment. Aunt Stell couldn't read, so she probably just threw it in the garbage. It would be interesting reading now.

I thought that I knew New York City and felt pretty confident. I didn't have a plan because my quick departure from Old Forge really caught me by surprise. The bus stopped at the Port of Authority. It looked kind of creepy. I walked over to Times Square. When I got there, I realized I did not know this part of New York City.

When I had lived in Brooklyn, before the Fourth of July, the kids in my neighborhood would gather up all of their money and give it to me so that I could buy fireworks for them. I would take the subway over to Manhattan, and then walk to Chinatown where I would buy the fireworks. But now I realized that I didn't know the rest of Manhattan. Times Square was full of bars, honky-tonk joints, and peep shows. I was intimidated by the scene at Times Square. I walked back to the bus terminal and tried to figure out my options. I couldn't go to Aunt Mary's, but maybe I could find a recruiting office. I slept on a bench in the bus station.

In the morning, I took the subway to Greenpoint. Wow! My neighborhood had changed in five years. All our houses were gone. A big four-lane highway replaced Oakland Street. I did not know where any of my friends had moved. I wondered what I should do. Maybe I would go to the recruiting office and enlist. But then I thought that I could do that anytime. Maybe I should just get a job. The Sullivan family was still on India Street, and I was sure that I could stay there until I found a job and rented a room.

Then I remembered that at Dad's funeral, Artie had told me that if I was ever in trouble, I could count on Commodore Perry at the Larchmont Yacht Club. I wasn't in any trouble, but maybe I should find this yacht club and see what it was all about. Artie had lived there a few years. It was a long shot, but I didn't feel ready to join the military. I could always come back to Greenpoint. I had options.

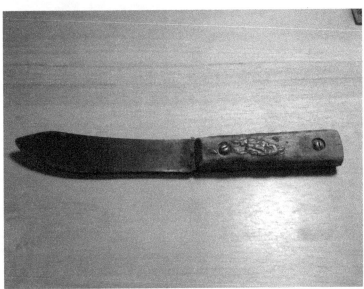

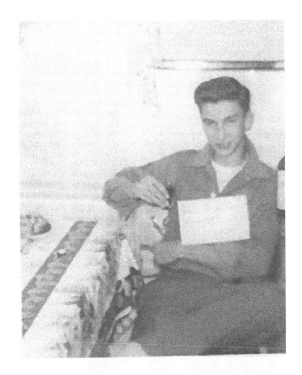

CHAPTER 3

From the Farm to the Larchmont Yacht Club

The Larchmont Yacht Club

Moving from the countryside in Pennsylvania to a yacht club was another huge change for me. I picked up a road map at a gas station and found Larchmont on it. It was not far north from the city. I took three subway trains to the end of the line. I then hitched a few rides to Larchmont and walked to the Larchmont Yacht Club. It was a prestigious, classy, elegant club on Long Island Sound. Later, I learned that membership was limited to five hundred very select families. (See photos: The Yacht Club dusk, Commodores and Officers lined up)

I went up to the front desk and asked where I could find Commodore Perry. The man at the desk asked someone to take me up to the commodore's room on the third floor.

"Hi, I'm Larry Garrahan's brother, Dave," I said. I felt comfortable and relieved to be in his small room. He obviously was no commodore. He was the club's electrician. He had been at the club so long and was so well-liked that they had made him an honorary commodore. On weekends, he would dress up in his commodore uniform and direct parking for the members. He spoke with a British accent.

He asked me how Larry (Artie) was doing. I explained that I had only seen Artie once in the past five years, and that we didn't write letters. I could tell from his voice that he liked Artie. I told him about my situation and asked if I could work and live there. For a few seconds, he just looked at me and my life's belongings, which were in my suitcase. He said he would speak to Mr. Carney (Robert F. Carney was the older brother of Art Carney, who was on television with Jackie Gleason in *The Honeymooners*. I had never seen it because we didn't have a television at Aunt Stell's).

Commodore Perry told me to wash up down the hall while he went to find Mr. Carney. When he came back, he told me that Mr. Carney would speak with me in his office in one hour. "Be sure to tell him you can paint, mow grass, and maybe be an ice boy like Larry."

Mr. Carney was a tall, distinguished looking man with white hair. He was very formal, stating that most of the yachts had refrigeration on board. He continued, "But they could use a hand getting their suitcases and gear down to the dock. Actually, it might be good having you posted at the icehouse. Some members still use ice, and now they have to phone the boatyard when they need someone to cut them a block of ice.

"You will stay up in the monkey house and take your meals with the help. How long will you need to stay here?" I told him that I did not have any plans. "You better talk to Mr. Perry about that. We don't have much work during the winter." Wow! I was in.

I took my suitcase and walked up to the monkey house. I immediately saw how the building got its name. Everyone housed there was an immigrant of color. Dimas welcomed me. His wife and five children lived in Puerto Rico. He sent them money from his earnings as a busboy. He went home once or twice a year. I mentioned to Dimas that I hadn't had breakfast or lunch and that I was pretty hungry. He said that he was going over to the help's kitchen and that I could come with him. He introduced me to his coworkers, who were eating.

(See photo: Jorge (Brazil), Vincente, pot washer (Mexico), me with my arm around Antonio, dishwasher (Argentina), and Dimas, who barely made it into the picture, with rum and coke.)

The photo was taken in 1960. By that time, I was out of the monkey house and living with the assistant manager and special club members in the main building. But I never forgot about the guys who had welcomed me into their monkey house home. I treated them to a tour of Manhattan and a feast in Spanish Harlem. For some, it was the first time they had ever been served. I doubt that any of them had been to Manhattan.

I quickly learned how to cut a 150-pound block of ice into smaller blocks and to place them in a wagon. I pushed the wagon down to the dock where I handed it off to a launch man, along with the member's other luggage and gear. The launch man took the members and their things out to their yachts. I would usually receive a tip from each member. Soon I learned I would also receive a regular paycheck from the club. What luck.

One day, I mentioned to Mr. Carney that I had too much downtime between customers and that I did not like sitting in the icehouse. He gave me a few small painting jobs, which I finished in a day or two. I then suggested to him that the Pandemonium, which had been built in 1902, could use a good painting before it started to crack and peel. I told Mr. Carney that I did not want any extra pay, but that I just liked to work. He was skeptical but said, "See Mr. Dempsey. He will set you up with a ladder, a brush, and paint, but keep your eye on the icehouse. I don't want any complaints."

The following morning a retired club employee, Mr. Bill Lynn, who had worked at the Club for more than 50 years, was dropped off by his daughter at an opening in the fence to the rear of the garage. Mr. Lynn who had started at the club as a stable boy; and later worked in the garage for many years, would sit atop his old wood desk in the garage for an hour, and then walk down to the icehouse. This was his routine. He would sit with me, smoking his pipe and talk to me. Mostly, it was talk about the good old days when this was 'a yachtsmans' club. Mr. Lynn seemed to think that swimming and tennis were distractions. He cheerfully greeted passing members by name, and then occasionally share a private comment about the individual. A week or so later, Bill asked me what I would do when I got around to the Sound side of the Pandemonium and would not have a view of the icehouse? He answered his own question, by taking a brass whistle from his pocket. "When I blow this whistle once, get down from the ladder because a member is approaching the icehouse." It worked! It took about six weeks, and the Pandemonium looked great with a fresh coat of forest green paint. Mr. Carney was pleased with the results, and my work ethic.

Saving Money for College

I had written a letter to Aunt Mary, letting her know that I was living and working at the yacht club. She must have written to Artie because he sent me a letter. He wrote that since I was getting free room and board, I should save all my money and apply for admission to college. Commodore Perry and Mr. Carney also encouraged me to go to college.

I wrote a letter to East Stroudsburg State Teachers College. The college sent me an application and requested a transcript. I returned the completed application along with a letter stating that I would bring them a transcript in September.

I needed to save a lot of money. Mr. Carney told me that I could roll the gravel tennis courts and reline them with white powder every morning at 6:30 a.m. and that he would pay me an extra twelve dollars and fifty cents a week.

Several members got to know me at the icehouse. Mrs. Legler was the first to ask me if I would prep her yacht for weekends. I charged seven dollars for her boat, and twelve dollars for her friend's larger yacht. This was fun for me. After supper, I would row out to their yacht. I would polish all the brass, clean the refrigerator, sink, and toilet, scrub the galley, and wash the salt off the exterior.

I was completely unaware that the Norwegian men in the boatyard had a monopoly on this work. They did not like the fact that I was cutting in and charging a lower fee. I asked Mr. Perry what he thought I should do. He spoke with Captain Toby. The boatmen then left me alone. However, I was so impressed with boatman, Tommy Thompson's understanding of my situation that I decided that I would not take on any additional boats. By the end of the summer, I had saved over $475! [Flash forward to 1965: My wife and I were visiting the 1964-65 World's Fair in Queens, and among the thousands of people I recognized Captain Toby and his wife. I told him that I had graduated from college, and was pursuing a doctoral degree at Columbia University. I asked him about Tommy, Bernt, and Commodore Perry. Sadly, Mr. Perry had passed away.]

Working Three Jobs

From 1957 through January 1961, the club was my home. During my Easter vacation in 1958, I sat down with Mr. Carney to discuss my coming summer work. In short, I had to convince him that I could do three full-time jobs by myself.

This is how I would do it: I would place a sign above the telephone in the icehouse that read, "Please Call Beach Grill for Ice Service." While cleaning tables at the grill, I would position myself on the patio in front of the beach grill, which was midway between the icehouse and the service dock. Whenever the phone rang at the grill, whoever answered it would lift his white hat off if the call was for ice service. I would be at the icehouse within one minute. While standing outside the grill, I had a clear view of the service dock, and could see when a boat was coming in for service. I would have to take my apron off and get over to the dock in time to tie up the boat and provide it with fuel and fresh water.

As I write this, it seems beyond belief that I had the gumption to ask Mr. Carney to give me three full-time jobs. However, the ice boy position was not really a full-time job because most yachts now had refrigeration. And the beach grill was easy.

Mr. Carney seemed annoyed as he said, "Are you saying that you want all three jobs? What about Billy and Dennis?" I responded that I knew I could handle all three jobs and that "those two guys live in Larchmont and don't need the money." To my surprise, he gave me the three jobs but warned me, "There must be no complaints." I would have to drop my tennis court work and give up the two yachts that I had been working on. He knew that I was a terrific worker and that the members liked me.

Near the end of that summer, I was in my usual position out on the beach grill's patio with my eyes on the service dock when Mr. Attilio, the maitre d' in the dining room approached me. He said, "I've been watching how you move among your three jobs. I can use you upstairs."

I responded that I liked what I was doing and was making good money but that I'd think about it. Back in the monkey house, I asked Dimas what his busboy job was like and how much money he made. We talked. He told me there was a good chance that Mr. Attilio would promote him to be a waiter soon. A few weeks later, I noticed Mr. Attilio watching me from the dining room above the grill. He came down to the grill and told me that whenever I stayed at the club during my holidays, I could team alongside Dimas in the dining room and that I would have regular work all year.

I thought, *Attilio gets a great worker, Dimas gets the waiter's position he has dreamed of, and we both make more money.* Attilio also said, "You will have to learn to speak proper English." Coming from a self-educated Cuban, that sounded strange to me. Subsequently, I learned that a busboy doesn't converse with members. He is mostly silent, deferential, respectful, and courteous, only interacting verbally as a function of his role.

I'm a Busboy

In 1959 on Thanksgiving eve, Norbert, a waiter, gave me black trousers, a white shirt and a black bow tie. Miss Mandeville who operated a laundry-service room on the third floor, gave me two white busboy jackets. I had to learn to carry, above my head, a large oval metal tray stacked with dirty dishes. This required some practice because the kitchen was downstairs and a good distance away.

"No conversation with the members. Butter on this side. Never put your arm in front of a guest. Stand off to the side with your eyes on your tables. Remain silent." I learned quickly. I worked all the holidays during my years attending college. The Larchmont Yacht Club was my home, away from my college home.

I knew the head bartender, Gene. I had done him favors like cracking ice and bringing it up to the bar, which was directly above the icehouse, and slicing up lemons and oranges for him. Sometimes he would ask me to go down to the kitchen and bring up a couple of trays of clean glasses for him. I was like Gene's unpaid bar boy.

Tom Saunders, the assistant bartender, spoke with a raspy voice. He told me that he had burned his vocal cords drinking a liquid that had contained some alcohol. He mentioned some bad times he had. One time he had woken up in Mexico City, and couldn't remember how he had gotten there. He had lost his job on Wall Street. I asked him, why, after all that, he had become a bartender. He said it was the safest place to work for a reformed alcoholic.

He told me about other workers at the club who were reformed alcoholics. Herman, I already knew about. Once I was up on the stage in the Pandemonium behind the curtains with a member's daughter, Jill. Hearing footsteps, I peeked through the curtain and saw Herman going from table to table, drinking whatever was left in the empty glasses. There had been a party, and the tables had not yet been cleared. He must have heard a noise from the stage, as he put his flashlight around the curtain and called us out. Knowing that it was very improper for me to be with a member's daughter, and thinking quickly, I said, "Everything will be okay...I'll pick up all of the glasses and take them down to the kitchen." He understood that I was aware… we both had a secret. That was a close call for me.

Then Tom dropped a bomb. He said, "Mr. Carney is an alcoholic." He told me that Mr. Carney had brought all these workers from his AA meetings to work at the Club. I kept my mouth shut.

The following year, Gene, the head bartender, was terminally ill and in a hospital. Mr. Carney visited him, and told me that Gene would like to see me. The request sounded a bit odd, but I went to the hospital. Gene whispered, "I trust you. There's a false bottom in the bar. On Monday, please remove everything to your car and get rid of it." I did as he asked. I also realized that Don, the quartermaster, had known Gene's secret. Shortly thereafter, Don resigned from his position. (See photos: Mr. Carney; Quarter Master Don; Chef Louie; Albert; Maitre de Attilio; Head Bartender Gene. I must have been well-liked to get these individuals to leave their duties, so that I could photograph them.)

Now I'm the Quartermaster

Attilio was not pleased to lose me from the dining room, but Mr. Carney gave me the position as the club's quartermaster. I think that Tom who replaced Gene, probably suggested to Mr. Carney that I would be a good replacement for Don. I would carry my small round tray of drinks out along the veranda that overlooked Larchmont Harbor. I served the special *men only* room and a large room inside room just off the veranda where members socialized.

I also worked the large parties in the Pandemonium where all of the waiters and I split a percentage of the beverages we served. Once, it was necessary to bring in union waiters for a large wedding party. I noticed something odd going on behind the bar. A union waiter was standing behind the bar, hunched over a metal sink.

Walking behind the bar closer, I could see he had a 1.5 liter bottle of champagne turned upside down in each of the sink's four corners with a napkin draped across the top of each bottle. I asked him what he was doing. He said this was a "hell of an easier way to make money than running around the Pandemonium topping off champagne glasses." I didn't stop him, but I did have his name removed from the list of approved union waiters for our club.

Mr. Carney Needs an Assistant Manager

The club had hosted Race Week since 1896, featuring hundreds of racing boats from distant ports. Race Week runs for nine consecutive days. The club library was outfitted with tables, typewriters, and telephones. Reporters from all the major newspapers had tables with the name of their newspapers on them up front. It is difficult for me to describe the hectic atmosphere during those nine days. There were strangers all over the place: at the bar paying cash, in the locker room, on the docks, and in the dining room.

Mr. Carney asked to speak with me in his office. He seemed a little edgy. He told me that he had a big problem. "Jay, his assistant manager, left this morning. He took a position at the Winged Foot Golf Club. Race Week starts in ten days. I need an assistant manager. Dave, you know the work that Jay did. Do you know someone who could take his position very quickly?" I said that the only person that I knew who could possibly do it was my friend Guzzi. He and I had successfully executed a big job in college. "He's smart, personable, and very organized."

Mr. Carney called Hartley, the switchboard operator, into the office and told him to find Dominic Guzzi in Old Forge, Pennsylvania. He said, "Try to get him on the phone." Soon Mr. Hartley said, "I have Mr. Guzzi on the line." Mr. Carney asked him to put the call through to his office. He told me, "Dave, talk to your friend about the position. When you're finished, hold the line open and open the door."

"Guz, are you working? No? Great. Listen. Mr. Carney, Art Carney's brother, needs a new assistant manager real quick," I said. Guzzi replied, "Are you kidding? The only boat I've ever been on was a canoe, and that did not end well." I told Guz that I knew the club and Mr. Carney very well. "I'll help you. Talk to Mr. Carney." When the call was over, Mr. Carney said, "He's never managed anything, but he sounds intelligent and honest and he speaks well. He'll be here tomorrow afternoon for an interview."

Out of the Monkey House

Never could I have imagined the lifelong bond that would develop between Guzzi and Mr. Carney. Guz had studied briefly to become a priest. Mr. Carney was a devout Catholic. Later they would pray together. Guz knew where to look for Mr. Carney when he 'fell off the wagon'. This was a great match for everyone.

Mr. Guzzi was given Jay's large room in the main clubhouse. I suggested to Mr. Carney that if I was in Guzzi's room, I could easily brief him on who was who and what was what. He agreed. I was out of the monkey house and into the clubhouse.

Only Mr. Ogilvy questioned what I was doing living among club members. This did not entirely surprise me. I recalled sitting at my ice house post one day, and I overheard Mr. Ogilvy talking with a member in the locker room behind me. He was being critical of Mr. Carney. I recently Googled Stanley Ogilvy so I could find the correct spelling of his name. I learned that in 1993, Stanley Ogilvy wrote a book. It was titled, *The Larchmont Yacht Club: A History, 1880–1990.*[3] Now I can better understand why he thought it was improper for me to live in the club house.

Mr. Carney and I had about eight days to get Mr. Guzzi acclimated to the Club's buildings and grounds. I introduced Guz to Tom, Mr. Deneke, Chef Louie and Oscar, Captain Toby and Tommy Thompson, et al. Mr. Carney covered the details of his responsible position. Race Week was a challenge for seasoned employees. For Mr. Guzzi, it would be 'a baptism of fire'. Guzzi was a fast learner. Most importantly, he and Mr. Carney 'clicked'. We survived Race Week.

Years later, I asked Guz how Mr. Carney was doing. He told me that Mr. Carney was divorced and selling used cars in Yonkers. What a sad ending for a prince of a man. Guzzi visited Mr. Carney throughout his life. Guz died in 2017.

[Flash forward to August 2018: Returning from a Lemko Association meeting in Ct. with my wife, and son, I asked if they might be interested in visiting the Yacht Club. It was a busy Sunday, but I was able to park legally in a handicapped spot directly in front of 'the monkey house' which had been renovated and repurposed. We walked through it, and out to the boatyard, and then down to the icehouse. And to the right, was the Pandemonium that I painted in 1957! It had been renovated, including a new bar with a view of the harbor. Then on to the great bronze elephant where we could see the dock where I had placed members' gear when I was the ice boy. Later, with cocktails, my wife and son made themselves comfortable in chairs overlooking the harbor. While there was an empty rocker next to them, I could not get myself to sit there. I had served Arthur Knapp, Rudi Schaefer, Stanley Bell, Mr. Monte-Sano, and other great yachtsmen in these chairs. (See photos: Larchmont Yacht Club; Larchmont Harbor; the side bar where I stood ordering drinks for members; Lea, Norbert, Liz the Iceman's daughter)

As we were leaving, I stopped at the desk with a question, and the manager, John Wall, engaged me in conversation. Soon we were enjoying the Club's special drink with him, reminiscing …Race Week…Miss. Mandeville…Vic Zoble, the head of the large salt-water pool. Every Fourth of July, to the sound of music, he would climb up the ladder to the very high diving board—light himself completely on fire, and dived into the pool. It was spectacular! The Club looked and felt as it did in the 1950s.] As we drove to my son's home in Hastings-on-Hudson, I thought about the wonderful people that I met there. I thought of the beauty and magic of Larchmont Harbor and how it may have affected me. Over the years, most of my homes have been on water…the beautiful Delaware River…Moodna Creek…the Pascack Brook….Indian Creek….and now Patrick Henry Lake.

It should be noted that while the first person that I met with at the Club in 1957 was Commodore Perry, it was Arthur Knapp who was responsible for my being at the Club. In the 1930s, my father worked at a hardware store in College Point, New York. Arthur Knapp, living in nearby Bayside, frequented the hardware store. He and my father developed a casual friendship. And many years later, my father asked a favor, and Mr. Knapp was responsible for both me and my brother becoming ice boys at the Club.

The Larchmont Yacht Club was a turning point in my life. I had always been self-confident, but now I was comfortable talking with important, wealthy people. Even when I completed my college degree requirements, I considered becoming a fulltime employee at the Club. And, it was not an idle thought, as I remember calculating that I would earn $2,000 more at the Club, compared with my teaching salary!

Chapter 4

I'm in College

There were several turning points in my life. Being a college student coincided with my work at the yacht club. Both were learning experiences in different ways. Both were transformative, and each gave new direction to my life.

All my relatives were working-class people. None went beyond elementary school. I expected college to be very difficult. I had never read a book in my life. There had been no books in our apartment in Brooklyn. There had been no books in Aunt Stella's home. I had never even been in a library. So I was entering a new world. This was also true of the yacht club which was also a mew world for me.

I was not intimidated and had already dealt with significant challenges. I had confidence in myself. I had had several very good teachers at Old Forge High School, including Mrs. Wozniak, who had taken chewing gum from my mouth, rubbed it into my hair, and slapped my face so that she could teach me English. She quickly found a way to get me involved. Every word in a sentence has a role in the sentence, just as in mathematics, every number and symbol has a role in an equation. Algebraic equations are mathematical sentences. She taught me to diagram compound-complex sentences, as if they were equations.

[Flash forward to 1975: After I delivered the commencement address to the graduating class of Old Forge High School, Mrs. Wozniak approached me and said, "Congratulations! You were the smartest troublemaker in all my years of teaching." Now I will endow a scholarship in her name.]

Remedial English, Remedial Math, and the Speech Clinic

As evidence of my confidence, I decided to graduate with a double major—mathematics and the physical sciences—with a minor in social studies. For some reason, the college put me in remedial math and remedial English. I was also required to attend the speech laboratory. I went to the lab twice a week. Mr. Dunning would put different sized marbles, which had a colored string hanging from each one, in my mouth. He would read words from a card as he tugged the different strings. I had to pronounce the words properly.

I thought that this was a stupid waste of my time, but guessed they had not had many students from Brooklyn. I was aware that I talked with a Brooklyn accent. The guys in the dorm would tease me because I would say 'dees', 'dems', and 'doughs' instead of these, them, and those.

I was not very interested in college and thought about joining the Air Force. I actually went down to the recruiting office and took a test. I was told that I would qualify for electronics training if I signed up. I also did not appreciate having to take non-credit courses in English and Mathematics.

There were activities though, that I really enjoyed on campus. Going into the cafeteria, being able to select from so many food choices, and eating as much as I wanted was great. There were only eight buildings on campus. I was assigned to the Shawnee dormitory. It was impressive. The bathroom had about fifteen showers and sinks. The toilets were private and clean.

But I'm Too Smelly

In my room, I was given clean sheets and towels every week. Each room housed three students. We shared one closet. One of my roommates asked to be reassigned during my first month. I asked the other guy, Larry Hardinger, why Ralph had left. He opened the closet door and said, "Just smell." It did not smell too bad to me, but I got the message.

The problem was that I only had one suitcase of clothes. But I quickly solved that problem. Students took their dirty clothes to the laundry building. Our clothes would be washed, dried, folded, and placed in a cubbyhole that had the student's name on it. I hung around outside the laundry room waiting for a guy to go in without dirty laundry. If he was about my size, I would look to see where his cubbyhole was. The next week, I'd take his clothes, but only wore his underwear and socks. It worked really well.

But when winter arrived, I wrote to Bulldog and told him I needed a pair of shoes and a winter coat. He brought a good gray suburban winter coat and a pair of shoes to me at college. He worked in the Maxson Plant and got my things there. I could always count on Bulldog.

In Brooklyn, in college, and everywhere else, I had always solved my own problems. When I was a child, I had learned that I could never depend on anyone. In 2018, college students can now retreat to a safe room. Recently, I read that some colleges have crying closets. Clearly, this does not prepare students to cope with the inevitable life problems they will encounter in the future. Retreating into a crying closet will likely exacerbate one's psychological problem.

Meanwhile, I got a job in town washing dishes and a job in the college library, which paid seventy-five cents per hour. In my library work, I came across a publication entitled *Writer's Market*. It delineated hundreds of magazines that paid for accepted articles. I submitted two articles, both of which were accepted for publication. I do not have any record of the magazines or the subjects of my articles. I do recall the compensation was meager. They paid pennies per word. I did not submit additional articles.

Always keeping my eyes open for opportunities to make some extra money, I spotted an item on a bulletin board. The Pocono Mountain Art Club was seeking a male model. I removed the ad so that I would reduce my competition. I wasn't even sure that I wanted to do this work. Me, a male model? Wait until Bulldog reads this. I obviously never told him.

The art club was located three blocks from the restaurant where I worked three nights a week, and they met on a night when I didn't have work. So I became a model. At the end of a sitting, they would pass a can around for my night's pay. Once they were practicing some kind of new chalk technique, and the sitting lasted more than two hours. That night the can had fourteen dollars in it!

One night as I was getting ready to leave, I asked a man, "What happens to all of these sketches of me?" He told me that most of them were probably thrown out or the backs of them were reused. He asked me if I would like some of the ones that he had painted of me. The next week, he brought in two pictures of me: one was in black ink, and the other was in colored chalk. The man signed and dated each picture. His name was Shorty Widmer. The drawings were pretty good, but I never hung them anywhere. After boxing them up for various moves, I finally discarded them.

Recently while reaching for my East Stroudsburg 1958–1959 college catalog to refresh my memory about my college costs, a bookend fell on the floor. As I picked it up, I noticed something on the bottom that surprised me. Written on masking tape in my handwriting, it read, "ESSTC 1959, I'm Flushed!"

(See photo: My college bookends)

The bookends had survived my moves to twenty different homes across the country during fifty-nine years, and I had never noticed this note on the bottom. Because it had been seated on bookshelves, the masking tape had been protected from oxidation. In 1959, I had considered myself to be flushed with money to the point that I could make the first nonessential purchase of my life. My guess is that the set of bookends may have cost two or three dollars. My savings reflected the fact that during the summer of 1958, I had been working three full-time jobs at the yacht club.

Later I purchased a slide-rule which I had noticed other students using in physics and spherical trigonometry. Now I could compete with my classmates, particularly on 'timed tests'. It proved to be a valuable instrument which I proudly hung from my belt in a leather case.

What? I Have to Go Home?

It was the Thanksgiving morning of 1957. I walked down from my room. As I walked past Dean Martin's office, I heard, "Garrahan, where are you going?" I answered that I was on my way to the cafeteria for breakfast. He said, "It's closed. The college is closed. It's Thanksgiving. Now get going home."

Stepping into his doorway, I said, "I don't have a home to go to." He sat me down, and I explained my situation. I did not know that colleges closed for holidays. I had never talked to anyone who went to college. And besides, I had paid all of my fees for the first semester which included room and board. I was shocked. I felt that I was being cheated and let Puffer Martin know that I had paid cash, and that I thought that the college would be 'my home'.

He knew that I was ticked off. He picked up the phone and called Dean Eiler. He asked Dean Eiler if he and his wife, Betty, were having relatives in for the holidays. The answer was "Yes, but he can stay here. I'll drive over and pick him up."

As I was leaving to wait outside for Dean Eiler, Dean Martin yelled out, "And Garrahan, remember, you better find a place to stay for Christmas and all the other holidays." My home away from college, from now on, would be the monkey house at the Larchmont Yacht Club.

Free False Teeth

Mr. Kovarick, my remedial math instructor, told me he was going to have me transferred into his regular college algebra class. That pleased me, as I did not like taking non-credit courses. Later Professor Fritz asked to speak with me after class. First, he gave me a note to take to the dean of instruction, Francis McGarry, requesting that I be moved into a regular English class. Then he said that it appeared to him that my upper teeth did not fit properly. He was right. Several times, I had been embarrassed when my teeth had fallen out when I was eating in the cafeteria and students had noticed. I had grown since the dentist made those teeth several years earlier.

He told me he knew a good dental mechanic, who could make me a new set of teeth that would fit properly. I told him I could not afford the cost. He replied that he would be happy to pay for them. I hesitated because I suspected he might be a homosexual. But I accepted his offer, knowing that I could handle myself in that situation. He drove me to a dental office in Washington, New Jersey. The dental mechanic took an impression. A few weeks later, I had my new teeth. They were the right size and color and fit perfectly. Professor Fritz was just being a very good person.

In January, a girl whom I had often seen in the library asked me to take her to the annual Turn-Around Dance. She told me that this dance was different from other school dances. If an upper class girl asked a freshman boy to this dance, the guy had to accept the invitation. The only dances I knew were wild Russian polkas, but I accepted. We became friends, but it was obvious to me that her overly strict religious parents did not approve of me. However, three years later, Janet and I were married.

Some Recognition

My physics professor, Dr. Gessner, made a recommendation to the department that I receive the annual award for achievement in physics. It was a special surprise, especially coming from him. The word on campus was that he had been a member of the team that had worked on the Manhattan Project in Los Alamos. The award turned out to be a 580-page, leather-bound book of scientific tables and formulae. My name was embossed in gold on the cover.

People were beginning to know me on campus. I was studying inorganic chemistry, and I really got into it. I wrote a letter to the American Chemical Society to inquire about the possibility of forming a chemistry club on our campus. They mailed me the paperwork. I met with the Dean of Student Activities, and I became the founding president of the Atomium Club. This club provided our members the opportunity to become affiliated with the American Chemical Society.

In my junior year, I was inducted into Sigma Zeta Tau, a national honorary science society for third- and fourth-year students who had reached a high level of achievement in science and mathematics. I enjoyed spherical trigonometry but did not care much for calculus. I even managed to wiggle Janet into the yearbook photograph of Sigma Zeta Tau. Years later, I figured out a way for her to receive two tuition-free graduate degrees from Columbia University while she was caring for our three young children. (See Appendix: Atomium Club; Sigma Zeta Tau)

My Best College Experience: The Proposal and Big Rewards

The best experience I had in college did not take place in a classroom. Rather, it was because of my job at the library. I was bored as I shelved books in the stacks and covered the front desk. I noticed that the library director, Mr. Emele, was doing a lot of pacing around and chain smoking. He seemed edgy, and was meeting more frequently with the two assistant librarians.

I asked him if something special was going on. He explained that in anticipation of the new library, the Dean had asked him to prepare a comprehensive plan to move hundreds of thousands of books, periodicals, art work, microfilm, et al. from the existing library into the new library building. Then he asked me an odd question, "What do you think, Dave...do you have any ideas"? I asked him what kind of plans they were coming up with. He answered, "Al wants to put it on the department heads to get their stuff over there, but I can see that getting all screwed up. Mr. Riebel thinks it would be better if we did it by moving one department at a time, but we don't have that much time left."

I thought about it as he was talking, and I said that it would be necessary to start by doing an inventory of all of the library's holdings, including their current location, and the measurements of the space that they currently occupy. He seemed interested. I asked him if it would be possible for me to use my regular work hours to do an inventory. He agreed. As I write this, I wonder how I would have even considered myself being capable of solving a problem that professionals had been struggling to figure out.

I got my friend, Guzzi, interested in the project. He was a senior, very conscientious, and well organized about everything he did. Together, we came up with some good ideas. Fortunately, there was a newly constructed unoccupied building within close proximity of the current library. (actually this building later was incorporated into the new library). Mr. Emele got the okay for us to use the building on a temporary basis.

The library was located in the basement of Stroud Hall, which was the girl's dormitory since the college's founding in 1893. Over the years, as the college grew, the library was expanded by occupying adjoining basement rooms, and various storage areas, as well as two sub-basement rooms. Two points were obvious, the college needed a new library...and this was going to be a complicated project.

We decided to do an inventory by categories, location, and measured space. We started with the 'card catalog" and using the Dewey Decimal classification to get an overview of what we were dealing with. We developed eighteen categories, and color-coded each. There would be corresponding color coded locations in the new library. Next, we measured the distance between the two buildings, taking note of the number of steps coming up from the old library and the steps entering the new building. The maintenance workers would build the necessary ramps.

My proposal called for student workers to transfer the holdings in library carts in a chain starting from the old building and continuing unbroken into the new building. The chain would continue twenty-four hours a day, until the entire job was complete. Students would work in four-hour shifts. We determined the number of library carts that would be required, and made provision for temporary lighting. In the event of rain, tarps would be placed inside a covered staging area where there would be chairs for student relief workers. Guzzi and I conducted trial runs with loaded library carts between the two buildings, recording the number of minutes it took to make a round trip.

After several weeks, we met with Mr. Emele in his office and reviewed the plan. He was impressed, and scheduled a meeting for us to present the plan to the entire library staff. Guzzi and I were able to answer their questions, and we made a few modifications to the plan. Then Mr. Emele reviewed the plan with department heads, and maintenance personnel, before submitting the proposal to the Dean. The proposal was approved.

Mr. Emele saw me as some kind of a hero. I received perks: I no longer had to punch my time card in and out. I simply had to write down my total hours and give them to Mr. Emele at the end of each week.

But that was just the beginning. I had no idea that Mr. Emele was president of the Belvedere Board of Education in New Jersey. When my future wife, Janet graduated, the Belvedere Board of Education appointed her to a second grade teaching position. Later Mr. Emele created a teaching position for me.

Have Car, Can't Drive

My home for all holidays during the school year and summers was the Larchmont Yacht Club. Mr. Carney always found work for me to do. However, it would take me at least five hours to get from the yacht club to the college. I had to walk a mile from the club to the train station and wait for a train to bring me to Grand Central Station. From there, I would have to walk to the Port of Authority bus station and wait for a bus to East Stroudsburg. Finally, I would walk a half mile to the college. Every weekend, I would arrive back at college at 7 a.m. on Monday and ready myself for my 9 a.m. class. I really needed a car.

So I hitched a ride to Old Forge. I asked Uncle Huggy if he would take me to Moosic Motors to buy a car. He asked if I had any money. I told him I had eight hundred dollars in my pocket (As quartermaster, I was making some serious money). He helped me buy a black Pontiac.

(see photo: my first car)

Then I asked Uncle Huggy if he would drive the car off the lot and park it on Moosic Road. He wanted to know why. I told him that I didn't have a driver's license, and did not know how to drive. We left my car on Moosic Road. Uncle Huggy dropped me off at Bulldog's house. Bulldog and I went down and got my car.

Bulldog drove it up to the top of Bald Mountain where he taught me how to drive in one day. The following day, Sunday, I drove very slowly back to the college. I knew I had to be careful because I didn't have a driver's license, and it was only my second day of driving. I've been driving sixty years and have never had an accident—not even a fender bender in a parking lot. Having a car opened new opportunities for me.

CHAPTER 5

College Graduate, Married, Mom's Out

College Graduate

I did the first quarter of my student teaching at Mount Pocono High School where I taught geometry, physics, and social studies. Then I taught chemistry at Stroud Union High School with Mr. Regan as my cooperating teacher. I did not learn anything from him. Mr. Regan just used my time so that he could have his free time in the teachers' room.

My final post was to East Stroudsburg Junior and Senior High School where Mr. Dimmick was my cooperating teacher. I taught algebra and trigonometry. I learned a lot by observing Mr. Dimmick teach. He really took his cooperating teacher responsibilities seriously, and I appreciated that.

For example, he had built a podium with five shelves in back. For each of his five classes, he had placed that day's lesson plan for each course and the corresponding textbook on the appropriate shelf. *What a great idea*, I thought and did the same thing when I started teaching.

I completed all the requirements for my degree in January of 1961, and graduated with honors in Math and Science. It had taken me three and a half years. The dean of instruction, Dr. McGarry, had given me special permission to carry an extra load of twenty-two credits during each of my last four semesters. I had received no financial aid.

January is a difficult time for an inexperienced teacher to find a job. However, I was certified to teach all of the subjects offered in mathematics, the physical sciences, and social studies. I interviewed for four positions, and was offered employment by all. I accepted and signed a contract with the North Burlington High School district in New Jersey. However, Mr. Emele contacted me with an offer. I met with the Burlington superintendent, and explained my situation, and told him that I was prepared to honor my contract. He replied that with your wife already teaching in Belivere, it would be difficult for you to give us your total effort. He released me from my contractual obligation. Mr. Emele had created a position for me teaching mathematics and earth science. My teaching career was launched.

Married

Looking back, there were two consequential voids in my life. I had never felt loved by anyone. Having never experienced it, I did not know the meaning of 'being in love.' Second, I had never enjoyed a safe, happy life at home. This potent combination led me to make a bad choice for my wife, and the ultimate failure of the marriage when I did stumble upon love.

There were days when I felt that Janet was not the right choice. I should have been patient, and played the field a bit. This was my first relationship with a girlfriend. She did have a wholesome family, Most Sundays, family members would gather around the dining room table and enjoy a great meal. Then they would sit together in the living room for conversation and laughter. I was envious of this homelife. I did perceive that Janet's thinking and values were often superficial, and at times, insincere. Yet, I did not have the courage to reject her advances.

Janet and I had to receive matrimonial instruction at the Stroudsburg Methodist Church. Janet's family had held leadership positions for several generations in this church. Near the end of our instruction, Reverend Stimson said, "David, I will ask you if you accept the Lord Jesus as your savior and redeemer, and you will answer, yes." I told him that I didn't believe that and would not answer "yes." He explained that college students often question their faith. He asked me to step behind the altar, and we made a deal. He said, "When I ask you the question, simply bow your head and speak softly to yourself about anything. The congregation will understand the emotion." It worked. Janet and I were married.

I invited four of my Russian uncles to the reception that was held in the basement of the church. They were shocked. No bar? No whiskey? This was unbelievable to them. They had never been to a dry wedding. I told them that was the way her family lived. Later, I noticed that two of my uncles went out for a smoke. When they returned, my other two uncles went out. They had found a VFW three blocks from the church.

Life on the Delaware River

Janet and I found a great house on the Delaware River in Bangor, Pennsylvania, which was only two miles from

Belvidere. It cost nine thousand dollars. We had no savings, but I convinced the owner to rent it to us for eighty-five dollars a month, and I would maintain the property as if I owned it. There was a PP&L plant about half a mile up river, which took in water, heated it for steam to generate electricity, and released it back into the river. This made the river swimmable through October.

I built a dock, and bought a boat for fifty dollars. I borrowed a tractor and cleared out the beach to reveal clean sand. Then I plowed the entire property, planted a lawn, and created a garden where I grew melons, cantaloupes, and cucumbers.

(See photos: Maintaining our rental. My first melon and cantaloupe!)

I rebuilt the wall that had deteriorated from the river flooding and freezing.

We had three surprise visits during this time that stand out to me. Commodore Perry from the yacht club came out of nowhere. It was a surprise visit. Apparently, I had sent him a letter about my college graduation, my marriage, and our address on the river. He had been very helpful to me, from the first moment he had seen me walk into his room saying I needed a job and a place to live. I think it made him feel good, to see how well I was doing. We had a great visit. (See photo: Mr. Perry and Neja)

Then Artie and his wife, Terry, drove out from New York City. He had sent me a letter letting me know that they were coming. We swam in the river, cooked some meat on the built-in fireplace on the patio, and enjoyed a few 'shots and beers', In the photo on the patio, one can readily discern 'who has the attitude'.

(See photos: Artie and I at my rented home)

Then we had another visit. I think that Artie must have told Loretta about the great property Janet and I had. Loretta visited us. We enjoyed swimming and jumping off the floating dock that I built. She was an airline stewardess. Later, she would marry and divorce an airline pilot.

[Flash forward to 1991: In March, I was in my office on the phone when I was interrupted by the operator with an emergency intercept. Loretta was upset. She told me that an intruder had broken into her home while she had been sleeping, threatened her with a knife, and had raped her. She assisted the police in their investigation and had just returned from the hospital.

She asked me what she should do. I told her to take a hot shower and to go to work. She seemed to want more advice. I immediately had my secretary book a flight to DC, where I rented a car and drove to Loretta's home in Silver Springs, Maryland.

When I arrived, the door was locked. A neighbor walked over and told me that Loretta had gone to work and showed me the very small window where the rapist had gained entry. I went to Home Depot and bought a steel plate and some headless bolts, to seal that opening.

I was waiting outside the law firm where Loretta worked when she walked out. She was surprised to see me. Loretta, always direct and honest to a fault, said, "On the phone, you sounded like rape was no big deal and blew me off." When Loretta had phoned me, she had intentionally not asked me to come down; I had intentionally not indicated that I would fly down.

She had me search the house before we entered it. We talked as I installed the metal plate over the window from the inside. We ate supper and talked. She brought out a fifth of scotch.

When I realized how traumatic the rape had been for her, I suggested that she consider selling the house and buy a condominium. In the morning, I dropped her off at her office and flew back to Newark. Several years later, a rapist was arrested in New York City. Loretta's rape kit confirmed his identity as her rapist. She chose not to attend the trial where he was convicted.]

About a month after my visit, Loretta wrote me several letters. I quote from one: "I am sorry to tell you that I believe Janet to be a very small-minded, seedy, sleazy person, who conceals these unsavory characteristics under a cloak of Christianity and motherhood." Her tone and assessment did not surprise me, but the letter did.

Janet's name was never mentioned during my visit with Loretta. Moreover, Janet and I had been divorced for about ten years. Loretta could pack a lot in one sentence. She was gifted with the sharpest intellect among her siblings.

[Flash forward: Sadly, years later during a rainy windstorm, a tree fell on the roof of Loretta's home in the middle of the night. She was killed in her sleep.]

[Flash forward to 1997: My partner, Eileen, and I were browsing around a craft show in a church on Court House Square in Prescott, Arizona. I was looking at a vendor's handmade greeting cards when she looked up and asked, "Are you Uncle David?" It was Loretta's daughter, Marlene, I had not seen her in several years. I said that the last time I had seen her had been when I had visited her at Bryn Mawr College. She explained that she was now a student at Prescott College and that Bryn Mawr had been too elitist! Interestingly, she and her boyfriend, Steve, were living in a garage just two blocks down the dirt road from my home. Eileen and I took them to dinner at the Hassayampa Inn.

Subsequently, Eileen and I drove to Colorado where Marlene and Steve were living in a commune. We took them to Boulder where we enjoyed learning about their interesting life, as we enjoyed dinner.]

Back at Our River Home

Each day, I would drive home after teaching, grab something to eat, and drive to Lehigh University for my classes. Several times, I noticed two men sitting in folding chairs on our beach fishing. That was okay, until it was not. I noticed that they were leaving beer cans and metal pull- tabs in the sand.

The next time that I saw them fishing, I went inside and took out my thirty-eight caliber revolver. I shot the revolver, emptying every chamber while making certain the bullets went over the men's heads and into the river. They jumped up and ran, leaving their chairs and poles behind. I would have done the same thing had they been white fishermen. Their chairs and poles disappeared, but the men never returned.

Igor, a Ukrainian Lemko who owned an adjacent lot had given the gun to me. I had helped him dig an outhouse and build a cabin. What are the odds of two Lemkos living so close together in this relatively remote spot on the Delaware River? Four or five years later, Igor contacted me, asking me to help his son Georgie get into college. I guided him into Utica College and later into Syracuse University. Igor repaid me by giving me a motorcycle, which he brought to my home in Demarest, New Jersey, in the back of his truck.

[Flash forward to 1992: I stopped at Igor's place on the Delaware River. A fisherman pulled his boat ashore. It was Georgie! He offered me a beer from his onboard six-pack and showed me a summons he had just received for consuming alcohol while on the river. He knew that his Dad and I frequently enjoyed a few beers on the river.

I was surprised to learn that Georgie had earned an MSW degree at Columbia University, but had not enjoyed the social work profession. So his Dad had hired him as his helper in his heating/air-conditioning business. When Igor passed away, Georgie took over his father's business.]

In September of 1961, I was admitted into a master's degree program at the University of Scranton. It was a 130-mile round-trip! My sense was that the professor did not know enough about his subject. He never went beyond what was in the textbook. I talked to my principal at Belvidere High school, Mr. Stoutman, about the situation. He said that Lehigh University in Bethlehem had a great reputation and was a lot closer to my home.

I was admitted to a graduate degree program in guidance and counseling at Lehigh. That summer, I also completed eight graduate credits in vocational psychology and counseling under a National Defense Education Act grant at Rutgers University.

I taught Janet how to use the .38 revolver, and moved into a dormitory for eight weeks at Rutgers. Being newly married and living right on the Delaware River, I wonder why I was taking multiple graduate courses at two universities during the summer months.

However, I was getting my money's worth at Lehigh University. I took five courses that Professor Scanlan, who had earned his doctorate at Harvard University, taught. He was a brilliant, chain-smoking professor with a photographic memory. Frequently, he would cite passages from memory of the various books we were using. Besides the textbook, we were required to read a different book each week.

I took a course with Professor Milan, and wrote a paper on the psychological origins of religion. When the course was over, I convinced him to engage in an open debate with Professor Scanlan, who held contrary views on the subject of God and religion. They debated before a capacity audience.

[Flash forward to 1974: After they appointed me deputy chairman of the department of applied psychology at Columbia University, I had access to all departmental files. Snooping through my student folder, I read the recommendation Professor Scanlan had written to support my admission into the doctoral program at Columbia. With one exception, all of his comments were positive: "an intellectually gifted graduate student."

One sentence baffled me. He had written, "He is physically immature." Why would this brilliant, Harvard-trained professor of psychology call attention to my physique in a letter of recommendation for a position that didn't require heavy lifting? To this day, I have no idea.]

Mom Is Out!

I was finishing course work at Rutgers when Aunt Mary contacted me. She said that Uncle Joe had somehow gotten Mom released from the Brooklyn State Hospital, and had taken her to Philadelphia. Uncle Joe had just been released from the Graterford State Penitentiary after completing an eight-year sentence. He had apparently convinced hospital officials that he owned an apartment building and a dress factory in Philadelphia. He told them his sister, Mom, could have her own apartment or live with him and his wife and work in his factory, if she wanted to. Uncle Joe did not own a factory, a home, or even a car. He had a well-developed con artist's personality.

I drove to the address Aunt Mary had given me. Mom was living in an SRO (single resident occupancy). She was still attractive, but her hair had turned completely white, and the pupils in her eyes danced constantly. I asked her about that. She said that it did not bother her and that it was probably from all the electric shock treatments the doctors had administered to the sides of her head.

We had a good long talk. It had been nine years. She told me that Joe and Sybil, who had a wooden leg, had gone off to work with a circus. I told her that she could come and live with Janet and me or that I could find her a nice place in Old Forge. Her response was quick and definitive: "You have to live your own life." She told me that she had a job washing dishes in a restaurant.

The next day, we went to a realtor who showed us a small apartment. As Mom looked around and out the windows, I could tell that she liked it. The apartment was in a private house. It was located close to a bus stop that stopped on the corner near the restaurant where she worked.

While Mom was at work the next day, I went back to the house and met the owner, sharing a little bit about Mom's situation. We worked out an arrangement whereby Mom would pay him a little rent each month and I would send him a check covering the larger balance. He also agreed to help Mom furnish the apartment. I had my checkbook with me. I signed a blank check and told him he could fill in an amount for all expenses. We exchanged phone numbers. I was comfortable that Mom would be okay there. I visited her every two or three weeks. After about six months, the restaurant gave her a job at the counter, waiting on customers. Later she would become a waitress and served tables.

Now I Have a Stepfather

Mom surprised me when she got married. I don't know where or how she and Carl met. He had been a police officer in North Carolina, but had been dismissed for shooting a Black man without cause. Artie did not like him from the beginning, but I decided to cut him slack if Mom was happy. They took in a stray dog, Nega. During several of my visits, I observed Carl mistreating the dog. I told Mom that Nega would have a better life with Janet and me in the country. Nega turned out to be a terrific pet.

(See photo: me and Nega enjoy the Delaware River)

Later, Carl became abusive to Mom. Artie finally decided that he and I should go to Philadelphia where Artie would smash Carl's kneecaps with a ball-peen hammer. After asking me several times, I finally said, "All right. Get your hammer, and let's drive down." Artie backed out, which didn't surprise me. He had never confronted the Kent Street guys. He was all tough talk.

I drove down by myself. Mom was at work. I started an argument with Carl and took a baseball bat from my trunk with the intent of breaking one of his legs. My first swing missed him by inches. Carl deflected my second swing and grabbed the bat from my hands. I managed to get into my car and take off. I did stop at two or three phone booths, dialed 911, and reported being assaulted by Carl Wilson at 1918 East Willard Street (I knew Carl had been convicted of armed robbery in Philadelphia). During my next visit, Mom told me that the neighbors said several police cars came to the house from both directions on the one-way street. He was arrested for disturbing the peace.

Oddly, Carl and I developed a better relationship after that bizarre encounter. A few years later on one of my regular visits to Mom, Carl was in severe pain and pleaded with me to take him to a hospital. I called for an ambulance, but since he was breathing and not bleeding, two hospitals refused.

However, I got the police to respond by mentioning that my stepfather was a former police officer, and was in critical condition. As the two officers lifted Carl out of his chair, they saw his gun. Mom explained that he always kept a gun nearby and that it was because of his police days. They took him to the hospital where he died the following week. Interestingly, Mom was unaffected by his death and lived another thirty years.

Mom bought an urban-renewal home for $3,500. Mom and the family in the adjoining building were the only white people on the block. When Artie got out of the navy, we took turns visiting Mom at least once a month. I cannot remember one visit when she did not insist that I take "this money," which was usually between fifty and one hundred dollars every visit. Artie and I decided to open an account to save this money for her future needs. She lived to be ninety-four. The total amount she had given us was $70,000! [Flash Forward to 2003: a pancreatic specialist at Sloan Kettering Memorial Hospital studied my cat-scans. One told me that they looked like tumors, and said, "If these were my scans, I would schedule surgery."]

Apparently, I shared this condition with my brother. One evening, he phoned me and asked, "What happens to Mom's money if one of us dies"? My reply was immediate, "If I die first, you take care of it, if you die first, I'll take over." Fifteen minutes later, he called back, and told me that his wife, Terry, thought that maybe my children should take over my responsibility. I thought, that's odd…the money belongs to Mom…my children lived in distant states. Accordingly, I rejected the suggestion, and said to leave the agreement as it was. Several years later, Artie was diagnosed with liver cancer, and given no more than sixty days. I told Artie about a friend of mine who had liver cancer, and paid to receive a liver transplant at a hospital in Pittsburgh. I offered to give my brother $200,000 to have a liver transplant at the same hospital in Pittsburgh. I forget his reasoning, but he did not want to have that surgery. I continued visiting him, and knowing that he was too weak to go shopping, I brought him six cases of beer and two bottles of whiskey. He enjoyed some, but soon was hospitalized. Terry and I visited him regularly at the V.A. hospital.

When I saw that he was nearing death, and realizing that Artie never told me whether he was investing Mom's money or where it was, I asked him about her money. I could hardly believe my hearing when he said that he didn't recall any agreement? Turning to his wife seated at the foot of his bed, I asked, "Terry, you remember that night when Artie called me twice." Her weak reply was, "No, not really." With anger in my voice, I said "Artie, on your deathbed you good Catholics are both lying to me, and you will burn in hell for eternity." I left. A week before he died, he confessed, and told Terry to give Mom's money to me as we had agreed.]

(See photos: Visiting with Mom in Philadelphia in 1989. Visiting Mom on her ninety-third birthday!)

Our First Plane Ride, A Master's Degree, and Leaving Belvidere

Meanwhile, I enjoyed teaching at Belvidere. My first year, I taught algebra, earth science, and senior math. In my senior math class, one of my students, Dale Ricks, had a two-year-old son.

During my free period, the director of guidance gave me the opportunity to meet with Dale in the guidance office. I discovered that teenagers felt comfortable talking with me. I decided that I would like to become a guidance counselor.

Janet and I even went on our first airplane ride, which could easily have been our last. While having a cigarette with the shop teacher, Mr. Wildguy, we talked about John Glenn's space flight. Wildguy was surprised that I had never been in a plane. He invited Janet and me to go up in his plane.

He lived on a large farm. There was a little bit of snow on the ground. He pulled his plane out of the barn with a rope. Janet and I climbed in. She had to sit on my lap behind the pilot's seat because it was such a small, skimpy plane. I tapped the sides and was shocked that they were made of canvas.

Wildguy grabbed a propeller and pushed it down until the engine turned over. He had to crank it several times before it started. I had a vision of Wildguy not getting into the plane in time and Janet and I driving away without him. But it got much worse, once he was in the plane and we were at the proper altitude. I didn't know it then, but Wildguy was very reckless and something of a show-off. He showed us too many of his maneuvers! We were very relieved when he landed.

In my first teaching position, I engaged in all assignments with a seriousness of purpose and youthful gusto. As a rookie teacher, I was given unpopular assignments, which included manager of the annual magazine campaign, chairman of the self-study committee in preparation for state evaluations, and adviser to the FFA (Future Farmers of America) club. I took the FFA students to the state agricultural fair in Harrisburg. On route, we visited an artificial insemination facility. We learned a lot while watching the men stimulate the bull to ejaculation. After collecting the semen, the tubes were labeled, dated, and placed in a freezer. Then they showed us a video of an experimental technique employing an artificial vagina.

On the way back from the fair, we stopped at the Hershey facility. Back on the bus, I explained to the students the method for calculating the amount of chocolate in one Kiss by using calculus, but the students were more interested in discussing the artificial insemination procedures. On December 14, 1961, the Warren County Teachers of Agriculture awarded me the degree of honorary chapter farmer. (See Appendix: FFA)

(See photos: Teaching senior math. The tall guy was a father already! I rewarded four students with a visit to Manhattan.)

I did manage to get on the wrong side of our school superintendent, Colonel Belet. I had been put in charge of the annual magazine campaign, an assignment I had not sought. Two competing magazine publishers wanted the contract: the company that had held the contract the previous year (A Publishing Company) and Curtis Publishing Company in Philadelphia.

One day, the A Publishing rep asked me to leave my car unlocked. After school, I saw that he had put a case of beer and a fancy wood planter stand inside my car. I compared both companies' respective proposals and decided on Curtis Publishing Company. Mr. Stoutman had mentioned to me that the colonel had wanted to stay with A Publishing Company, but I recommended Curtis Publishing Company, and they got the new contract.

I learned there was a lot of money to be made having kids go door-to-door and signing up customers in order to win a bike. I had organized all the homeroom classes at each of the four grade levels to compete against each other. The students broke the school record for the number of subscribers signed up.

Principal Stoutman called me into his office and told me that Superintendent Belet had objected vehemently to my frequenting a bar on Main Street in Belvidere. It seemed like he was being vindictive. I agreed to stop but thought the businesses I frequented after work should not have been any of the superintendent's concern.

Soon I found a way to strike back. I was asked to be the chairman of a self-evaluation committee, prior to the five-year state evaluation of the high school. I worked diligently organizing the committee's responsibilities. One of several recommendations my committee wrote in the self-evaluation report was a need to replace the old, uncomfortable oak chairs in the guidance office.

During the opening reception for the state evaluators, it was my role to present our committee's report. Earlier that morning, I had stopped in the guidance office and had been surprised to see new, comfortable chairs. I asked where the chairs had come from, but no one knew. The Guidance Director had previously had his request for new chairs rejected. I was ticked off.

While presenting the recommendations in our report to the visiting state committee, I called their attention to the recommendation concerning the need for new chairs. I told them that morning I had noticed new chairs in the guidance office that had not been there the previous afternoon. I stated that I had not been able to learn how the chairs had gotten there or how long they would be there. I suggested to the state evaluators that that was something they might want to have clarified.

Colonel Belet had introduced the visiting evaluators to the entire staff. I was later told that his face flushed red when I had made those comments. It had been a stupid cheap shot. Mr. Stoutman let me know that my job was in jeopardy.

I met with Mr. Emele, but did not mention my difficulties with Superintendent Belet. I told him that I had received my master's degree in guidance counseling from Lehigh University and was ready to move on.

I applied for a counseling position in Hackettstown, New Jersey. Although I had an excellent interview with the superintendent, I didn't get the job. Apparently, the Hacketttown superintendent had phoned Superintendent Belet who likely mentioned that I was a trouble-maker. I decided to look for an out-of-state position. Janet and I applied for positions in the Washingtonville Central School District in upstate New York.

Now I'm a Guidance Counselor

Dr. Donald Wagon, the superintendent of schools interviewed Janet and me separately. Charles Wieland, the director of elementary education, also interviewed Janet (Charlie became my lifelong friend and gave me invaluable career assistance twenty-five years later). They offered both of us positions. Janet would teach second grade in a three-room Salisbury Mills school. I would join the guidance department in the high school.

We moved from our Delaware River home to a small cottage on eighteen acres in Salisbury Mills. The owners lived in a large house on the front of the Orrs Mill Road property. The owner gave me permission to plant a vegetable garden and to use his tractor on the eighteen acres.

[see photo: Plowing for a garden and waiting for the mailman to deliver Columbia University's decision!]

By my third year at Washingtonville, I had gained favor with the board and the superintendent and was well established in the community. Dr. Wagon advertised for a new position of assistant superintendent. I immediately phoned my former principal, Mr. Stoutman, in Belvidere and asked him if he might be interested in the position. He told me that he had just completed his doctorate at Temple University and that the position would be a timely and appropriate promotion.

I had formed a personal bond with Dr. Wagon. It began when he and I had been discussing an important district-wide matter in his office when his secretary had interrupted us with the words, "President Kennedy has been shot." Dr. Wagon closed the office door; walked over to the fireplace, and with his hand on the mantel, became emotional. Later, I become involved when the band director had put his hand on Dr. Wagon's son's leg during a bus trip to a band competition. The band director was dismissed from the district.

So I felt comfortable talking to him about my former principal. Dr. William Stoutman of Belvidere was appointed to the position of assistant superintendent! I don't know where I learned to do things in this way, but it had become a pattern. Maybe it started when I helped Guzzi become Mr. Carney's assistant manager at the yacht club.

My employment as guidance counselor proved to be the most satisfying work that I would experience in my life. Several young students have stayed in touch with me for years, and one student for thirty-five years! I met him on my first day of work as a high school guidance counselor on August 15, 1963. I was busy organizing my office when the director of guidance, Mark Clark, rushed in. Pointing out my window, he said, "You see that kid? His name is Seth Grodson. He's no good. He broke into Alex's barbershop and stole the cash register. His parents own the local lumberyard. They sent him to Israel so that he could not be prosecuted. I know he should be your counselee, but I'll take him." I replied, "I became a counselor to help troubled students. I'd like to work with him." And he answered, "Okay, but you will be sorry."

Seth stepped into my office, dressed in an army fatigue shirt, which was mostly unbuttoned and revealed his hairy chest. I made a benign introductory comment, as he took out a cigarette and tapped it on my desk. My guidance work had officially begun. I said, "Seth, I'm a smoker. This is my first day of work, and I decided to not light up until I learn what the rules are." He put the cigarette back in the pack. We talked for half an hour, and then Seth said, "Come on over to the lumberyard. We'll have a sandwich and beer, and you'll meet my parents." I worked with him for a very long time, but was never sorry.

The following year, I asked Mr. Grodson if I could work in the lumberyard on Saturdays without pay. He looked at me and questioned why I would work for no pay. I explained that I just wanted to learn about the lumber business. He liked that, and I got the job. A few years later, Mr. Grodson and I went on a weeklong trip to Virginia, looking for acreage to jointly buy. I really got involved with my counselees and the people in the community.

One night, Seth's father, Julius, came to my home. It was close to midnight. He said, "Seth took the truck and drove it right through the gates. He has a bottle of whiskey. You have to go find him before he hurts someone."

As I left, I asked Julius to phone Dr. Pavorsky, a psychiatrist Seth's parents had taken him to several times. Hours later, I returned with Seth. The four of us sat down at my kitchen table and drew up an agreement, which Seth and his father signed at 6 a.m.

[Flash forward to 1970: Seth knocked on my door in the Bronx. He had recently returned from Vietnam. He looked terrible. He told me he had a court hearing in a few days and needed to get cleaned up. He stayed with us until his court case. Judge Samuelson sentenced Seth to 364 days in the Orange County Jail.]

[Flash Forward to 1996: I had retired to Prescott, Arizona. Seth's father, Julius, phoned me. His wife was suing him for a divorce in Texas. He told me, "David, I need you to meet Seth in Austin. He will give you power-of-attorney papers. Just remember, Alicia doesn't get the house in Round Rock and I have no assets."

Seth and I met with her lawyers at their ranch. It was a tough job. I knew that Julius had $900K in bearer bonds. Back then, these bonds were unregistered and not traceable. I told the lawyers that Mr. Grodson had no assets. The lawyers said that they were prepared to spend $50K with a firm that located assets.

The bottom line was that, after three days of negotiating, we had an agreement. I signed the house over to Alicia. Her name was not on the deed. Julius never spoke to me again! In retrospect, I did not represent Mr. Grodson's interests well. It was entirely inappropriate for me to have injected my personal viewpoint regarding his home and his wife's needs. I understand why Julius never spoke to me again.]

After Julius died, Seth arrived unexpectedly at my home in Prescott, Arizona. We drove to Las Vegas in his new truck, where Seth, despite my forewarning, lost $15K the first night playing poker. He thought he could win it back the next day, but I prevailed. We drove to Costa Mesa, California, and visited two of his buddies from his Vietnam days.

In 1967, we had a great trip to Montreal where we attended the world's fair. In 2006, Seth drove to Narrowsburg, New York, when I was building a home on the Delaware River. Then in 2008 when my wife and I returned to Manhattan from a visit to Seattle, there was a message on our phone from Seth's wife, Joanie. Seth had passed away in a VA hospital in Pittsburgh. I had phoned him before we left for Seattle, and he had sounded optimistic. He said that if he didn't make it, I could have Joanie. Seth was a very good friend.

Another counselee was Andrew Batch. His father was General Batch, who was stationed at Stewart Air Force Base. For some reason, General Batch took an interest in me and had me flown out to the Air Force Academy in Colorado Springs for a week. That was a long, exciting flight. Our in-flight dinner was filet mignon!

Later, he was instrumental in having Janet and I admitted to a special program for married couples at Vassar College. He knew that I understood Russian culture and was able to communicate in Russian. The program trained couples to speak Russian fluently. There was speculation about the intent of the program. None of the married couples had children. I think it was a Defense Intelligence Agency initiative. We were paid eighty dollars each per week.

Casey Krupa was yet another of the several hundred counselees I got to know. His Dad was a colonel at the air base. One day, Casey came into my office and said, "I just got my college board results and can't believe how great I did." I told him that I had also noticed and was thinking about calling the College Entrance Examination Board. "Oh, yeah, that's a good idea. Maybe they got my results mixed up," he said. A month later, the CEEB informed me that a handwriting analysis revealed that Casey had not taken that exam. Casey explained to me that he should not have had his girlfriend, the future valedictorian of the class, sit in for him. Despite his two college acceptances, Casey enlisted in the army after graduation.

Two years later, he came into my office in uniform to show me an article in a military paper that noted his heroism. He had been wounded while holding off the Vietcong as his team scrambled into a helicopter. He had been awarded the Silver Star Medal. Later, he graduated from a college in Vermont with a degree in business.

Serving as a guidance counselor was a wonderful experience. As I page through a yearbook, I am reminded of all the good that a high school counselor can accomplish. As I look at their faces, I realize I can write an interesting book. These kids were amazing. The Class of 1966 expressed their appreciation in the dedication of their yearbook (See appendix. Notice my silver lunch pail sitting on the radiator in the background).

What if in 1968, I had decided to remain in Washingtonville as a guidance counselor? We had built a new home. Artie was building a home directly across the road. We were well-liked, and established in the community. I certainly did not need a doctorate. The quality of life would have been better for our children. But I was driven to earn more degrees and to keep climbing the ladder of achievement. In retrospect, it seems clearly related to my life experiences during the 1940s in Brooklyn.

Actually, Janet had enjoyed Washingtonville so much that ten years later, following our divorce, she applied for a teaching position there and was reappointed. She taught there until her retirement.

CHAPTER 6

Doctoral Study, Building a Home, and Columbia University

My Admission to Doctoral Study

In 1963, I applied for admission to a doctoral program at Teachers College, Columbia University, the nation's first and largest graduate school of education in the United States. I had my academic records forwarded to Columbia University from East Stroudsburg State Teachers College, Rutgers, Cornell, the University of Scranton, and Lehigh University, as well as my scores on the Graduate Record Examinations and the Miller Analogies Test. My sense was that the interview with Professor Morris had gone well. Soon I learned that a follow-up meeting was necessary.

Professor Morris told me that the committee had decided to offer me admission to their MEd program, and if I performed well, I would likely be admitted to the doctoral program. I declined, explaining that I had already completed a master's degree at Lehigh. Professor Morris puffed on his pipe and asked me to tell him about my personal background. When I finished, he asked one question, "Have you been in psychotherapy?" I told him that I had not, and he ended the meeting, telling me that he would take my application back to the committee and that I would receive the final decision directly from the Office of Doctoral Studies. To me, that sounded like he was distancing himself from the final decision.

I was on the tractor plowing the field behind our house in Salisbury Mills when Janet brought a letter out to me from Columbia University.

(See photo: Plowing for my garden)

We sat down on the back steps. The letter began with a one-word sentence, "Congratulations." That night we went out to dinner to celebrate. Years later, I learned that my personal background had influenced the committee's decision.

Building a Home

Meanwhile, I used to stop at a Black bar in Washingtonville and had gotten to know a school bus driver, Larry Peterson. I hired him to cut the trees and pull the stumps out on an expensive lot I had purchased in Mountain View Estates. Larry got a mason to pour the basement and build a block foundation. Within six months, Janet and I moved into our own new home.

I had taken out a construction loan to cover the $20,000 cost of the house. Out back, I built a screened-in patio, which overlooked a concrete pond that I had constructed. I lined the deep pond with heavy plastic and channeled all the rainwater from the roof down into a conduit underground and into the pond. Fish were able to move about beneath the ice in winter. Professor Morris and his wife, Kate, even made a surprise visit to our new home one Sunday afternoon. Chuck was always intrigued with my various adventures.

(See photo: Mark and I visited the home I built)

Getting into the Stock Market

It is interesting to note that while I was building my home, I developed an interest in the stock market. I had already explained to Janet that it didn't make sense for us to save money in a bank account because in twenty-five years, my salary would likely be ten times greater than it was. Therefore, the three hundred dollars we were saving now would be relatively insignificant in 1990. She said it was okay.

I had never spoken with anyone who had owned stocks. I would eat my lunch in the car while driving to Newburgh and then watch a group of older men looking up at a ticker tape that moved across the top wall of a room in a stockbroker's office. They would take notes and at times, go over to a broker's desk. They were not a sociable group, but one of them answered a few of my questions and said I should "follow the news in the business section of *The New York Times*."

I took that advice and found the daily fluctuations in stock prices to be very interesting. I focused on the daily list of stocks that had reached new highs and lows for the year on the previous day. Trying to figure out why some stocks had hit a low was extremely difficult back then, but I opened an account with $300. It was a baptism by fire because I lost more than I gained but learned a good deal. I stayed in the stock market for the next fifty years. For the most part, I searched for stocks that had been beaten down to new lows. I was a 'bottom fisherman'. Years later with the arrival of the internet, it became relatively easy to find abandoned treasure at the bottom, and understand why their stock prices were at a low.

[Flash forward to 2015: My new wife thought it would be wise for us to let a financial advisor do our investing. We found a reputable firm in our new community. Between April 30,

2015, and March 1, 2016, our account went down $275, 472! I'm now back in the market and am recovering our losses.]

(See photo: I'm back with my Wall Street Bull in a bull market!)

[Flash Forward: Years later, I took my granddaughter, Sarah, to the financial district in New York City. I had to show her this piece of guerrilla art because he and I both came from Greenpoint, Brooklyn. I learned this tidbit when my friend in Israel, Chaim, asked me for a favor. He wanted me to go to his storage unit, remove a particular bronze, bring it to Crosby Street in lower Manhattan, ask Arturo to please buy it back, and wire Chaim the money. As I came in from the street carrying one of his sculptures, Arturo asked me lots of questions, including where I was from. When I said Greenpoint, he said that was where my bull was from. The foundry that cast his Wall Street Bull was in Greenpoint.]

Commuting to Columbia University

It was a 120-mile round-trip drive from Washingtonville to Columbia University. I formed a car pool with three other people from Washingtonville who were working on their doctoral degrees. I sat in the front seat of Charlie Weiland's (our director of elementary education who became a lifelong buddy) car. Frank, our school psychologist, and Don, our assistant principal, were seated behind us. It was winter, and we had a tough drive on Route 9W.

Later, I learned that Frank had already been washed out of his doctoral program. Once, on the sixty-mile ride back to Washingtonville, Charlie said, "Hey Frank, what did you learn in class tonight?" It was a cruel question because we knew Frank had just driven down with us and then sat in the library for a few hours. Later I learned that it is not uncommon for doctoral students to reach the point of writing their dissertation, and either not complete it, or fail the oral defense of their dissertation defense. These individuals are referred to as ABD's (All But Dissertation).

After this, I learned of others who had post-traumatic doctoral syndrome. One unfortunate guy would pace back and forth in front of his former department with his head down, mumbling to himself. I asked Professor Morris if he knew anything about him. He told me that he had been a doctoral student in that department, but had washed out in his final year. I remember thinking, *Why the hell doesn't someone offer some assistance to the guy?*

Dr. Westervelt: Warrior Professor

Professor Morris was my advisor. At times, he gave advice that I would have preferred not to receive. For example, he told me to register for a course in statistics. I resisted, reminding him that I had already completed a graduate statistics course and had received an A and that Lehigh had primarily been an engineering institution. "Yes, that's fine, but you need Columbia's statistical inference course," he said. I took it and received an A+ (Professor Morris said that he had never seen an A+ in this course, which was taught by Professor Lindeman). Having had an undergraduate major in mathematics and a Lehigh statistics' course gave me an advantage over my classmates. It was the most difficult course that I ever took. And Professor Morris was right. My Lehigh course never went much beyond chi-square, and Columbia's course included statistical modeling and probability which prepared me well to analyze sophisticated empirical research (See Appendix: Statistical Inference).

To offset my tuition fees, I became a teaching assistant. Professor Morris suggested that I meet with Professor Westervelt, who was looking for an assistant. Word among doctoral students was that 'assisting' was one way departments could assess one's doctoral potential. It was one of the several hurdles.

I agreed to be Professor Esther Westervelt's assistant. Her students feared her. She had been a pilot and a member of the Women's Airforce Service Pilots of World War II. I learned she had an influential friend in Washingtonville who was active in civic affairs and knew who I was. I had been her grandson's guidance counselor. That was fine by me because I knew that my counseling skills were exceptional.

I sat to the right of Dr. Westervelt in front of the class of doctoral students. During one class, a student boasted that he had been named man of the year in a publication that he held in his hand. Professor Westervelt cut him off, stating, "You should take your materials and leave. You don't have what it takes to earn a doctorate here." He gathered his papers, walked out, and never returned.

At the completion of my academic year assignment, I thanked Professor Westervelt for giving me the opportunity to work with her. In her response, she mentioned that when she had been considering which doctoral student might work well with her, she had remembered that her friend in Washingtonville had said that I worked in a lumberyard on Saturdays, and that had struck her as being different.

Later, I took a required course, which was only taught by Professor Westervelt. Our major assignment was to identify a psychological construct (a phenomenon not yet supported by empirical research), read everything that had ever been published about it, and then write a report that could not exceed two typewritten pages. I selected empathy and dutifully read everything I could get my hands on. I even had to pay someone to translate an article that had been published in a German journal.

My first draft was fifty handwritten pages in length. It was a real challenge to reduce it to two typed pages. Professor Westervelt gave me an A on my paper. Her written comment suggested that it was worthy of publication. The article was published in the 1968 *Journal of the New York School Counselor Association*.

Shortly thereafter, Professor Westervelt was diagnosed with brain cancer. Professor Morris asked me to drive with him to visit her at Goshen Hospital. It was a difficult visit. She forced a smile and thanked us. She passed away the following month. She was no ordinary woman.

Psychological Consultation Center and Professor Roger Myers

The following year, I was offered a part-time position as an associate in the renowned Teachers College Psychological Consultation Center. I have no idea how this came about, but I learned a great deal. I enjoyed free tuition and a small stipend. More importantly was what I learned working with Roger Myers, Hank Kavkewitz, Jean Jordaan, Robert L. Thorndike, and others. We met periodically to discuss an active case. The depth of the analyses and the perspectives from their specialized expertise and experience was enriching.

I was asked to present a case. I was counseling a Catholic priest, at the time, who had been born in Ireland and had been sent to Italy for preparatory religious training at the age of thirteen. Father Mac, who was a few years older than I, was seeing a lady friend, and was torn between this relationship and his calling. Over a period of months, I had developed a healthy rapport with him.

It should be noted that, at this time, I had come under the influence of Albert Ellis, a Teachers College, Columbia University graduate. Albert Ellis had launched a new branch of psychotherapy: rational emotive psychotherapy. This behavioral approach was not embraced at Columbia.

Father Mac's defenses had been penetrated. The tape I played for my colleagues showed the priest rising to his feet, ripping his clerical collar from his neck, throwing it to the floor, and stomping on it. I had risen and embraced him, saying, "Your demon is gone. You'll feel better now."

Roger Myers was the first to speak. He asked, "Is he suicidal?"….. "No."…… "Are you in contact with him now? Tell us about the depth of your relationship with Father Mac."

"We were together in the moment. There was unconditional acceptance and near perfect empathy." On the way out, Roger whispered, "Nice work, but you took a hell of a risk."

[Flash forward to 1980: Father Mac left the priesthood, married, had two children, and held an important position in Connecticut working in educational program development. And in 2011, as the president of a small catholic college, Father Mac facilitated the late admission of my stepdaughter!]

Professor Blackman and I had developed good working relationship. Our thinking on social issues was usually aligned. However, once in private conversation, I asked Professor Blackman his view regarding the recently released Moynihan Report. he replied that he believed that Professor Moynihan was intellectually dishonest. I kept my thoughts private. In fact, I was in complete agreement with Moynihan that the 'matriarchal structure' of the Negro family and the increase in 'welfare dependency', together, were significantly related to the plight of disadvantaged youth. My beliefs, in this regard, have not changed.

Blacks, Puerto Ricans, Chicanos, and Native Americans

The chairman of my department, a gifted Black professor, Rudy Blackman, briefed me on a Ford Foundation/CEEB project that he was in charge of. I had noticed that Dr. Blackman had arranged for the external project monitor, Sam Catchman, to teach a Saturday morning course in our department as a guest lecturer. It struck me as a curious appointment and suggested that the project might be in trouble. The two individuals running the project had accepted out-of-state positions.

Chairman Blackman gave me the keys to a storefront on Amsterdam Avenue and asked me to assess the status of the project. I was shocked at the lack of progress. The project had been generously funded by the Ford Foundation and the College Entrance Examination Board. I reported my findings to Professor Blackman, stating that there was no usable work product. The project would need to begin anew. He asked if I could take over the project. I would have two office workers and part of the remaining $12,000 from the funded grant. It would be a challenge, but I agreed.

Having recently read about an upcoming meeting to be held at Antioch College of individuals who represented Blacks, Puerto Ricans, Chicanos, and Native Americans, I flew to Ohio. The first day, I embarrassed myself by referring to one group as American Indians. I was corrected. "We are Native Americans."

I spoke to David Hillfeather at the end of the session. He introduced me to the leaders of each minority group. Offie White mentioned that his office had extensive files on most of the college programs for disadvantaged students. That evening I explained to Offie the reason I had invited myself to their meeting. I made a deal with Offie: He would give me access to his files, and I would recognize him for his contribution in my report's introduction. By the third day, this group became the founding members of the National Association for Minority Education (NAME). Hillfeather agreed to send me his copies of documents on Native Americans that he had accumulated on his Oklahoma campus. The following week, I drove to Trenton and met with Offie. He did have a treasure trove of documents, journal articles, and reports on each of the minority groups.

Back at Columbia, I prepared a two-page survey, which was mailed to every college that had a special program for minority students. My office workers summarized the results as I compiled a draft project report from all the information that I had acquired. It took me approximately two months. Several nights, I slept on a couch in Dr. Blackman's office.

Professor Blackman assembled a group of seven individuals to review the draft. We met at the Barbizon Plaza Hotel on Central Park South. The group offered critical observations, but recommended that the revised draft be published for widespread circulation. The 575-page project report was completed, including an introduction acknowledging the contributions of each minority leader who had entrusted their materials to me.

(See Appendix: Study of Collegiate Compensatory Programs for Disadvantaged Youth)

Doctoral Residency at Columbia

We sold our new home in Washingtonville and used the $12,000 profit to finance my residency at Columbia. In1968, doctoral students were required to sign a statement agreeing that we would not be employed full or part-time during our one-year residency. We were expected to be on campus every weekday, and each of us was assigned to a doctoral cubical.

For my doctoral dissertation, I conducted an empirical study analyzing the behaviors of Black college students under various degrees of stress. My self-developed data-collection instrument (Powerlessness Scale) was administered to minority students at Essex Community College in Newark, New Jersey. The instrument was validated as a reliable measuring device. The actual study was conducted using Black students enrolled in the Urban University Program at Rutgers University.

I would be remiss to not acknowledge the assistance provided by Chairman Blackman. My research necessitated the administration of a 'sensitive instrument' (Powerlessness) to group of Black students enrolled in special programs for disadvantaged youth, and subsequently subject these students to conditions of stress. As a young white doctoral student, I would never have been given access to these subjects. Professor Blackman introduced me to the key administrators at both Essex Community College and Rutgers University.

One month after the instrument was administered, the students were subjected to real-life stress conditions of varying degrees of frustration. I was given access to the students' academic records as well as any disciplinary reports. All data was entered into a computer at Columbia. The results indicated that all four of my hypotheses were rejected. In a state of disbelief, I hired a statistics professor, Dr. Rockwar, from City College to conduct an independent analysis of my data. The results were the same. I was stymied. Even after a couple of months had passed, I had visions of myself pacing the halls mumbling about my results.

Roger Myers and I had developed a good relationship at the Psychological Consultation Center. We often played handball on the courts that were in the basement. One day I met Roger in the cafeteria, and he asked me how my dissertation was going. I was embarrassed, but told him about my results. He urged me to have a sit-down with Chuck.

I made an appointment with Professor Morris and told him about my disappointing results. He asked if he could take my dissertation home and look over my data. A week later, he called me into his office. He explained that by virtue of 'unintended consequences', my data showed significant results. In short, my results had answered important questions that my study had not hypothesized. It made sense, but could I defend it in my oral examination? Puffing on his pipe, he said, "It happens occasionally, but be prepared to explain why you did not ask those two important questions."

As I entered the oral examination, Professor Winthrop Adkins whispered to me, "Dave, just remember that you know more about locus of control than anyone in the country." Though I appreciated his words of encouragement, I knew that Julian Rotter was the nationally recognized authority on locus-of-control. The examination lasted an hour, and then I was asked to step outside. Finally, the door opened, and the chairman called me inside, and read the outcome. I had received the highest possible score!

Two weeks later, I received a letter from the Office of Doctoral Studies. It was addressed to Dr. David P. Garrahan. The opening sentence was one word, "Congratulations," and informed me that my degree would be conferred in May. However, I could begin using my doctoral title prior to graduation.

It had taken nine years (1963-1972). My children were now three, four, and five years of age. My dissertation research was published in a national peer-reviewed journal.

(See photos: Mark likes pasta; Dad builds a playhouse and readies the bath water; Susan shows some leg; Later, Mark plays with a python!)

What if in 1963, I had applied for admission to the doctoral program at Rutgers University where I had already completed eight graduate credits? It would have been significantly less rigorous than Columbia University, which arguably was the most competitive graduate school in the nation. The cost would have been one-fifth of Columbia's. It would have been a much easier commute. Again, my only explanation was that I was driven to eradicate the psychological damage of having been retained in grade one.

It should be noted that holding a doctorate from Columbia University did open doors for me. I had instant credibility with government agency officials, as well as with prospective employers.

Social/Political Activism

I became active in politics in the mid-1960s when Seth's parents introduced me to Phyllis and Sears Hunter—Washingtonville residents. At the time, Sears was the Democratic party chairman of Orange County. He had introduced me to Robert Kennedy at a fund-raiser in Goshen.

Later, I urged Congressman Helstoski to move forward with the Nixon impeachment initiative in the House of Representatives. Years later, I would develop a relationship with Bob Dole, and he would nominate me for a position on the RNC's advisory board. While following the Dole-Kemp campaign for the presidency, I learned that as a result of his WW II injuries, Senator Dole used a buttonhook to button his shirt. I had the perfect buttonhook for the senator. A man, whose son had been killed in action, had welded the shank of a buttonhook onto a WWII brass cartridge as the handle. Then he had fastened one of his son's medals to the handle very artistically. Senator Dole expressed his appreciation for the perfect buttonhook in a letter to me (See Appendix: Correspondence with Helstoski, Kennedy, Dole, and Governor Corzine advising me at a birthday party).

I have always had a natural inclination to side with the socially disadvantaged. Beginning in 1962, I addressed the needs of forgotten students at Rutgers, got involved with the neglected aged population, became active as a Title IX consultant, and supported maids employed by Columbia University. The latter involvement could have cost me my degree because it erupted just weeks before my oral examination. I wrote a letter of support on behalf of the maids who were on strike at Columbia.

My involvement had begun when I refused to cross the maids' picket line. Holding court at the famous West End Bar where liberal professors and students met, Professor Morris sent word to me, saying, "I better get myself into the building," with was an implied, 'or else'. Without crossing the picket lines, I went to my office and dictated a strongly worded letter to departmental secretary, Elinor King, and mailed it to President McGill.

Elinor must have mentioned it to Professor Morris because he stepped into my office and asked me if it was true. I handed him my carbon copy (which did not survive the fracas). Reading it, he became as agitated as I've ever seen him. I paraphrase him here: "Do you understand that President McGill has responsibility for all of Columbia, the colleges of journalism, business, medical/dental, engineering, and law? Do you think he has time to address your concern about the treatment of maids?"

In retrospect, I should not have written the letter. President Lincoln had a practice of putting his letters, written with emotion, into his desk drawer. Most were not mailed after he read them the following day (See Appendix for President McGill's reply).

Dr. Garrahan/Professor Garrahan

Professor Morris asked me what my plans were. I had not given it much thought but was confident I had good options. He said, "Professor Blackman wants to keep you at Columbia." (Rudy Blackman was the chairman of the department of applied psychology). He did not offer any specific reason.

Soon thereafter, Dr. Blackman invited me to lunch. "The college is prepared to offer you a full-time, tenure-tracked, professorial position in the department of applied psychology." This possibility had never entered my mind. "Dave, you have had life experiences that no professor here has had. You can leverage your disadvantaged life experiences to address critical issues in society. You can create a new course based on your personal history."

Expressing my appreciation, I told him that Janet was looking forward to having a home for our children that was outside of the city, but that I would discuss it with her. Janet liked the idea, saying, "We can find a nice home over in New Jersey." For the most part, I believe that she liked the idea of her husband being a member of the graduate school faculty at Columbia.

I gave it a lot of thought. I knew I was not one of them and had never belonged there—not as a student and certainly not as a professor. Chairman Blackman had designed numerous programs for disadvantaged youth. He was bringing in disproportionate amounts of money to Columbia through grants from government agencies and various foundations. He had once mentioned to me that as a child in North Carolina, his family had been permitted to shop in white stores because of his father's prominence in the community as a Black physician. Professor Blackman had no personal experience with poverty. I knew why he wanted to keep me at Columbia. With serious reservations, I accepted the appointment to the graduate faculty of Columbia University. Now I was in the major league of academia. Janet and I bought an old home on a large lot in Demarest, New Jersey. (See photo: 37 Brookside Ave with Fieldstone Wall)

Inside My Alma Mater

Chairman Blackman followed up on his commitment and had me create my own course. I developed and taught Educational and Vocational Implications of Ethnic and Social Status Differences. (See Appendix: TG4111)

The following spring, Dr. Blackman received a federal grant to offer a summer program for directors of inner-city poverty programs from across the country. In May, he asked me to design a program for them. In length, it needed to be two hours a day for six weeks, which would be my summer teaching assignment. This was a tall order on such short notice, but I knew my role at Columbia as the 'white nigger' on the faculty, as Roger Myers had told me.

I correctly assumed my students would be minority group members. They were older than I and, were from Detroit, Newark, and Los Angeles, and had expectations for the summer—some with an attitude.

I used my TG4111 course outline to design their program. The topic for the first week was understanding poverty: the thoughts, feelings, and behaviors of the impoverished, spiked with empathy. Week three was empowering the powerless from a locus of control perspective. One hour, each day, was devoted to best practices and program development, where they learned from each other. Wednesday nights, they could join me at the Cotton Club in Harlem, the storied West End Bar on Broadway at West 114th Street, or Paddy Murphy's.

[Flash forward to 2016: Two weeks after I sent my daughter, Susan, a copy of *Transition America*, in which I addressed poverty, foreign aid, and dependency relationships[4], I received three new books on poverty from her. I checked the authors' poverty credentials, skimmed their contents, and donated them to the Kingsport Library.]

At the end of my first semester, I asked Professor Morris for some feedback. His sage advice began with, "Encouraging students to address you as Dave suggests an inappropriate familiarity. The faculty and staff call me Chuck, but I've never been called Chuck by a student. Professor connotes more authority, wisdom, and experience than doctor." Upon meeting with a new class, I would write on the board, "Professor Garrahan," although I was not yet comfortable with the title.

Then he suggested that I was lacking in gravitas and said, "But that will come in time. You are the youngest member on the faculty." Desiring to speed up the process, I cultivated a beard and began puffing on a pipe. However, after receiving some unsolicited feedback and becoming the butt of too many jokes, I shaved. For my daughter's birthday, I put on a one-person magic show at her party. With all of her friends gathered on the back terrace of our home in Demarest. I told them that I could disappear for two minutes and come back as a different person. Stepping inside the garage where I had set up my razor, I quickly shaved my beard off, put on a clown hat and glasses, and opened the door. Abracadabra, I was a different person.

When my colleagues began ribbing me about my 'identity crisis', I explained how I had saved a hundred dollars by not hiring a birthday clown. I had to dump my pipe and return to cigarettes.

Students Dropped by Their Sponsor

During my second semester, I sponsored the first of fourteen doctoral dissertations, which were all successfully defended at oral examinations. A few were challenging (see Appendix). Infrequently, a professor would discontinue sponsoring a student's dissertation. That presented a huge challenge for the candidate, as well as the professor who accepted the student at that late stage. In retrospect, I suspect that Professor Morris thought this would be a good way for me 'to cut my teeth'.

Chuck stepped into my office and said, "I can't work with Joyce any longer. It's too frustrating." Joyce was a middle-aged Black woman, I asked, "Where's Rudy on this?" …. "He couldn't deal with her, and pushed her off on me."

I asked Chuck how she got into our doctoral program. He explained that several years ago, Blackman had accepted her on the basis of a telephone interview. I thought, *What the hell was he thinking? I'm the one with the reckless reputation.*

"Dave, if you take her on, you'll have to carry her on your back. If she passes the oral, hopefully, she'll get some kind of

Christian education position in Texas and never mention that her degree came from Columbia."

Given the circumstances under which Joyce had been accepted, Teachers College had some responsibility for her progress. I met with Joyce, telling her, "If I take you on, you will have to do everything I tell you to do. There will be no discussion." Within a year, Dr. Joyce went back to Texas.

Chuck used the same line later when he said, "If you take Sam, you'll have to carry him over the finish line." Sam actually got down on his knees in my office and pleaded with me, explaining the difficulties he and his family would face if he returned to his country without his doctoral degree. His government had funded his six years of study at Columbia. Nigeria was even more violent and corrupt in the 1970s than it is today. He was actually a much stronger student than Joyce. Sam returned to Nigeria with his doctorate.

[Flash forward to 1998: Sam mailed me copies of five articles that he authored, which were published in education journals in Nigeria.]

Calvin, a Black doctoral student in his last year, was not dropped by his sponsor…but he was dropping his advisor! Cal had based his dissertation on my 'locus of control' research. I was his dissertation sponsor; Professor Morris was his advisor. One evening, he and Chuck got into a nasty exchange. While I could hear their angry voices, I didn't know what the issue was.

Cal bolted into my office, and slammed the door shut. "That man is a f…. racist…. I'm finished with him…from now on you're my advisor." Placing my hand on his shoulder, I asked him to sit down and calm down. "Cal, I don't need to know what just happened, but Professor Morris is not a racist….. doctoral students don't fire their advisors….you're finishing your dissertation, and I'll be at your side at the oral exam, but

I will not be your advisor." I told him to go home and discuss this with his wife. And that they had both made many sacrifices to reach this point, and he owed it to himself and his family to 'bite the bullet' and finish his doctorate. He did, and expressed his appreciation in a copy of his dissertation that he gave me. (See Appendix for Cal's dissertation)

During my first year on the faculty, I completed two relatively small consulting contracts for the Leonia and the Hackensack school districts in New Jersey. In 1973, Chuck was a 'finalist' in pursuit of a large contract to evaluate a federal program in the Norwalk, Ct. public schools. I was a member of Chuck's team. The final step in the selection procedure was a meeting with the Norwalk school administrators. During the meeting, an administrator asked us, "Will you be using tests of statistical inference in your analyses, and if so, what tests will you use?" Chuck turned to me and asked, "Dave, will you take this question?" I replied that we would use inferential statistics if the preliminary data indicates that necessity. And that the statistical tests used would depend on both the preliminary data, and the research questions being addressed, and therefore the specific tests used was unknowable at this point. As we drove out of Norwalk, Chuck said: "I like the way you handled that smartass." I think I thanked Chuck for forcing me to take Columbia's statistics. Chuck was awarded the contract. And it did become necessary for us to use inferential statistics.

Sexual Orientation at My Alma Mater in the 1970s

When I was moving into the office across from Chuck's, I asked him whatever happened to Professor Klimp, who had had the office before me when I had been interviewed for admission in 1963. Chuck responded that he had probably sensed that he would not receive tenure because colleagues had suspected that he had likely been a homosexual. I was surprised to hear this about Columbia University. Professor Klimp subsequently became the provost and dean of faculty at the Bank Street College of Education.

Several years later, Chuck cautioned me, "You're not helping your Columbia career by working with students like Maurice." I had invited Maurice to my home to meet my wife and children.

He and I had gone out for a drink at a bar in River Edge. Sitting at the bar, he said, "Dave, there's something I need to tell you. I'm a homosexual." I was really surprised. He was a Robert Redford look-alike, who had been raised on a large farm in the Midwest. "I had to leave. My parents don't know. My brothers don't know." I thanked him for sharing, but cautioned him to be careful on campus.

One weekend he took me out to Fire Island. I knew of the island's reputation. We had a great time darting around the island in water taxis. Maury knew where all the interesting parties were—lots of drugs, alcohol, and interesting dancing.

As I prepared to leave Columbia and join the faculty at the University Maryland, I took great care in finding a colleague who would take Maurice through his oral exam. Professor Manis, who held a doctorate from Harvard, and was a sensitive, religious, family man, agreed to work with Maurice.

[Flash forward to 1990: I received a phone call from Elinor King, the department secretary, asking me whether I would consider opening an incomplete grade that I had given a student. I said, "Sure." Then I took the opportunity to ask about Maurice.

"He didn't make it," she said. Damn. One's sexual orientation is a deeply personal matter. A doctoral student must clear numerous hurdles. Sexual orientation should not be one of them, not then and not ever.]

Subsequently, I began serving as an oral examiner at college-wide exams. I gained a reputation for my skill in analyzing research design and statistical methods. Apparently, I was too severe in my examination of one candidate.

The morning following that oral examination, Chuck stepped into my office to tell me that Professor Oldclass was upset because I had blindsided him with my critique of one of his students during an oral exam. The candidate had never established the validity and reliability of his instrument. I told the candidate that it made no sense to discuss his results, because of that critical defect. Of course, I was right. Professor Oldclass obviously had not read his candidate's research very carefully.

Moreover, Oldclass should have made a more studied judgment of my posture as an oral examiner, since I had previously fired a shot across his bow. In that case, the student he was sponsoring had used an analysis of covariance model, which I knew to be an inappropriate statistic for his study and would cause misleading results. It was clear that I was not one to turn a blind eye, regardless of the candidate's sponsor's status.

Too Much Partying

Over the next five years, I made presentations at professional conventions in Detroit, Miami, San Diego, Boston, and Chicago. The one in Chicago was unforgettable. I always tried to have my presentations scheduled for the beginning of a convention so that I could then relax and enjoy my surroundings. In this case, I did make my presentation the first afternoon. Then I took the subway to an antique store where the owner had glass buttonhooks. I found the place and bought all three, but then got off at the wrong subway station.

As soon as I exited the station, I realized that it was not the right neighborhood. There was a bar at the top of the exit. I went in for a drink and directions. It was a Black bar. I took a seat and put money on the bar. The bartender saw me but ignored me. I said to the guy on my right, "What do I have to do to get a drink?" "Go somewhere else," was his response. The guy on my left, however, called the bartender down, and I was served. I also got directions to the Palmer Hotel where I knew that a party was going on. I found it and got involved, forgetting that we were interviewing an applicant for a psychology department position the following morning. When I woke up on the floor and looked around, there were six or seven Black people in the room. I asked the woman who was closest to me, "What time is it?"

She said, "My watch is in the top drawer." When I opened the drawer, the watch was on the wrist of a black artificial arm. The face of the watch was not visible, so I had to turn the arm over. I was late for the 10 a.m. interview. I got out of the room quickly and ran through the revolving door to the sidewalk. I ran to Teachers College's suite in our hotel, which was nearby. I paused at the door, gathering my wits and composing myself.

Roger Myers opened the door and looked at me with his small, dark, piercing eyes. "The interview is over. The candidate left ten minutes ago," he said. I nodded my head and walked inside and up to a window without even looking around the room. I just peered out, as thoughts raced through my mind. Then my colleagues exploded with laughter. Yes, I was thirty minutes late. However, the applicant had missed his flight in St. Louis. We didn't interview him until four o'clock. The way in which Roger greeted me at the door had been perfect. Man, he got me good!

Roger had a great sense of humor that most people were not aware of. One day, he, Jean Jordaan, and I were gathering for lunch. Jean asked, "Where's Win?" (Professor Winthrop Adkins) Roger answered, "He's working on his Dick and Jane series," referring to Adkins' Life Coping Skills model, which involved a series of questions designed for unemployed subjects. The fact that Roger cracked an inside joke of that nature in my presence suggested that he considered me a trusted colleague. Still later, Roger and I were showering up after some handball, and he shared with me that at times, professors had referred to me as the college's 'white nigger'. Of course, I understood and chuckled.

There was a special room which was named for a benefactor of the College. It had mahogany walls, a large carved table, and a special carpet. I held an end of course, gathering for an exceptional group of ten doctoral seminar students. The following morning Chuck steps into my office. "Did you have a party last night in the Watson Room?" I said yes. "Did anyone spill wine on the carpet?" I said that it was a small gathering, and I didn't notice anything unusual. Chuck: "Well Professor Stanton did." Within minutes, Professor Irish came in. "Relax, I'm Professor Stanton." While I was relieved, I did not appreciate the humor.

Teachers College had been involved in educational development in Afghanistan between 1954 and 1978, publishing textbooks for school children and other activities. Teachers College also ran programs in Africa, Asia, and Latin America. It was widely believed that the Afghan Project was also a base for national intelligence personnel. We also knew it as an assignment for faculty who had drinking problems or sexual relationship issues. It was common on college campuses for female students to take advantage of professors. The Me

Too movement has recently exposed numerous situations on campuses across the country.

During my tenure, four of my colleagues accepted assignments in Afghanistan. They had little choice in the matter. They had to accept the assignment or resign their position. One professor in my department refused to accept being assigned to the Afghan Project. He resigned his tenured position at Columbia and joined the faculty of a Florida university.

Roger had cautioned me, "Keep it up, and you'll wake up in Afghanistan." This comment had come after a meal with my colleagues at the West End Bar. We had stayed too long. While crossing Broadway, Andy stumbled into a parked car, cutting his forehead. Jean and Chuck grabbed him under a shoulder and walked him back onto campus.

As we were entering Horace Mann Hall, President Creman was exiting. He opened the door to leave, and there we were. He just stood there and stared at us in disbelief. Jack Foley and I had tried to hide behind Chuck, Andy, and Jean. President Creman said, "Charles, I'll speak with you in my office in the morning."

The following morning, Chuck stepped into my office. "How did it go?" I asked. He said, "I've got to get Andy into a program or he's going to Afghanistan." The next year, Andy was posted to the Afghan Project. I talked with him once after he returned. Afghanistan was a tough place to live if one was a drinker. Teachers College reported Andy's death in a newsletter and quoted his wife: "He died from liver cancer."

Jack Foley didn't fit in with the Columbia faculty. The first time I met Professor Foley, he was in his room in the women's dormitory. I knocked on the door, and his voice invited me in. Jack was overweight and reminded me of Santa Claus with his full head of white hair and his long beard. He had a remote in his hand and elevated his mattress to a sitting position. We hit it off. He said, "My wife threw me out, so I'm staying here temporarily."

One night, I joined him and his doctoral student Ryan down at Paddy Murphy's, which was an Irish pub located a block south of St. John the Divine Cathedral on Amsterdam Avenue. After a few drinks at the bar, Ryan was coaxed into doing some kind of old Irish skit called "The Face on the Barroom Floor." He obliged.

The bartender collected a dollar from each person sitting at the bar. Then he opened a bottle of Irish whiskey and handed it to Ryan with a glass. Ryan took a drink standing in the middle of the floor and began reciting some Irish lyrics. Every two or three sentences, he would pour himself another drink. Soon he was leaning against the wall, reciting his lyrics with more gusto. Eventually, Ryan poured himself his last drink from the bottle and fell facedown on the floor.

It was my intent to turn him over, but Jack stopped me. He'll be all right. I could not understand why anyone would do this to his body. Months later, Tommy Irish and I walked down to Paddy's, and Ryan was against the wall finishing his lyrics.

[Flash Forward to 2017: In 2017, my wife and I visited Columbia University, enjoyed lunch at the West End Bar, and drove over to Paddy Murphy's to have a drink. Unfortunately, our pub is now a Hispanic bodega.]

Riding with and for Chairman Blackman

Professor Blackman would often ask me to accompany him on professional trips. When going to Rutgers to deliver a speech to a large group, Blackman drove. As he drove, he dictated his speech, and I took notes. He then asked me to prepare a bullet-point outline. I sat with the audience as he delivered a well-received speech.

On another trip, we both drove to Providence, Rhode Island. Professor Blackman was a consultant of some sort for Sesame Street and PBS. It was a long ride with lots of time and questions. "Did you read Professor M's book?" he asked. "Yeah, *Counseling and the Self Concept*," I replied. "Give me a synopsis," he said. "You'd have to look at the bibliography" I replied. "Why do you say that, Dave? My response was, "I don't recall any original thinking." Blackman continued to press on, saying, "I see. Any thoughts on his commitment to disadvantaged people?" "Skin thin," was my curt reply.

Chairman Blackman valued my perception as well as my directness. Professor M had his eye on the position of deputy department chairman, however, his contract at Columbia was not renewed. In 1974, I was appointed deputy chairman of the department of applied psychology.

On my last trip, Chairman Blackman asked me "to go in his place" to a memorial service in Great Barrington, Massachusetts, for Shirley Graham Du Bois (wife of W. E. B. Du Bois, who had predeceased her in Ghana). Shirley had passed away in China.

I got into the car with three Black men whom I had never met, and we drove to Great Barrington. It was an uncomfortable ride. Apparently, Blackman did not tell them anything about me, and I had no interest in revealing my background to strangers. There was no GPS, and we got lost. There was some yelling.

We knew it would be awkward if we arrived late, but we just made it in the gate. Heads turned to see who the almost latecomers were. I was one of three white people at the Mahaiwe Cemetery. At one point, I found myself looking up at two linemen at the top of a telephone pole doing some work on the wires. The guy next to me, leaned over and said, "If you don't have an FBI file, you'll have one next week."

The ride back to New York City was more comfortable. The men were certain that the guys atop the pole had a camera on us. We talked about that. I revealed that I was one of the founding members of NAME. Interestingly, two of the guys knew about the organization. By this point, they must have been curious about who I was: Du Bois memorial, NAME, young white guy? I considered sharing that I was Columbia's white nigger. However, I chose to not disclose.

While I knew nothing about Shirley Du Bois, I had read a lot about her husband, W. E. B. Du Bois and joined in the conversation with my car mates. He had been the first Black person to receive a doctorate from Harvard University. He had been a member of the Communist party, as well as a serious social activist. He had also been a scholar, writer, professor, and historian.

I served Chairman Blackman well on that trip, and yes, I assume that I have an FBI file. Several folks at the Palmer Hotel struck me as being more than serious Black activists. The NAME group certainly would have been fertile ground for surveillance.

Chuck's Gone

One day, Chuck stepped into my office and closed the door behind him. He had never done that before. I figured I must be in real trouble this time. He sat down and said, "Dave, I think I'm dying." He talked a little about his symptoms. Over the previous month or so, I had noticed that he hadn't finished his bagged lunch. Once, I had seen Chuck sitting on a Broadway curb while on his way to the bus station. He had not seen a doctor, nor had he told his wife, Kate.

I urged him to phone Columbia Presbyterian Hospital to schedule a diagnostic evaluation and talk to Kate that night. I visited him in the hospital and found out that it had been too late. He died in a couple of months. His body wouldn't process protein. Subsequently, his wife shared with me that I was the only person outside of the family whom he had allowed to visit him.

I had met most of his nine children. Mary had taken a class with me. Years earlier when I was a guidance counselor visiting colleges, Chuck had said, "Look in on my son John," who was a student at Parsons College in Iowa.

Chuck had interviewed me for admission to Columbia in 1963. He had driven up with Kate to see the home I had built in Washingtonville, had resolved my dissertation data problem, had mentored me as a neophyte professor, and hadn't seemed to mind the roaches on the couch where he and my mother had been sitting (she with a can of beer in her hand and cigarette in her mouth). I wonder if he ever told Roger about that visit. Chuck had ribbed me when I had become his boss as deputy Chairman of the department. He had steered me clear of trouble more than once. He had suggested the importance of some grandiosity and gravitas in my budding career in academia. He had been a good guy—a regular guy. I missed him. It would never be the same for me at Columbia.

Making Some Extra Money and Having Lots of Fun

During my tenure at Columbia, I was appointed to the adjunct faculty of the Union Graduate School (UGS) at Antioch College in Ohio. No one at Columbia was aware of my dual role—not even Chuck. Unlike Columbia, I had some colorful students in the (UGS) doctoral program.

My first student was Sy Weissman. I had interviewed him for admission to Columbia and concluded he would not gain admission. However, because he had twenty years of significant administrative achievement, I suggested UGS as a viable option. I sponsored his dissertation and held him to Columbia's standards. He received his PhD.

Other individuals I mentored through their doctoral degrees included Steve Aiello, who later served in the White House as special assistant to President Jimmy Carter on ethnic and urban affairs, and Harvey Darner, who became chancellor of the New York City school system. These were major league players. Luigi Maybe was not.

The colorful Luigi Maybe had immigrated to the US as a teenager and had spoken no English. I got to meet most of his family. He had several brothers and two sisters. My sense was that he was 'connected'. Whenever he visited my home in Demarest, he would give each of my young children a ten dollar bill. Once, he foolishly walked into my office at Columbia and handed me two sets of round-trip tickets to Fort Lauderdale. He said, "Go and take one of your friends. Relax and enjoy staying at my motel on the beach."

It was January. Professor Foley and I did indeed enjoy ourselves. Jack, while sitting on the top deck of the Paddle Queen, instructed our waitress, "Two Cutty Sarks on the rocks for me, and be sure I never have two empty glasses." That night it took three of us to carry Jack into our room. I sensed that Luigi's two sisters, who managed the motel, were not pleased with us.

When the time came for Luigi's oral defense, I knew his committee members. They were heavyweights: Colin Deer of

Brooklyn College, CUNY, and a retired Harvard professor. In my opening toast, I mentioned that I had been intrigued with how Luigi had gotten the bit part of cleaning up tables at the wedding party in the original Godfather. Luigi spoke to the roomful of guests attending his Ph.D. celebration at Mama Leone's in Manhattan.

Luigi did go on to become a successful entrepreneur. He established the Fordham Beauty School and the International School of Foreign Languages. He is probably best known for his *Italian Hour* radio program, which was broadcast from White Plains every Saturday. I Googled him recently, and was not entirely surprised to learn that he and an M.D. in Vermont are involved in the health-supplement industry.

My next venture started at Columbia. Chuck had stepped into my office holding a letter in his hand. "Professor, I could use a favor. The National Association of Trade and Technical Schools [NATTS], requests that a member of the graduate faculty serve on an accreditation committee to evaluate the Delehanty Institute off Union Square," he said. I could see why Chuck had passed it to me.

The two-day visit was boring, but I did like Delehanty's president, Tom Souran, and his Ukrainian secretary, Vera. When it came time for the committee to write the final evaluative report, I got the clear sense that this NATTS group was biased against Delehanty. I refused to be a signatory to the report. They reluctantly appended my minority report. When Tom received the results and cover letter stating that NATTS's accreditation was not being renewed, he invited me to lunch, telling me he appreciated my minority report.

I had learned that Delehanty was bringing in a lot of money. Somehow, Tom had acquired copies of the NYPD's promotion exams. Any cop who was eligible for a promotion to sergeant or captain was required to pass an exam. Delehanty was the place to go for the three-night class preparation. Tom Souran was a good friend of Sanford Garelik who was the first Jewish Chief Inspector in the N.Y.P.D.

I told Tom that it was not likely they would be reaccredited by NATTS. He put me on a $600 a month retainer to fix the problem. I had to learn a lot about the accreditation of proprietary trade and technical schools. I learned that NATTS was not the only option for Delehanty. I found an accrediting agency in Illinois that agreed to conduct a preliminary assessment.

I had Big John, the admissions director, clean up the recruitment procedures. I convinced Tom that there was no future in the school's radio-repair program, which was very weak. He arranged to transfer the few students to a tech school in Brooklyn, and eliminated the program. The police-training component was set off as a separate entity, which was not subject to accreditation purview. Delehanty received accreditation by the Association of Accredited Business Schools. I stayed on retainer for several years.

One day I received a phone call from Big John. He was now the director of the Eastern School for Physician's Aides at 85 Fifth Avenue, a few blocks north of the Delehanty Institute. His wife was friends with Angelo Daria, the owner of a worldwide aeronautical components company. Angelo bought the Eastern School and made Big John the director.

John told me that Mr. Daria wanted to meet me. I drove out to Copiague and had dinner with Angelo. I thought it curious that he did not ask Big John to join us, especially since he only lived two miles from the restaurant. I had previously met Big John's wife. I understood Big John's issues, as well as his managerial limitations. Angelo told me that he had paid $3

million for Eastern and made it clear that he wanted to keep
the school and keep Big John in the city.

The Eastern School for Physician's Aides had lost their
required New York State charter. Angelo was paying all of
the bills because the school had lost all government funding.
There are two conditions that could be fatal for a private school;
the loss of accreditation and the loss of a state charter. Loss
of accreditation can be fixed more easily because accrediting
agencies need schools to monitor. States have no such need. The
loss of one's state charter requires a high level of professional
intervention.

Angelo put me on an $800-a-month retainer to fix the
problem. On Columbia letterhead, I wrote to the N.Y.S.
education department's head of vocational education in Albany
requesting an appointment (an example of where a doctoral
degree from Columbia helps in opening doors). We met and
reviewed the list of deficiencies. I asked the director what his
department's preferred remediation was for each deficiency.

The following week, I sat down with Big John and developed
a plan. It was my studied judgment that if we remediated the
deficiencies in the prescribed manner, Eastern would get its
N.Y.S. charter back. The school's dental technology program
had too many issues to remediate. The instructional staff for
the three medical assistant programs was very weak and would
be the most difficult deficiency to deal with. The fact that the
school had no library would be relatively easy to bring into
compliance.

I found a retired hematologist, Dr. Mangrum, who had
authored a book on hematology, which became the textbook for
our course. Dr. Mangrum was hired to teach the course. I also
hired two Russian medical doctors, who were studying so that
they could be licensed to practice medicine in New York. They

were excellent. It was a stretch, but the state issued me a license to teach a medical assistant course. (See Appendix).

Number five on the list of deficiencies was the fact that the school did not have a library. No problem, we had an extra room. Students brought in any medical-related books they owned. With Eastern's credit card, I went on a buying spree at the nearby Strand Bookstore.

I had to convince Big John that it would not be cost effective to bring the dental technology program into compliance. We stopped admitting new students and phased dental technology out of the school's offerings. On weekends, I had the school painted, replaced the ceiling light fixtures, and carpeted the floors.

I intentionally had no contact with Angelo. Rather, I encouraged Big John to keep him apprised of our efforts. It took about four months to bring the school up to the state's standards. I was intent on leaving no margin for failure, knowing that if I succeeded, I could write my own ticket.

I wrote a carefully crafted letter to the vocational head in Albany. Enclosed with the letter was a single-page delineation of the improvements we had completed at the school. In the letter, I asked for his department's guidance as to our next steps. Albany sent two staff members down to reevaluate the school. The Eastern School for Physicians Aides got their charter back.

During my second meeting with Angelo, he gave me a tour of his facility. It was a huge air-conditioned warehouse of aircraft parts. It had hundreds of shelves with bins that contained every part. These parts were labeled and numbered to a master index. Essentially, it was an Amazon of aircraft parts.

Angelo was born in Argentina and was a self-made multimillionaire. I assumed the triangulation among Big John, his wife, and Angelo. As I was leaving Angelo said, "Just keep

John busy in the city and make sure he doesn't let the school get into any more trouble with the state." I got it.

Then Mr. Daria bought the entire second floor in the adjoining building (87 Fifth Avenue). This was a huge financial investment. He obtained a New York City permit and removed the two walls between the buildings.

Eastern was expanding and became the Eastern Technical School. I developed new programs in graphic design, licensed practical nursing, and business office management. I stayed on retainer with ETS until 1983. Even during the year I lived in Maryland, the monthly checks continued.

As I was writing this section, I wondered if Big John was still alive. Knowing that he had a son named John, I Googled him. When I found someone who would be about the right age, I phoned him and left a message. He returned my call. Big John had passed away in 2015, and his wife had predeceased him. His son remembered his father talking about some activities he had worked on with a Dr. Garrahan back in the 1970s. I shared a little with him as well. John Jr. enjoyed our conversation.

(See photos: The Delehanty Institute with my second floor corner office facing Union Square. The Eastern Technical School at 85 Fifth Ave and the expansion into 87 Fifth Avenue).

CHAPTER 7

From Columbia University to Frostburg State College

Back at Columbia, Roger and I had a serious talk. I don't recall what prompted our discussion, but I asked him candidly how I was being perceived at the college. "You're very good at what you do, but you're a hustler. You spend a lot of time off campus in your private consulting. You're never on campus on Fridays. Everyone likes you, but there's talk." Roger was spot on. I enjoyed my consulting more than I did my professorial responsibilities.

Professors at the graduate level carry a light teaching load. I taught three courses in the fall and two courses in the spring, which equated to ten clock hours of instructional time each week during the academic year. This was not enough work for me. However, in addition to the teaching load, professors were expected to publish, conduct research, bring in grant funds, serve as an advisor to students, sponsor doctoral dissertations, serve as oral examiners, and maintain national visibility. I learned how funding agencies scored proposals and developed agency contacts.

Our department's gerontology program was aligned with the Office on Aging in Washington DC. Seeking more options, I completed a training program to become certified as a Title IX consultant. By the mid 1970s, the feminist movement was advocating full equality for women, with lawsuits being filed against corporations and institutions across the country.

Consulting opportunities abounded. My specialty was training human resource personnel to comply with the relatively new legal mandates. I was also doing consultations with public school districts. Teachers College, Columbia University had the reputation as the place to turn to when a district had institutional problems. These were demanding projects that required one's presence during the workweek to make observations and collect data. I completed studies for Leonia, Hastings-on-Hudson, Metuchen, Ridgefield Park, Hackensack, Teaneck, Great Neck, Norwalk, and others. Unlike the private proprietary schools, these were challenging. They typically required me to give a public presentation of my findings and recommendations to a polarized audience.

I thought that the money and fun was in private school consulting. Through my work for Delehanty and the Eastern School, I developed a reputation within the tight-knit, private trade and technical entities in Manhattan, Brooklyn, and the Bronx. I could easily have made this my full-time employment.

Often these institutions presented ethical challenges. For example, in my role as special assistant to the president of the board at 110 Livingston Street, I was in a position to facilitate the referral of thousands of students from the city's vocational schools to the for-profit, private technical schools. I never crossed this line. Depending on the incentives, the line could become blurred.

In the business world of private entities, the incentives were difficult to ignore. Readers will be spared the specifics. I was, however, devoting almost as much time to consulting as I was to Columbia.

Another variable in my career decision-making was related to a student who I had never taught. Her doctoral dissertation necessitated the use of sophisticated inferential statistics. Her sponsor's (my drinking colleague, Foley) expertise was limited to simple descriptive statistics, at best. Her cosponsor, professor Dave Bilder, understood canonical regression analysis, but misused his position to curry favor. Cleverly, she had discreetly taped one such encounter at a restaurant on the Saw Mill River Parkway where he threatened to attack her research at the oral … unless. I became involved, critiquing her design and statistics from Frostburg, Maryland. It became personal. I was just outside as she took her oral examination and successfully defended her research.

While it was obvious that Janet and I were not a good match, it was my intention to hold the marriage together until all of our children went off to college. I thought it would be wise to distance myself from New York City, both in terms of this personal relationship, and my over-involvement in private consulting, although Chairman Blackman was entirely comfortable with my consulting and encouraged me to stay at Columbia.

However, Chuck was gone. The few faculty members that I had related to—Foley, Tom, and Andy—were gone. As much as I enjoyed the Big Apple, it made sense to reset and relocate. After pondering the matter, I asked Roger and Ed, both of whom had national reputations, to write letters of recommendation. Blackman wrote, "His colleagues at the college and in the profession readily turn to him for leadership."

Roger wrote, "It is my strong hope that he remains at Teachers College, Columbia University, and were he to do so, I would readily accept him as a member of the department of psychology faculty." (See Appendix: For Roger Myers and Edmund W. Gordon letters of recommendation)

I applied for a position at Frostburg State College, a unit of the University of Maryland, and resigned from my post at Columbia. At Frostburg, I was appointed as an associate professor of psychology, and the director of counseling psychology, guidance and counseling, and social work programs.

Fast Start

It was something of a culture shock when I moved from Columbia University in Manhattan to Frostburg State College in the mountains of western Maryland. Getting off to a fast start, I rewrote the fieldwork placement guides in social work and guidance and counseling. I strengthened the curriculum by adding three new courses and dropping others.

My faculty had their offices scattered about the campus. One professor had his office in a teacher-training facility, which included an elementary school for children. He brought his dog to his office every day. They each had reasons for being where they were; they were comfortable. Three professors objected to having their courses dropped. I explained the importance of having departmental offices in one location, both for the convenience of students as well as for the development of 'program identity'. My words fell on deaf ears.

Quick Finish

With the approval of Vice President Bablon, all course changes and office reassignments were implemented by the end of the first semester. One professor appreciated what I was trying to accomplish. I took Otto to the American Psychological Association's convention in Washington, DC, where we made two presentations. The rest of the faculty remained uncooperative, attempting to undermine my initiatives. In retrospect, it is clear that I moved too quickly and in a heavy-handed manner. I also missed the vibrancy of New York City.

I resigned at the end of the first year. Even though I had been in Manhattan two to three days each month maintaining my ties with the Eastern School, the Delehanty Institute, and 110 Livingston Street, I had missed the pleasure of wandering the neighborhoods of the Big Apple.

At this time, Janet and I decided to get a divorce. There was no love in our marriage. We both knew that the relationship was wrong. Something important was missing. Later, my second wife, would teach me what love was.

Janet and I began by going to a stationery store where we bought a divorce kit. Together, we prepared a divorce agreement. It included both alimony and child support. When we were both satisfied with our agreement, we hired an attorney, Al Barney, to execute it. He strongly advised against representing both of us, but finally agreed.

Janet was granted custody of our three children, but there was a restriction of how far she could move the children away from me. Mr. Barney charged us $2,100 (the legal fee for my last divorce was $45,000). I assisted Janet in buying a home in New York where she lived until her retirement.

Mr. Barney called our attention to the fact that we had made no provision for the college educations of our three children. Janet wrote a codicil that stated that we would share all college expenses in proportion to our respective incomes at the time. Her handwritten page was appended to the divorce agreement.

When the three children went off to Alfred University, American University, and Salem College, Janet refused to honor the provision that she had written. To avoid litigation, I assumed financial responsibility. I did require Susan and Mark to take out student loans, so that they would feel invested in their own college education.

It should be noted that prior to going off to college, my children, Susan and Dean, asked me if they could come and live with my wife, Eileen, and me. We welcomed them into our home in Pearl River. My children have maintained lifelong relationships with Eileen.

Chapter 8

From Frostburg State College to New York City

I'm a Guidance Counselor, Again!

I phoned Dr. Weissman and told him I was coming back to New York City and that I needed a position with flexible hours to cover my expenses until I found employment. Sy came through. This time, I thought about how I had enjoyed counseling high school students. Eileen pointed out the advantages of a state pension. She loaned me money to buy back eight years of out-of-state service.

Passaic Valley High School in New Jersey hired me as a guidance counselor. I was back to where I had been in 1963—working with teenage students. The other four counselors in the building tried to convince me to stop meeting the incoming school buses in the morning to greet my counselees by name. They got over it. It was a very good use of my time because I could touch a lot of bases with a dozen of my kids each morning. I was totally into doing a great job and enjoying my work with my counselees. I was the butt of a few their jokes…. "Is that what they taught you in your doctoral studies, to say hello to your counselees getting off the school bus in the morning."

Later, however, on staff- development day, they asked me to conduct a workshop. I welcomed the opportunity. Being a strong proponent of using empathy as a necessary relationship tool in counseling, I presented a full day workshop on the topic for the guidance counselors, school psychologist, and social worker.

Defining empathy as a person's ability to identify with the client...to see through their eyes....to feel the anger, frustration, fear, anxiety, and self doubt of the counselee. I explained the natural use of 'tactile communication' between counselor and counselee to foster a feeling of understanding the issue being shared. I demonstrated that a gentle supportive touch engenders feelings of acceptance, caring, and trust.

During the afternoon role-playing, it became apparent that the older counselors were uncomfortable putting their hand on the arm of a troubled student. During the critique portion, they summarized their conclusions: there is a difference between intellectually understanding a student's problem, and feeling the psychological impact that the student is experiencing.... one cannot teach a counselor to be empathic, as it is related to one's personality, culture, and past experiences. It was a day well spent.

It was very satisfying for four years. However, I seemed to be driven to lead, which was probably a result of the leadership roles I had held after receiving my doctoral degree.

I'm a Director of Guidance

Teaneck High School advertised for a director of guidance. A decade earlier when I was a young professor at Columbia,

Teaneck had hired me as a consultant to conduct a district-wide assessment of their guidance services. It had been a comprehensive study with recommendations for improving and reorganizing their system of guidance services. Now I would have the opportunity to implement some of my own recommendations.

I was appointed director of guidance. During my first week at Teaneck, I posted a benign schedule with the names of college admissions counselors who would be meeting with students the following month. The day after I posted the schedules on the school's bulletin boards, the principal walked into my office and threw the schedules on my desk. "Don't ever put anything up in this building without my approval" (his tone of voice was worse). I made a quick diagnosis that he would not be amenable to personal counseling.

At the end of the day, I spoke with the school psychologist, who had been a doctoral student at Columbia. She confirmed my assessment. Given my work style and his psychological transparency, it was clear that one of us would have to go (See Appendix: Director of Guidance Resigns).

I'm a Director of Pupil Personnel Services

In a February Sunday issue of *The New York Times*, I spotted a listing for director of pupil personnel services in the Northern Highlands Regional High School District. I applied. There were three inside candidates. I knew that if the competition was open and fair, the position would be mine. It was fair. I was granted an early release from my Teaneck contract. In March, I took over as director with the responsibilities for guidance, school psychology, social work, and special services. This was a wonderful opportunity in an affluent community.

I decided to also carry a caseload of fifty students as my counselees—doing what I enjoyed most. One of my counselees was Beth, the daughter of Bernie Arnold, who was the district's president of the board of education. As we approached the end of my first very successful year, Mr. Arnold spoke privately with me. He shared that he was not satisfied with the performance of our district superintendent. He delineated his numerous concerns. "I want you in his position," he said. I explained that it would not be possible because I was not qualified. Moreover, I could not be certified by the state because I did not have the requisite six years of administrative experience in New Jersey. I had not taken the required courses for state certification, which included school administration, school finance, and education law. Bernie was persistent.

Not Qualified and Not Certifiable

One day, I was attending a meeting in the county office. During a break, I found the smokers' room. A lone woman was inside enjoying a cigarette. She mentioned that she handled certification issues for the county. I thought that if I applied for state certification, I would obviously be rejected, and this would put the idea out of Bernie's head. So I asked the woman about the procedure for applying, mentioning that I lacked almost all of the state requirements.

She asked about my professional background. Then she suggested I assemble all of my credentials and mail them to a specific individual in the Office of Academic Credentials in Trenton. "Do not request a waiver of requirements or any course substitutions," she said.

I mailed the package. Within a month I received my certificate in the mail. *This is crazy and not possible*, I thought. I asked my friend Dr. Goldstein to contact the state and ask what positions a person would be eligible to hold with certification as a 'school administrator'. The shocking answer was, "Any and all school district administrative positions in New Jersey."

As I reflect back on this encounter in the smokers' room, my guess is that the woman thought that I wanted to be certified as a superintendent. I did not want or expect that outcome. She probably told her contact in Trenton to see what he or she could do to help me out. There is simply no other reasonable explanation to explain the outcome. Just think, a cigarette with a stranger, a brief casual conversation, and my life is changed.

What? Are They Crazy in Trenton?

What should I do? I enjoy challenges, but this would be beyond the pale. I did not know anything about running a school district. Mr. Hopkins, the superintendent, had been the founding superintendent. He had led the school district since its inception in 1963. He was tenured in his position with twenty-two years as superintendent of the district.

Bernie Arnold was one of a kind when he learned that the state had certified me. He went into action. Mr. Hopkins took early retirement. The board offered the position to me. The salary was great. I accepted (See Appendix: Superintendent's appointment).

CHAPTER 9

District Superintendent Garrahan

Allendale and Upper Saddle River

The Northern Highlands Regional High School District (NHRHS) serves the residents of Allandale and Upper Saddle River, New Jersey. It is an affluent community populated by corporate executives, lawyers, and bankers—most of whom commute into Manhattan. For some reason, the district also attracts a disproportionate number of major league athletes, including Lawrence Taylor, Lou Piniella, Jim Burt, and Bill Parcells. Former FBI Director James Comey graduated from NHRHS.

I thought this would certainly be an interesting place to work. I expected the position to be a challenge. Soon I would learn that the challenges exceeded my expectations. Board president, Arnold, made it clear to me when he said, "I want you to clean house and make NHRHS one of the top ten high schools in the United States."

I thought, *Does he know that there are more than 25,000 public high schools in the country?* Mr. Arnold had set the bar high. Expectations in the community were also elevated. I was well aware of my own unqualified experience for the role of district superintendent and made no pretense to the contrary.

Upon entering the superintendent's office, I pulled open every file drawer in each of the file cabinets. Yikes! There was not one folder or piece of paper anywhere. Someone had removed everything. Dropping in new hanging folders, I labeled three of them: State Education Dept., County Education Office, and Teachers Union. This was the extent of my knowledge about being a superintendent. Typically, an incoming superintendent will work together with the departing superintendent for thirty days. Obviously, this was not to be.

A few months into my new position, Charlie, my carpool buddy from Washingtonville called. He asked, "How does it feel to be a member of an elite group of superintendents?" I had no idea. Charlie explained that ten or twelve years ago, my predecessor had formed a special group of five superintendents, who had been well connected, to discuss current issues and salaries and to socialize. They called themselves the Mini Rounders. I told him that I had heard about them, but had not had any contact with them.

A year later, the Ridgewood superintendent phoned and invited me to attend the Mini Rounders' meetings as his guest. I attended three meetings and quit. I felt their contempt for me. I was not one of them. I had not come up through the administrative ranks. I knew nothing about school finance or New Jersey school law. What was worse was their belief that I had been involved in the unfair ouster of their leader, Superintendent Hopkins, founder of the Mini Rounders. At times, they would ask my position on some arcane feature in school law or the projected impact of a new corporation in my town on my district's mill rate. I thought, *I don't need this crap. I'm out*, and I withdrew from the Mini Rounders.

Interestingly, three years later following the national recognition of NHRHS, my board gave me an 11 percent increase in salary when the average increase for superintendents in Bergen County that year was 2.5 percent. My board president mentioned that he had received two phone calls from area board presidents saying that my salary increase was being used by their superintendents during salary negotiations.

It is important to note that in the history of the district, the board had never developed a job description for this number one leadership position. More interesting is the fact that during my ten years as superintendent, I never had a contract. This was at my request. When the board offered me the position, I realized that I didn't even know where to start, so I told them I did not want to tie them into a contract. I explained that if at any time a majority of the board became dissatisfied with my performance, they should just tell me, and I would resign.

[Flash forward to 1995: As I prepared to retire, I went to Trenton to meet with a retirement counselor. The young woman was shocked to learn that I had never had a contract. I thought, *What's the big deal? I just want to make sure that I will receive a pension.*

She conferred with a superior, who came in to confirm that I had never had a contract and asked if I had any vacation days left. I told her that in my ten years, I had never taken a vacation. To my surprise, I was told that the district would be required to reimburse me for each of my unused vacation days at my current salary. It came to $120,000! My board was also shocked. I couldn't do this to them, but who throws that kind of money away? I cut a deal with them.]

Start with a Controversy

My appointment was very controversial. A prominent, outspoken, community leader threatened a lawsuit on the basis that no female or minority applicants had been granted an interview. Others charged that there had been no search conducted at all. In silence, I agreed with the disgruntled taxpayers. However, state officials ruled that my appointment was legal.

A week into my new position, I received a phone call from a reporter for *The Scranton Times*. He had written an article entitled, "Trouble Maker Student Now Heads School District," and wanted to verify several points before publishing the story. I have no idea how the newspaper learned about me (It it quite possible that the reporter's information could have come from Mrs. Wozniak and/or Guzzi, who was the principal of Old Forge High School). Within a week, the article was in the hands of Allandale and Upper Saddle River residents, some of whom had opposed my appointment. Most people understood that teenagers could do dopey things and get into trouble. I sure did! (See Appendix: Appointment Controversy).

First Week: Two Very Important Lunches

My first week in the position, I took the chief of police, Frank Parenti, and the editor of the *Town Journal*, Mary Service, to separate lunch meetings. It seemed like a good idea. Chief Parenti was most appreciative, mentioning that the former superintendent had not spoken to him in all his years as chief.

I established good rapport with these two important community people. For example, a few years later when kids were pulling the fire alarm once a week and we had to evacuate as firemen searched the building, I met with the chief, explaining that when the alarm went off, my security person would reset it. I told the chief, "This will take a few weeks until I can have cameras installed to monitor every alarm box" (Later I would learn that it was not only students who were setting off the alarms!). Frank had a private conversation with the fire chief.

Later, when my vice principal, Rocky Head, was arrested on a DUI with an underage female in the car, Mary called to give me a heads-up that the story would be in the next issue of the Town Journal. I asked her to reconsider. She said, "I saw the video of him slobbering all over the police station." I pleaded that this story would be damaging to our school and community. With great reluctance, she killed the story. Vice Principal Rocky rode a bicycle to school for a year.

During my first few weeks, my friend Charlie who was now a superintendent in a neighboring school district, sans doctorate, gave me a heads-up. He told me that my business administrator, Kowalsky, might become a problem. Charlie said, "He's very headstrong and doesn't accept guidance from his superiors. He's also a drinker."

After work one evening, I asked Kowalsky to join me for a drink at the Ramada Inn. Sitting at the bar, I mentioned that I asked questions because I needed to learn about tax rates, contracts, vendors, etc. He replied that he was the district's business administrator, and implied that he didn't want me nosing around. I said something stupid, "You will follow my orders?" John reminded me that I didn't know anything about school business. Sensing that he was challenging my authority, I said that he would have to follow my directives, or else.

"Or else what," he responded. Looking at him, I said, "You f*** with me, and I'll bring someone from out of state to blow your legs off." Staring at me, he said, "You're crazy," and he left. At the time I didn't know that Kowalsky was a Ukrainian Lemko (nor did he).

We worked very well together until he retired. One time, John was at my home in Pearl River. He was out on the side deck talking to my son Mark. I was inside doing something. Later, Mark asked me, "Dad, did you ever tell Mr. Kowalsky that you would have someone shoot his legs off?"

I said, "I did."

My Initiatives Are Not Well-Received

I met with the department supervisors, asking them to review their course offerings and to submit copies of all teacher evaluations to me. Their reaction was that this had not been done in the past, and was unnecessary. I saw it as an opportunity to see the quality of their work, and to learn more about the individual teachers.

I initiated the practice of meeting with all of the district's administrators after school on Fridays in my conference room. If we had a public event during the week, I would lead a critique of the event. Their posture: If it isn't broken, don't try to fix it. However, I believed that there was always room for improvement.

Later, I dropped Latin from the curriculum and added a computer education course. The teachers union objected. It was, however, a board prerogative. The Latin teacher retired, and I phased Latin out of the curricula. I engaged a consultant to design a required computer education course in concert with our business and mathematics teachers.

Another initiative involved having some of our top students taking college courses. A senior executive of Ingersoll Rand Corporation (IR) lived in Upper Saddle River. With funding from IR and support from the president of Ramapo College in nearby Mahwah, we established the Rand Scholars Program, whereby selected seniors received college credit for courses which they would take on the college campus during their senior year. The administrators and supervisors resisted the program because of the logistics and paperwork involved in transporting the students to the college, adjusting their schedules, and calculating their grade point averages.

Soon I could sense that my initiatives were not being well received. I knew that my leadership style was autocratic. Several years later, I attempted to change my style by forming a decision-making council. It took us days to reach a decision. I withdrew from the council. It was just not my style. However, I sensed that the staff's attitude toward me was rooted in something beyond my leadership style.

An Interrelated Faculty and Administration

I talked to the board president, Bernie. He gave me a historical perspective. Our current board attorney had been the town's attorney back in 1962. He had advised the mayor and council to hire a consultant to lay the groundwork for the new school district. The consultant that they had hired had been the father of Mr. Hisson, our current principal.

To my surprise, Bernie told me that my principal had been the only other candidate the board had interviewed for my position. This consultant recommended to the town council that my predecessor, Mr. Hopkins, be the district's first superintendent. Mr. Hopkins had hired every employee in the district. So Mr. Hopkins and Mr. Hisson had been employed by the district since the very first day and had hired the entire staff that I inherited.

The big picture was becoming clear to me. My staff was interrelated by personal and family relationships. Obviously, a healthy institution is enhanced by the recruitment of individuals with solid professional credentials and who are not necessarily connected to administrators and supervisors. Now I understood why cooperating with me was not high on their list. This job was going to be more challenging than I had anticipated.

Drug Use, School Security, and Rudner

During my first year, I designed a drug use survey and had it administered to all students. From the results it was clear that we had a drug problem. While I refused to make the results public, I told the board that we needed a school security program. It was a hard sell in 1985 in an affluent school district. On a split vote, the board agreed to hire two security officers.

I met with Chief Parenti. He suggested that I hire two retired policemen who knew the community. I am not sure why, but I decided on a twenty-two year old graduate from our high school. Knowing he would be a hard sell with the board, I met privately with Bernie. I told him that I needed his help in getting the board to approve my recommendation. Bernie knew the young man. It seemed that everyone knew Rudner.

Bernie said it would be better if I followed Chief Parenti's suggestion, but I persisted. I recall Bernie telling me, "David, if this doesn't work out, it's going to be bad for you." However, he pushed the appointment. The board passed the resolution. Rudner turned out to be the best hire I ever made.

After the security program had been in place for three months, Rudner issued the first school security report. This report delineated the number and nature of incidents that had resulted in the arrest of several individuals from outside of our two towns. These individuals had been arrested for selling drugs to our students on the school's campus. Rudner knew the students, and when and where things were going down.

We continued the drug survey for three years. One finding unexpectedly related to the factors that might influence a student not to get involved with drugs. Surprisingly, it was the students' concern with their health, specifically, with their personal appearance.

One day, I phoned Bernie to tell him the Waldwick Fitness Center was upgrading their equipment and auctioning off their existing equipment the following night. Bidding was to start at $25,000. Bernie directed me to get the money from Kowalsky, our business administrator. We bought everything for $35,000. Absent our board's prior approval, this purchase was illegal.

We tore down a wall between two classrooms near the gym and installed the fitness machines. The kids loved it. Years later, I wrote an article, "The Application of a Systems Approach to Substance Use Prevention: Linking Interventions to the Infrastructure." The article was published in the *Journal of Alcohol and Drug Education*. The longitudinal data from our study was subsequently incorporated into a meta-analysis in the Netherlands.

Banning Foreign Travel

Some of my decisions sparked controversy in the community. My unilateral ban on all student group trips to foreign countries caused an uproar. We had sister schools in Germany, France, and Spain. The board backed me, but several teachers, on their own, began planning foreign student trips. Later, I learned that teachers were eager to sponsor these trips because they enjoyed a visit to Europe cost free. The company that managed the trips covered teachers' expenses. I probably went too far by ordering teachers not to discuss the travel ban or other plans during class time. Some parents wrote letters to the editor of the Town Journal stating that my order was unconstitutional (See Appendix: Banning Foreign Travel; Leaching Life Blood from Foreign Travel).

Focusing on enhancing the education our students were receiving, I recruited a cadre of exceptional teachers. They were young, and at the bottom of the salary scale. They replaced teachers who I had pushed out who were at the top of the salary scale. These new teachers were not part of the old guard. They even supported the idea of lengthening the school day!

Implementing an Eight-Period Day

It was just common sense that if students had the opportunity to take an additional course, they would learn more. I anticipated resistance from most teachers and the union, as well as an outcry from students. Some teachers began wearing sweatshirts with "No 8-Period Day" emblazoned on the front of them while teaching. In the good old days, I recall a teacher who came to school wearing a turtleneck shirt being sent home to put on a shirt and tie. Now teachers have free-speech rights that cover their clothes. While I had publicly supported an increase in teachers' salaries to compensate them for the additional class and the lengthened school day, apparently, it had not been generous enough. When teachers protested by refusing to enter the building, I was forced to close the school for a day (See Appendix: Implementing an Eight Period Day).

No Confidence in Superintendent Garrahan

The union took out a full-page ad in the *Town Journal* censoring me with a vote of no confidence (See Appendix: No confidence in Superintendent Garrahan). Students presented a petition to the board, which had been signed by half the student body. Even parents objected to increasing the demands on students and putting them under additional stress. My response was that the school is a good environment for students to learn how to cope with stress.

The union and the board negotiated a salary increase. We added an additional period and lengthened the school day. Teachers received a hefty increase. Obviously, I had underestimated the power and ruthlessness of the teachers' union. I moved on to my next challenge.

It should be noted that school superintendents would never "self initiate" these educationally sound changes—knowing that such initiatives would invite conflict and controversy. And I did not endear myself with my fellow superintendents.

NHRHS Seeks National Recognition

Every superintendent received information concerning the Federal Secondary School Recognition Program. I was reminded of Bernie's desire to have NRHRS as one of the top ten high schools in the country. At the next meeting of the Bergen County superintendents, I learned that New Jersey had never participated in this national competition. Superintendents perceived this competition as an unwise and time-consuming distraction.

I discussed the competition with the board. They asked why excellent high schools in Princeton and Ridgewood had never entered the competition. No high school in New Jersey had ever entered. I told the board that we would probably learn what other good schools across the country were doing and that it would require some extra time.

"I'm good at preparing reports. I think we should compete." As soon as word got out, superintendents began calling me with words of discouragement: all that paperwork and boards pushing them to enter the competition. They were right. Other school districts pushed their high schools to enter the competition.

NHRHS was one of the eight schools in New Jersey that made the first cut. We moved on to the national competition. At the time, there were more than twenty-five thousand high schools (See Appendix: NHRHS - in Top 8 schools in New Jersey).

We received notice from Washington DC that we had qualified for an on-site evaluation. The evaluation team would consist of educators from across the country. I was responsible for getting groups of teachers, supervisors, parents, and students ready to meet in evening sessions with the visitors. During the day, visitors would observe classroom instruction, gather test scores and school records, and conduct private one-on-one interviews within the building. I was directed to reserve a block of rooms at a motel that had conference/meeting rooms. Our visitors came from Nashville to Boston.

I had Rudner take the school van and pick up our visitors at the airport. The Department of Education funded most of our expenses for the visitors. Rudner was late returning from the airport—very late. Meanwhile, I walked around the campus and chain-smoked. Rudner could be a loose cannon.

Finally, the van arrived. Rudner, being Rudner, had decided to give our visitors a tour of Manhattan and to treat them to dinner in Little Italy. He whispered to me that they had enjoyed three bottles of Italian wine. "I loosened them up for you, Doc," he said. Rudner had a great sense of humor. He had likely entertained them with stories about Northern Highlands. Yes, I had rented potted plants and had met with the various groups to prepare them for questions they would likely be asked by the visitors. My sense was that the visit had gone very well.

National Recognition: We Did It!

I received a letter from William Bennett, the US Secretary of Education, saying that NHRHS had been selected as one of the exemplary high schools in the United States. I responded by doing something I rarely did. I went on the school's public address system to let everyone in the building know that it was official. I said, "We are one of the top schools in the country." I could hear the cheering throughout the building.

The newspapers covered it extensively. They said that property values would go up (*The New York Times*) and that our graduates would be even more attractive to the elite colleges. It was a coveted recognition. We were invited to Washington DC and greeted by Secretary Bennett. President Reagan praised our achievement in a Rose Garden ceremony. I met with Senator Bill Bradley. He is very tall, as are most NBA stars. Back home in Allendale and Upper Saddle River our residents were jubilant (See Appendix: NHRHS honored in Rose Garden ceremony in D.C. Garrahan leads to excellence) (See photos: Senator Bill Bradley; the Award Ceremony)

Declining Enrollment and Increasing Taxes

During these first few years, I had taken note of the school's declining student population and the seriously high property taxes. Many residents were paying more than $15,000 a year in school property taxes. I was concerned that these conditions would eventually have a negative impact on the quality of education being provided. It was obvious to me that regionalization was the answer. I had published several articles on the subject in leading state educational journals. If only we could merge our district with school districts in one or two of the contiguous towns.

One large K–12 school district would yield significant economies of scale: one superintendent of schools, one special education department, one school bus vendor, etc. Under one regionalized school district, each town would spend less money, and their children would receive a vastly superior K–12 education. Very importantly, we could streamline a K–12 curriculum. This is particularly important in foreign language and mathematics curricula. Property taxes would be reduced. At the time, there were 590 independent school districts in New Jersey, including seventy-seven separate school districts in Bergen County. This was plain stupid local politics. Allendale and Saddle River were both K-8 separate school districts which made them obvious candidates for a regionalized K-12 school district.

Rumors began to circulate in the communities where I was pushing for regionalization, that I was doing this in anticipation of becoming the superintendent of the new enlarged district. That ticked me off. However, I took that possibility off the table, by telling the *Town Journal* that if we regionalized, I would resign from my tenured superintendent position, and that I would not be a candidate for the superintendent position of a merged school district. They had to know that I truly believed in the merits of regionalization, and had no personal vested interest.

The bottom line was that none of the local school boards thought regionalization was a good idea. About twenty board members would lose their elected positions. A regionalized district would simply have one board of education. I realized that this idea of consolidation was a losing battle. This is an example of the government's waste of tax dollars. It was the most frustrating experience in my entire ten years.

For Sale: A High Quality Education

I convinced my board that in view of our recent national recognition, we could probably attract tuition-paying students from outside our district. We agreed on a tuition rate and that parents would be responsible for their children's transportation. I placed five or six ads in newspapers from Tuxedo Park, New York to Demarest, New Jersey. I actually went door-to-door in affluent communities, ringing doorbells and handing out an impressive twenty-three-page booklet describing our educational and student activities programs. We attracted thirty-two tuition students the first year, which brought in about $250,000. It was good but not good enough. Moreover, it took considerable time and effort to find these families.

Let's Make a Deal

I thought about the possibility of convincing an entire town to bus their students to NHRHS. I spoke privately with our new board president, Dr. Schmendric. He gave me the go-ahead to see what I could do. There was only one logical town, Ho-Ho-Kus, which was a very affluent town. For years, they had been sending their entire class of eighth-grade graduates to Midland Park High School. Midland Park was essentially a blue-collar town. My perception was that their tax base was reflected in the quality of their high school.

I phoned the president of the Ho-Ho-Kus board of education without telling her the reason for my call. I invited her to lunch in Waldwick where the likelihood of our being recognized was small. I let her know that our conversation must be kept private. Then I broached the sensitive subject. NHRHS's recent national recognition had been in all of the local newspapers. I noticed a sparkle in her eyes. She thought this idea had great potential. We agreed to discreetly seek feedback from key individuals in our respective towns.

A few weeks later, we met again. She said that the people she spoke to had been surprised to learn of the possibility. She thought that Ho-Ho-Kus would jump at the opportunity. We then agreed to meet in executive session, closed to the public, with our respective boards.

I designed a tuition model, which was both clever and inviting. It was an offer they could hardly refuse. The tuition during the first year would be $8,000. At the time, they were paying $9,200 to Midland Park. In three to four years, there would be a slight increase. Subsequently, tuition would become significantly higher, but would be subject to negotiation.

Her board wanted in. My board struggled with the implications. Board attorneys were engaged to work on the issues at stake. Midland Park's superintendent, Larry Presco, phoned me to say that he had heard a rumor and that surely, it wasn't true. I said, "It's true." Larry had a hot temper. I was determined. Ho-Ho-Kus was in the middle of a three-year contract with Midland Park (See Appendix: Ho-Ho-Kus merger in the news).

The contract issue became a huge story in the press. Midland Park superintendent Presco was quoted as stating that the tuition rates proposed by Northern Highlands were 'out of whack'. Of course, he was right. Our cost per pupil was $13,000 per year. The proposal I had offered Ho-Ho-Kus was $8,000 for the first year. I was playing dirty pool. Our board and the Ho-Ho-Kus board voted to consummate the proposal.

[Flash forward to 1996: I received a phone call at my home in Arizona from Jamie Plosia, who had been my last board attorney. "Dave, the supreme court just ruled in favor of Ho-Ho-Kus and dismissed Midland Park's lawsuit with prejudice," he said. It was nice of Jamie to remember who had initiated the merger that put the NHRHS district in a very favorable financial position. It should be noted that as of September 2018, Ho-Ho-Kus and the Northern Highlands Regional High School district are still contractually bound in what clearly has been a win-win relationship.]

No Martin Luther King Day at Northern Highlands

The more time students are in a classroom with good teachers, the more they learn and the better they will be prepared for the challenges of life. My board asked me to close the school for Martin Luther King Day. I refused. We had five or six Black students. If they decided to celebrate MLK Day, it would be understandable. If we closed the whole school, however, most students would not observe the holiday. Some of them would hang out at the Paramus Mall for the day.

Board members were concerned that we would be perceived as racist. Dr. Schmendric reminded the board members, "Dave has never seemed to care what people thought of him."

A week before the MLK holiday, Lawrence Taylor (LT of NFL fame) came into my office. He was a resident taxpayer. I explained my thinking to him. Reverend King was a notch above the Rainbow Coalition operator, Reverend Jesse Jackson and Reverend Al Sharpton of Tawana Brawley infamy. My mind would never change.

Two years later LT and I were on opposing basketball teams for a fund-raiser. When I was at the foul line to take a shot, he came up behind me and pulled my socks down. The crowd roared. It was a fun move by LT.

(See photo: Seconds before the pull down by L.T.)

While I respected King as a leader, I knew that he had plagiarized his doctoral dissertation. Two investigations had concluded that large portions of his dissertation had been lifted from other people's works and that he had presented the material as his own. Boston University should never have awarded him the doctoral degree. His history of extramarital affairs had also been documented. More importantly, I wanted our students in classrooms learning, and not driving around the area getting in trouble.

School was in session. I peered out my window at the protestors blocking traffic. During my ten years as superintendent, I had never closed the school for MLK Day. The protestors were doing what they believed was right, and so was I (See Appendix: No MLK Day at NHRHS).

UNANTICPATED PROBLEMS

VANDALS ATTACK NHRHS: It was about 2:30 a.m., when Chief Parenti phoned me: "Dave, someone is inside the high school wrecking everything." When I arrived, police were talking to the vandal, but were unable to apprehend him because they were separated by a floor to ceiling metal security gate which was locked. One officer had his gun drawn, as the vandal was armed with a pick-axe in one hand and a hatchet in the other hand. I unlocked the gate. The vandal ran, but the police apprehended him.

Assessing the damage, I walked by broken plate glass windows, electric wiring ripped out of switch plates, water running from broken fountains, shattered trophy cases and smashed trophies. He had chopped through two oak doors to gain access to the planetarium which he destroyed. At the time, NHRHS was the only public high school in the state with a planetarium.

I phoned my business administrator, Kowalsky, who was attending a convention in Atlantic City. He arrived on campus at 5:30 a.m. I called our bus vendor, Mike Ely, and asked him to prepare for a delayed opening. The district had never had a delayed opening due to the complexity of our bus routes. This time, however, I pushed Mike, and he made it happen. Soon our maintenance men were trucking in sheets of plywood, and two electricians were working on the wiring. I woke up Bernie Arnold, briefed him on the destruction, and told him that I anticipated a delayed 10:00 a.m. school opening. Then I asked Molly Wellen, Director of Pupil Personnel Services to phone the Education Testing Service in Princeton and reschedule that afternoon's Advance Placement Tests in chemistry and biology.

Staff writer for the Record, Laura Gardner, wrote: "...when students and teachers were allowed into the building, many expressed disbelief and shock at the Rambo-like destruction throughout the building. Police Chief Parenti said that when he asked through the security gate, why he did this, the vandal replied, "because I felt like it," turned his back, and yelled, "so shoot me." Police took the vandal, bleeding profusely from his hands and arms to Bergen Pines Hospital."

Months later, I testified at Danny's trial in Hackensack. Our insurance carrier covered $525, 000 of the damages. Danny was not a NHRHS student! (See Appendix: Vandal attacks NHRHS)

VICTORIA'S SECRET and PHONE CALLS TO POLAND: I had made it a practice to look at the District's monthly charges to the school's credit cards, as well as the telephone statements. A Victoria's Secret charge of $77 caught my attention. Knowing that one of my administrators had attended a convention in San Francisco on the date of the charge, I called him into my office. He was quick to acknowledge that he had bought his wife a gift. He reimbursed the District.

Likewise, my antenna went up when I saw several telephone calls to Poland. Knowing that the Director of Special Education had a young female au pair, I casually asked him if she was Polish. He acknowledged the phone calls and reimbursed the District. Two months later, his wife decided that the au pair had to be flown back to Poland.

A GOOD PERSON AND TEACHER WITH A PROBLEM: Carol, a former airline stewardess, was a good special education teacher, and an alcoholic. I had cut her some slack, as long as her condition did not affect her teaching responsibilities. When she ran her car off the gravel road back entrance to the high school at 7:30 a.m., I asked her to come to my office after she dealt with her car and insurance company. With sensitivity, I told her that recently a staff member told me that she was certain that Carol was drinking vodka in her classroom. Carol assured me that it would not happen again. However, at the end of our meeting, I placed her on an indefinite medical leave of absence. Two months later she phoned, and asked me if I would speak with her at her home. When we met, it appeared that her condition had deteriorated. Yet she asked me to reinstate her to her teaching position, and showed me a letter from the teacher's union which stated that it was up to the superintendent. I told her that I was not prepared to reinstate her at this time. I handed her the professional cards of two area physicians who I knew. I told her that I would reinstate her when one of these two individuals, or another medical professional of her choice, stated in writing that she was ready to reassume her teaching responsibilities. Approximately five months later Carol died.

SOMETHING BAD IN THE BARN: Police Chief Parenti phoned me at about 10 p.m., "Dave, you've got to get up here, there are EPA people all over the place…something bad is going on in the barn." I arrived to a bizarre scene, numerous emergency vehicles with lights flashing. There were several individuals cloaked in full protective outfits walking around like robots. I asked Chief Parenti who was in charge. He pointed to two men and said they were from two different agencies, and they were both giving orders.

I had an idea what had happened. Earlier in the week, Dr. Norton (Allendale superintendent) phoned me: "Dave, a woman is going to do something bad to you very soon. That's all I can tell you, so be careful." I hypothesized that this woman had heard about chemicals in the barn. Our chemistry teacher, Dr. C., had very poor vision and was unable to drive a car. I decided to observe him teaching a class. As a former chemistry teacher, I noticed debris in all the sinks, and when I turned on the gas jets there was no gas in the line. I met with him and he accepted early retirement. I removed about ten small bottles of outdated chemicals, which I judged to be inert. I placed them in a metal pail with a lid, then put them in a 50 gallon drum in the barn for future disposal. I explained this to the two EPA officials, and asked them to take the pail away. I was told that the chemicals had to be removed by a private vendor with an EPA permit, and that no persons would be permitted on the grounds until the chemicals were removed. They gave me the name of a company in Ohio. I phoned the company's emergency number and explained that I needed a very small tank truck to remove a pail of chemicals within the next four hours. I was put in touch with a company in New York City. I called the company. When I heard the total cost, I had them put $12,000 on a credit card, and said that they would receive the balance of the money when the chemicals were in their truck. By 6 a.m., the truck and chemicals drove off our property. The EPA officials then removed the yellow tape and road barriers.

I have no idea who the woman was, or what I might have done to cause her to take such radical action. The following week the barn was condemned by the town engineer and razed. I had Rudner save two beams for members of the Historical Society.

Anonymous Allegations

Meanwhile, the problem with the inbred staff continued to fester. It is difficult to imagine the extent to which some educators will go to protect the status quo. Someone shot a bullet through my window. Then Mary Service phoned me with a heads-up. The *Town Journal* had received a copy of an anonymous document that detailed my alleged misdeeds. I stopped at the *Town Journal* and picked up a copy. It was bad. It was now out in the community. It had been mailed to each member of the board, as well as to the mayor, and town council.

The document included allegations of misuse of public funds, inappropriate sexual conduct, drunken episodes, and my high salary. Bernie had decided not to run for reelection. The new president of the board, Ray Brian, called for an emergency meeting. The board would meet with me in an executive session that would be closed to the public.

It was two hours of discomfort for all of us. I addressed each of the allegations, separating fact from fiction. For example, one afternoon, my secretary called Rudner into my office. I was asleep with my head on the desk. Rudner, Rocky, and Ajalat managed to carry me in my chair out the back to Rudner's truck. I woke up in the bed of the truck and looked out from under the tarp. I thought, *Oh no, Main Street, Allendale.* They took me home.

I did enjoy a couple of manhattans with dinner at the Seven Seas in nearby Ramsey on the district's credit card. Kowalsky and I did this when there was an evening board meeting. These were twelve- to fifteen-hour days for me. Some were much longer. One unforgettable board meeting found me sitting at the conference table with one last member who insisted on going into extreme detail. The wall clock indicated that it was 2:15 a.m.

Mr. Goodman fell asleep at the table. I had heard that he suffered from narcolepsy. I phoned his wife. She advised me to make sure that he didn't fall and hit his head. Then she explained that Bill could hear and understand everything that was going on around him. She told me to continue the meeting, as if he was awake! I dutifully went on with the meeting, asking him questions and explaining my positions on the remaining issues. When Mr. Goodman woke up, he thanked me for calling his wife, and answered the questioned that I had raised while he had been asleep.

As to my sexual misbehavior, I described a business lunch that Kowalsky and I had with the district's bus vendor, who picked up the tab at the Spanish Fly restaurant in Allendale. I noticed a lone woman at the bar who appeared to be sobbing. Placing my hand on her shoulder, I asked her something. She said that it was her fortieth birthday and that she was alone. I invited her to join us at our table (Kowalsky was an entertaining raconteur), and we cheered her up. Yes, I drove her home and met her mother, who was wheelchair bound. Later I learned that the bar boy had been a NHRHS graduate, had recognized me, and had mentioned it to someone who had told it to a teacher.

I waited outside the conference room as the board deliberated. This was almost as difficult for me as waiting outside for the results of my doctoral oral exam at Columbia University. When I was called back into the session, there was recognition of what I had accomplished and confidence that I would continue to achieve at a high level. They told me that my personal life was just that, and to keep it personal. This was a courageous board. (See Appendix: Photo of a courageous Board)

Draining the Swamp

Now the gloves were off. I'm from Brooklyn. I convinced the board to pass a resolution promoting the longtime board attorney to the sole role of handling special education litigation.

His promotion was a humiliating demotion. I phoned Charlie, my old carpool buddy from Washingtonville, and asked him who the best board attorney in New Jersey was. Without hesitation, he said, "Jamie Plosia." The board appointed Mr. Plosia as our new board attorney. Three months later, our special education attorney retired. He had served as the school board attorney for twenty-seven years!

Then I made another call to Charlie. I explained that I had some personnel and organizational problems. I needed a reputable consultant who was open-minded, and might be able to see things my way.

"Take a look at Ravige Associates out on Long Island," was Charlie's reply. I convinced the board that we needed to hire an outside consultant to analyze our organizational structure. After sending out fifteen requests for proposals, I recommended Ravige Associates for the contract. The board awarded the contract to Ravige Associates.

When Dr. Ravige presented his findings and recommendations to the board, all hell broke loose in the school and community. Principal Hisson was quoted in the *Town Journal* as saying, "The consultant's work was a legalized hit-and-run job" (See Appendix: The Ravige report a "hit and run job"). The Ravige report made a strong case for the restructuring of the administration and a redeployment of staff. The taxpayers had paid for the study. It was now incumbent upon the board to follow through with the effort, and approve actions to implement the recommendations.

A public meeting was held, which drew a large agitated crowd including reporters for the *Bergen Record* and the *Town Journal*. Mary Service put it succinctly when she wrote,

"The *Town Journal* has talked to the participants in the dispute—what emerges is a deep division between the Superintendent, Dr. Garrahan, and the Highland's staff, and a resistance to change by the staff. At the same time, harassment has been directed at Dr. Garrahan's family, with anonymous letters saying that he won't have a job next year. Yet, Principal Hisson and two teachers stated that "Highlands is a family.""

She went on to write,

"The superintendent supports the consultant's recommendations. The Principal, Hisson, does not, nor do the teachers, nor does the president of the union, nor does the executive committee .... Dr. Garrahan would not speculate about the reasons for the staff's strenuous opposition to implementing the report ... nor could he suggest who orchestrated the campaign of harassment ... an anonymous five-page handout has circulated among Allendale residents the past few weeks, critical of Dr. Garrahan's yearly salary of $94,000, and questioning why Principal Hisson is being reassigned." (See Appendix)

After the dust settled, a dozen staff members resigned from their positions in the school district, including the principal, vice principal, director of athletics, director of computer operations, and four supervisors.

I Was Forced to Resign

Next, I went after remaining members of the old guard. Most accepted a monetary payout (illegal in New Jersey). A few others dug in their heels. The last holdout was tough. After placing a voice-activated recorder on the bookshelf in my office, I invited Mr. Banjo to come in to discuss his thoughts on his retirement with me. When I thought I had collected enough of our conversation, I suggested we think it over and talk the following day.

When he returned the next day, I played the tape. Banjo became enraged and ran from my office, yelling that I had taped him. He returned to my office the following day and asked for the tape. I reminded him that he had left the previous meeting without listening to the entire tape, and that he had made comments that he would never want others to hear. I handed Banjo a suggested letter of resignation and informed him that the tape would be destroyed once the board accepted his resignation. Two weeks later, the board accepted his resignation.

Subsequently, Banjo contacted Mary Service at the *Town Journal*, telling her that I had taped him, and had forced him to retire. At the next meeting of the board, Banjo had packed the meeting with his supporters. He read a letter aloud from his attorney and accused me of illegally taping a private conversation. Under these circumstances, he asked the board to rescind their prior action. The board held its ground and voted unanimously not to rescind his resignation. I cleaned house, Bernie. The swamp has been drained. Northern Highlands Regional High School was ranked 29th among the best high schools in the United States out of 25,000 high schools. And NHRHS is a Federally designated Drug-Free School. (See Appendix: Banjo Forced to Retire, "I was taped.")

National Recognition: A Drug-Free School

For three consecutive years, I had collected valid and reliable data relating to our students drug use. I requested literature from the US Department of Education and the Office of Safe and Drug-Free Schools. I was reasonably certain that few schools, if any, had approached student substance abuse from the perspective of 'substance use prevention', as NHRHS had.

We entered the national competition and won. NHRHS was designated a drug-free school. We were invited to Washington, DC where our host was to be Senator Ted Kennedy. However, Senator Orrin Hatch greeted us, and explained that his friend Senator Kennedy had asked him to meet with us. Senator Kennedy had a more interesting invitation.

(See photo: Senator Orrin, Hatch and I)

National recognition is always good for the local town. Our community was cited in an article in *The New York Times*, relating to the positive impact that an excellent school could have on the local community. Subsequently, the New Jersey State Education Department recognized me as a distinguished educator. (See Appendix: Drug Free School; Distinguished Educator)

A Battle Royale

Following the resignation of Mr. Hisson, I was tasked with finding a replacement. Our employment listing attracted fifty highly qualified candidates from across the country. I interviewed the top five contenders and decided to recommend Dr. William Woeman. He had impressive credentials, excellent letters of recommendation, and an engaging personality. The board interviewed Dr. Woeman. They appreciated why I had recommended him. Just as I had been appointed to be the school district's second superintendent, Dr. Woeman was appointed as the high school's second principal. As newspaper reports show, he was popular with students, staff, and parents. I cannot recall anyone who did not like him. He was a great choice ... or maybe not!

About three months into the position, I met with Dr. Woeman to discuss something (I don't remember what). During our conversation, one of his responses did not ring true to me. I thought Molly Wellen, the director of pupil personnel services, might be able to confirm what he had told me. After telling her what was on my mind, she stated emphatically, "That's simply not true." A red flag went up.

I confronted Dr. Woeman. His face flushed red, and he said, "Well, what I actually meant was—""No, Bill, you lied." I dropped the matter and moved on, but I didn't forget.

A couple months later, Rhoda Ferat, our social worker, spoke privately with me. She raised a concern about something she had heard from a student. "It's probably nothing, but I thought you should know." I gave a lot of thought to the implications of what Rhoda had shared with me. She was a very competent professional.

Then one night, I had a custodian get me into Dr. Woeman's office. The keys to his file cabinets were in his desk drawer. I found some personal correspondence that had nothing to do with Northern Highland. He probably should have kept this stuff at home. I was beginning to wonder if there was another side to Dr. Woeman.

While inside Dr. Woeman's office, I hid a voice-activated micro cassette recorder. His inappropriate telephone conversations provided me with convincing evidence. It was my duty to protect our students, and I did not want to have a potential threat to their well-being in the building.

This was a most difficult decision. I did what I believed was the right thing to do. New Jersey education law provides a superintendent with the inherent power to block any personnel appointment.

When it came time for the board to renew Dr. Woeman's contract, I invited him into my office. Everyone in the school and community assumed that his contract would be renewed. However, I explained to Dr. Woeman why I would not recommend his reappointment. It was an awkward conversation. He asked me if our conversation was being recorded. I replied, "Just tell the truth, and it won't make any difference."

The afternoon the board was to act on his reappointment, he came into the conference room where I was assembling materials for the evening board meeting. He had a phony smile on his face as he said, "You're not going to do this, right?" Wrong! He asked if I would remove the motion relative to his reappointment from the agenda so that he would have time to meet with an attorney. I agreed. As soon as word got out that Dr. Woeman's reappointment had been removed from the board's agenda, rumors began circulating in the community.

Subsequently, we met in my office. Dr. Woeman came with a high-profile labor attorney. I had asked our board attorney to be present. We all knew that in New Jersey, the board lacked the authority to overrule if a superintendent did not recommend an individual for a position. When it became clear that my position was immovable, our board attorney said something to the effect, "I know Dr. Garrahan well, and Dr. Woeman will be gone from the district by July 1st."

The two lawyers caucused in my conference room. When they returned, they explained that the situation called for a gag order, which they had prepared. Dr. Woeman and I, both signed the gag order. Shock, disbelief, anger, accusations, and lots of rumors followed. The newspapers covered the known facts. It was very frustrating for members of the community. The only people who could answer their questions were held silent by the gag order. Dr. Woeman resigned. I thought, *Why would an innocent man resign?* (See Endnote #6 and Appendix: Popular Principal Resigns).

Life Can Be Rough

One night, a police officer came to my home in Pearl River. He asked to step inside. He said, "Can we sit down? Your son Dean is dead. He took his own life." My life was changed forever. Dean had been twenty-six. He had a degree in environmental science. He was in the Florida Everglades doing work he enjoyed. His girlfriend had left him.

Mark and I flew down to Florida to Dean's home. After Mark finished cleaning his brother's facial tissue from the wall in the bedroom, he found a suicide note that Dean had placed inside a book on the top bookshelf. One sentence was etched in my brain. "Dad where were you, when I needed you?" In fact, I was mowing the lawn the night before Dean's death. Eileen yelled down to me from the bedroom deck, "One of your drunken teachers called..." I continued mowing. It was my son, Dean, reaching out to me. Eileen has refused to acknowledge her role in that phone call. It became an issue (See endnote #6 and Appendix: Popular Principal Resigns).

I had dealt with lots of problems in my life, but I couldn't handle this. I began drinking too much, smoking pot, and taking lorazepam to sleep at night. The people at Northern Highland were very supportive. I had hired competent professionals. The district could run on autopilot. My administrative assistant, Elaine, was capable of running the district office.

One night, I was at home sitting on the couch drinking vodka. My wife was in our bedroom. Three men in white uniforms came in the front door and walked toward the couch saying they were there to help me. When one went behind me, I stood up and resisted. They wrapped velcro straps around me, and carried me into an ambulance. I saw one preparing a hypodermic needle. I yelled, "I don't want to be injected with anything!" He stuck the needle into my body.

The Superintendent Is in the Psychiatric Ward

I woke up in the Frawley Psychiatric Unit of Good Samarian Hospital in Suffern strapped to a gurney. With no response to my voice, I managed to move the gurney into the doorway and hall. It was 3 a.m. on the wall clock. They rolled me back into the room. A psychiatrist began asking me questions. My sense was that I knew more about mental disorders than he did.

I made a deal: I would make no more disturbances, if I could phone my lawyer. He had a nurse bring me a phone. I called Rudner, my security director. "Hello, Mr. Rudner. I know lawyers don't appreciate calls at this time of the day, but I'm strapped to a gurney across from the nurse's station in the Frawley Unit at Good Sam. I need to get out of here as soon as possible. ... Okay, I appreciate whatever you need to do to get me out."

I thanked the doctor and nurses. I knew that Rudner had decoded my message. Within an hour, he walked into my room, and showed me the razor in his hand. I said, "Let's go." As we rushed out of the room, the nursed yelled, "You can't leave. You're not checked out. It's snowing out. You don't have shoes." We broke into a run for Rudner's truck and took off.

The next day, he got me an ill-fitting suit of clothes. In the evening, we went to my home. My wife refused to open the door. She would not put my wallet, medicine, and keys out the pet door. We left, but planned a forced entry for the following morning when my wife would be at work. The next morning, Rudner, one of his maintenance guys, and I waited out of sight across the road in the neighbor's driveway. She never left the house because there was too much snow. Our mission was aborted.

I knew a woman who was employed at the county courthouse in New City. Years earlier, I had helped her with some personal problem. She put me at the top of the judge's calendar. The judge asked me to stand in the crowded courtroom. I explained what I had been subjected to. He asked me which car I wanted. I replied that the Cadillac was Eileen's and that I would take the Volkswagen. The judge issued a court order to enter and live in my home. I had told the judge that the home was owned by my wife. He said that according to the law in New York, this was my home.

I arrived at 93 Pascack Road with Kevin, a locksmith in Pearl River, and a lawyer with a video camera. My wife came to the door. She denied me entry. The lawyer read the judge's order, but to no avail. I told Kevin to drill through the lock. My wife was screaming to someone on the phone, "They are drilling the lock." She unlocked the door. My lawyer handed her the court order. She packed up and left. I gave all of the liquor in the house to Kevin. The judge's order required me to remove all alcohol from the house.

About two months later, Eileen phoned me at night. She had fallen at a construction site and had injured her head. She stated that she did not need to go for X-rays, and that she just wanted me to come and bring her home. I brought her back to 93 Pascack Road.

Meanwhile, the board had met with me in an executive session. They were convinced that I was emotionally stable, and competent to carry out the responsibilities of my position. During my ten years administering in the district, I had never had a bad board. I returned to my district duties. Eileen and I divorced.

I resigned from my position on June 30, 1995. I was fifty-six years old and could have worked another ten or fifteen years. My salary was $150,000. But there was an emptiness in my heart. The Northern Highlands school board recognized my ten years of leadership in a special board of education resolution (See Appendix: Board Resolution).

For me, the most meaningful recognition was from the great police officers with whom I had worked closely with for a decade. The Allendale Police Department attended my retirement dinner, and presented me with a special plaque acknowledging our work for the community (See Appendix: Board Resolution and Allendale Police Department plaque).

CHAPTER 10

Starting Over

Life in Prescott, Arizona

Our school bus vendor offered me a condo in Park Ridge to live in as long as I wanted to. I stayed there for about two months. There was not one day when I did not think of Dean or meet someone who knew Dean. I knew that changing my geography would not change my feelings. Psychotherapy would be fruitless. I bought a cargo van and loaded it with my possessions. I left a lot behind, including every photograph of Dean.

I drove west looking for a place to live and to start a new life. I visited Colorado, New Mexico, Texas, California, and Arizona, staying several days in each state. The first time I drove into Prescott, Arizona, I had a good feeling about it. Courthouse Square, Whiskey Row, antique shops, and restaurants were there.

I rented a motel room and went to a real estate office. After riding around with the realtor for several days, she showed me a house that seemed right for me. I bought it, furnished it, and moved in. A young cat wandered by. I took her in. Maggie was a good buddy.

A few months later, my daughter, Susan, a senior project control engineer for NASA at JPL in Pasadena, came to visit me. She introduced me to her fiancé, Frank. For some reason they wanted us to meet with a priest and answer three pages of questions. I don't know what that was about. Frank was obviously very serious about his Catholicism.

The weather was great in Prescott, which had an elevation of over five thousand feet. That first winter, we got more snow than my son Mark got in Manhattan, where he was a client-relations manager at Moody's Investor Services. But my cold winter days were dry. I had great weather and good neighbors. Whenever I drove to California to visit Susan, Ron and Sue, who lived next door, would take care of Maggie.

My Website and Collections for Sale

I read something in *The Daily Courier* about a new device whereby one could access the Internet through the television, called Web TV. I drove down to Phoenix and bought one for a hundred dollars. Included was a book with instructions on setting up your own website. It was a great gadget. The television was my monitor. It had a wireless keyboard so I could sit and watch TV or switch to the Internet. I had no idea what to do with my website, so I just listed some of my collections and invited people to contact me if anything interested them.

I was more than surprised when a retired lawyer in Tennessee contacted me. He said that he had a tin photograph of his long deceased father. He thought one of my daguerreotype frames might be appropriate. It wasn't possible to put photos on my website, so I described one of my best frames to him. He mailed me $300, and I mailed him the frame.

Within days, a photography institution in Pittsburgh contacted me. I described my collection in detail. The caller told me what they would be prepared to pay. I flew to Pittsburgh. They bought the entire collection. I decided this could be fun.

The lawyer called back and said that the daguerreotype frame was not in excellent condition as I had described it. He said that it was in mint condition, and that he would like to purchase another one. I explained that I had already sold the entire collection.

Then I received an email from a woman in North Hollywood who was interested in buying my collection of vintage photographs of nude females from 1915–1950. When I understood that she only wanted to use them on her business website, and realized I really was not ready to sell these photos, I rented six hundred photographs to her for two weeks which she scanned to her website. She paid generously and gave me a membership to her website, Retro Raunch, in perpetuity. Several of my photographs are still on her website. At the time, my collection consisted of about two thousand photos.

[Flash forward to 2017: I sold one hundred nude photos by Alexander Baege for $9,000 to a vintage photo collector in Manhattan. Currently, I have five walls in my home decorated with nudes.]

(See photos: Daguerreotypes, nudes, button hooks)

A woman in Colorado then expressed interest in my buttonhook collection. She bought ten or fifteen of them. Months later, she made a surprise visit to Prescott with her husband. I invited them into my living room, and laid out my buttonhooks on a sheet on the floor. She bought $800 worth. An article that I wrote for the *American Collector*, "Buttonhooks in America: A Reflection of Social Class," attracted several buyers but not enough. Currently, I am negotiating a sale with a local dealer for the remaining three hundred buttonhooks.

My collection of racist postcards went for $5,000 to a New York City collector who had read two of my published articles: "Military Tradition: African Americans in Military Service" and "Cancelled Cards Document Racism in American Social History." He got a very good deal. (See Appendix: Included in resumé)

Back in the Stock Market

I had kept my hand in the stock market since the 1960s. My Web TV gave me the opportunity to buy and sell stocks in real time. I got into it and became a day trader, selling out of most positions before the closing bell each day.

Once, I got burned. I lost thousands of dollars on one stock. For some reason, I had executed that trade by phone with Ameritrade. They had sent me a brochure in which they listed the final steps that they took before executing an order. I was certain that their agent had not addressed one of the steps before he placed the trade. I asked for a copy of the tape recording. We went to arbitration, and I got most of my money back. I also switched brokers. I moved my account to Charles Schwab and continued in the stock market.

A Phone Call

One day, my ex-wife Eileen phoned me. She wanted to know how I was doing, what Prescott was like, and if she come for a visit. I told her that it was okay. We enjoyed the visit. Soon, she sold her home in Pear River and joined me in Arizona.

We frequently drove to Seattle to visit her daughter and to California to visit my daughter.

In Prescott, our next-door neighbor, Ron, had an antique store downtown. Whenever he went on a buying trip, my partner Eileen would work in his antique shop. She enjoyed that. We made some friends in Chino Valley and Skull Valley.

My house, built in the 1930s, was relatively small. Eileen needed more room. I hired a builder to remove the roof and build a second level on top. However, the project was not uneventful. The day that the builder removed the entire roof, we were awakened in the middle of the night by water falling from the ceiling onto our bed. Water was dropping from the ceilings in every room. (Later I learned that the monsoon had arrived early. I didn't even know about monsoons in Arizona!) I phoned the builder, described the situation, and asked him to get over here quickly, and bring tarps. I was surprised to hear that he didn't have any tarps, and would have to wait for Home Depot to open in a few hours. Eileen and I placed all the pots, bowls, and pails that we had around the house to catch the water. In the end, we were pleased with the addition to our home.

The additional space included a large bedroom with a walk-in closet. I lined the closet with cedar. I had bought an antique claw-footed tub somewhere on the east coast which we put in the upstairs bathroom. (I recall that after buying the tub, I stopped at Mom's home in Philadelphia to visit with her. When I was leaving, she walked me out to the station wagon and said, "What the heck are you doing with that old bathtub in the back?" I told her that I was taking it for my home in Arizona. I think she thought that I was crazy.)

We did have a great view of the mountains from that claw foot tub. We even built a small outside deck, which gave us a further view of the spectacular snowcapped mountains. The bedroom also had a direct view of Thumb Butte, which we often climbed when our children visited.

(See photos: The addition is larger than the house. Spectacular views. Doing some riding with our friend Rich on his ranch in Skull Valley and Maggie enjoys the view)

I had to hire a crane to lift a large outdoor hot tub and place it in back of the house. Later, I bought a house nearby as an investment. I rented it to a preacher and his wife while they were building their own home. After they moved out, I rented the house to a woman and her female partner. They were excellent tenants. Life was good.

Eileen and I enjoyed visiting many places: Bisbee, a historic town about fifteen miles from Mexico; Bullhead City, which had casinos and was located across the Colorado River in Laughlin, Nevada; Quartzsite, the world's largest flea market where one could even buy weed from a used-book vendor; Jerome, an old mining town; Cottonwood with its good German restaurant; and even several car trips to Puerto Penasco (Rocky Point) in Mexico.

On one of our more memorable trips to Mexico, we arranged to fly our children there for Thanksgiving dinner in a condo we had rented. Eileen prepared a feast of a dinner at home. I bought a large car top carrier for five dollars at a garage sale. We loaded the feast into the carrier. I tied the carrier securely to the rack of our 1995 Ford Explorer, with ropes coming inside the car through the windows. Off we went to Mexico.

That night we encountered a rainstorm, and I reached up to touch our carrier, but there was nothing there. I pulled off the road and tried to calm Eileen down. I said that we would take the kids out for dinner in Rocky Point. No, we had to walk back and look for it in the rain. Eileen used our flashlight. She yelled that she had found the carrier, which was in pretty good condition. I walked back to get the car. Then we had to unload the contents of the carrier in order to get it up on the roof. Then we reloaded the food. It was dicey in the wet darkness, but we did it. I tied it down more securely.

While enjoying Thanksgiving dinner, Eileen's daughter, Melissa, crunched on something in her vegetables and removed a chard of glass from her mouth. I explained that we had had a mishap enroute.

Eileen and I had lots of fun together, so it surprised me when she told me that she wanted to move back to New York City. Her primary reason was that there were not enough Jews in Prescott. I tried to change her thinking, mentioning the three generations of Resnicks who owned the jewelry business on Courthouse Square, the Navajo carpet salesman, Zelda and Rich with their horses out in Skull Valley. They were retired Jews from Long Island. There was also a temple on a ranch. But I understood that there was something especially unique about Jews from Brooklyn, the Bronx, and Manhattan. Eileen was also looking forward to the birth of her first grandchild in Manhattan. So she went back to find a place for us.

CHAPTER 11

From Prescott to Lincoln Center

Soon Eileen phoned and said that she had found the perfect co-op in Lincoln Center. I could see why she liked it. It was a corner unit on the fourteenth floor with a line of sight to Central Park, and the Empire State Building. It even gave you a peek of the Hudson River. "Will I be able to smoke?" I asked. "Yes, there is a wonderful twenty-six-foot terrace."

I ran a two-week garage sale in Prescott, which attracted many of the antique dealers in town. Some of them bought several of my collections, including vintage Hunter Case pocket watches, buttonhooks, black amethyst glassware, and more. That brought in nearly $2,000. It took me two months to sell both of my Prescott properties. Real estate transactions are quick and simple in Arizona and lawyers are optional. I broke even on my home, but made a substantial profit on the rental home.

I had always enjoyed Manhattan. However, I could see that the aspects I had liked most were disappearing. The little shops were being bought up. More skyscrapers were being built. I was never interested in concerts, opera, musical productions, and the like.

Near the end of July in 2001, we were enjoying the views from the rooftop garden of my stepdaughter Melissa's co-op. Holding my two-year-old granddaughter, Sarah, who was visiting from California, I pointed to the Twin Towers of the World Trade Center. Two months later, on September 11, I was eating breakfast while watching the TV news when I saw the plane crash into one of the towers.

Eileen drove me to West 23rd Street and 10th Avenue to the Chelsea Tavern where I was scheduled to hang a dozen framed female nudes on my wall inside (I had an arrangement with the owner whereby the tavern would receive 25 percent of my gross sales). While I was refreshing the wall with new photos, the bartender, who was in the process of setting up the bar, hollered, "Dave, another plane just hit the other tower." Climbing down off the ladder, I could see the scene on TV. I knew immediately it had to be a terrorist attack.

(See photos: Showing my granddaughter the towers in July 2001. Refreshing my photos in the Chelsea Tavern on September 11, 2001)

I gathered all my photos and placed them into a shopping cart. Pushing my framed nudes, I walked forty-three blocks north on 10th Avenue in the heat and confusion. I cannot imagine why I pushed this load when I could have simply left them in the tavern and picked them up at any time. I joined a stream of about a thousand people fleeing north out of lower Manhattan. No one knew what was happening, they just wanted to get far away from it. It was a surreal experience. People stood on the sidewalks offering us water and juice.

The following morning, Melissa's husband, Nelson, and I headed to their co-op to gather up items, including their infant son's medicine. However, we learned that people were not allowed south of Canal Street. We asked a soldier atop an armored vehicle for permission to retrieve the medicine. He checked with a superior who gave us permission.

We walked down to Houston Street where the white ash on the ground was about an inch deep. Nelson retrieved his stuff and closed the open windows. We walked another block south where Nelson took photos of the crash scene. I had a red bandana covering my nose and mouth. Then we headed for the Mercer Hotel where displaced residents had been given emergency housing.

Our friend Bernie Arnold from Northern Highlands lived across the Hudson River in Upper Saddle River. Not entirely satisfied with synagogue life, Bernie had started his own, calling it a 'havurah'. We joined and attended services each Friday night at the homes of different members.

Bernie began having difficulty swallowing his food. He was loyal to his ninety-two year old family doctor, Peter Mink. Unfortunately, the doctor misdiagnosed the problem. Bernie had esophageal cancer. He died. He had never smoked. At gatherings, he might have one glass of wine. Bernie was a man of conviction and courage, and the best family man I ever met. What a terrible loss to his family and community.

Building a Home on the Delaware River

Getting restless, I started looking for a place on the Delaware River. One day I stopped into the Penn-York Real Estate office in Narrowsburg, New York. The office had no listings for houses on the Delaware. However, an agent mentioned that she was going to be listing an abandoned commercial garage later in the week.

We went out to see it in five inches of snow. The garage had two long pits inside where mechanics had worked on the underside of vehicles. An official notice posted on the external door indicated that the EPA had condemned the property. The real estate agent let me know that the owner had saved the dirty oil to use as heating fuel. A few of the fifty-gallon drums had rotted, seeping oil into the ground.

I looked beyond that issue. The property was being sold 'as is'. The property itself was outstanding and had two hundred feet of frontage on the Delaware River. Across the River in Pennsylvania, one could see only trees and cliffs. From the rear of the garage, there was not a house in sight, but only nature. I entered the bidding by phone from Lincoln Towers. While I was prepared to bid up to $70,000, I got the property for $25,000! (See photos: Garage House, Family Room with steps up to the new addition, shooting pool in the village pub)

Narrowsburg is a sleepy, laid-back town. I received a building permit. I hired a local builder and converted the garage into a house with four bedrooms. The old garage became a forty by forty foot recreation room with a twenty-foot ceiling.

My first encounter with police began when I drove into Narrowsburg where a state police barrack was located. I was pulled over, and the trooper informed me that I had just driven through a stop sign, had not signaled my right turn, and was driving forty miles per hour in a zone where the speed limit was thirty. A few minutes later, he told me that I was driving an unregistered and uninsured vehicle!

The trooper asked me if I was a local. I replied that I owned a home on the river in the village, and that the folks at the Village Pub considered me a local. Then I mentioned that he and I had been the only two people (in a bar crowd of more than forty people) who had not dressed in costume at the Village Pub's recent Halloween party. That got his attention. I had asked Gale, the bartender, who the guy in regular clothes at the bar was, and she had said that he was the head of the state police barrack in the village, adding that he was a good guy, and that they rode together often because they were in the same bikers club. I had recognized his name on his nameplate.

We talked for a bit, and he told me to drive slowly (snow was beginning to fall)down the hill, to turn left, and to leave my car in the St. Francis's parking lot. He also said that in the morning, I should call the MVB in Albany and solve my registration/insurance problem. I left my car at the church and walked to the Village Pub where I chatted with Gale and her mother, Marge. At 11 p.m., against Gale's advice, I walked to my car in two inches of snow and drove slowly to my home in Lincoln Center. Three weeks later, I learned that someone had typed one incorrect digit of my VIN number on a form.

I frequented three bars in the area. The Village Pub in Narrowsburg was run by Gale and her mother, Marge. I never went by there without stopping in. One night, my buddy Charlie Wieland got into a disagreement with Tom P. (the well-heeled owner of the Narrowsburg Inn). When Tom's comments got nasty, I yelled down to him to knock it off. He barked back, "Who the hell are you, and where did you get your doctor's degree?"

I said, "Columbia University in Manhattan." He walked up, took the stool next to me, and told Gale to give Charlie and the good doctor a drink. He had an undergraduate degree from an Ivy League college. We became close, but it would take another chapter to capture the flavor.

A few years later, Marge and Gale sold the Village Pub to Richard from Paramus, New Jersey. He told me that his life's dream was to own a tavern in a sleepy, country town. He was a decent enough guy, but I observed that he didn't understand the local culture. And he was not good with people. The bar crowd got smaller and smaller until I was the only person at the bar. He was always sitting at a table playing cards with two guys. I stopped going to the village pub. Subsequently, Rich was found dead with his head on the bar. He had shot himself. I had already moved on. The pub had lost its atmosphere and there was no camaraderie.

I enjoyed good dinners at the Three Wishes over the bridge in Pennsylvania. Unfortunately, while they served alcohol, they didn't have a bar. I've always enjoyed sitting with locals at a bar. So I moved on to the Western Hotel in Callicoon, north of Narrowsburg, the oldest continuously running hotel/bar in NYS. This Victorian mansion dates back to 1852. They had good, classy dining. I enjoyed Joe, the owner, who wore a black vest, jacket, and bow tie.

However, he did a dumb thing one late Saturday night after he had closed. He sat at the bar with one of his waitresses and showed her a revolver. It discharged, killing the woman. A few months later, my son Mark and I went up to the Western Hotel for dinner. To my surprise, Joe served us. I ordered my usual manhattan, but Joe apologized, saying that he had temporarily lost his alcohol license. My son stood up to leave, but I asked him to sit down. I told him that this was no time to abandon a good guy. A few minutes later, Joe came over with a drink in a fruit juice glass, "I found some cherry juice in the kitchen." It was my manhattan!

[Flash forward to 2017: I took Erika up to show her my Delaware River house. We stayed overnight at the Western Hotel. A young Russian woman from Brooklyn had bought it. She told me that Joe 'was out', lived a few blocks up the street and stopped in often.]

Then the floods came. The first flood, a one-hundred-year flood, wiped out the ground floor of my home. I could deal with that. The next flood, however, was a five-hundred-year flood. I had assumed that this rare event would occur once in 500 years. The guys at the bar explained that it means on any day the chances of having a 500 year flood are 1 in 500? The raging river smashed out the windows on the north side of my home and pushed out the windows on the south side. My son Mark drove up from New York City and started cutting up the new carpeting, but his knife was not up to the task.

I went up to Tom P.'s house, also on the river, and asked him if he could spare a worker or two. He had six guys, two of whom were working in his wine cellar where Tom said at least $10,000 of his rare wine had been lost. He asked all six of his workers to help me. Six pickups unloaded in front of my home. They came in with tools and cut out and removed the muddy carpeting from my 40'x40' recreation room. Then they removed all of the soggy sheetrock. After carrying all the debris to their trucks, they refused to accept any money. I asked the leader of the crew what his name was and learned that his brother was the head of the state police.

The next day I withdrew money from the bank and went to the barracks. The lieutenant came out of his office. As I handed him six one-hundred-dollar bills, he looked up at the ceiling and said, "It's not going to look good on the videotape." He gave me his brother's address on the Flats and said that I should just put it under the mat at his side door. He said that he would call his brother and tell him to look for a surprise when he got off work. I wrote a piece about this experience, "The Meaning of Community," which was published in the *River Reporter*. (See Appendix)

Someone said that 'you've got to know when to fold them'. I listed the property at $465,000 but finally took $265,000. In 2008, the real estate market was in turmoil. With about

$125,000 in the property and plenty of good times, I was satisfied. My son Mark still goes up to *our house* to fish. My wife and I visited Narrowsburg in 2017. We hooked up with my old buddy Charlie. We sat on the banks of the Delaware River in back of my house.

(See photos: Delaware River 50ft. above normal; me and Charlie, Charlie and Erika on the riverbank, my riverhouse facing the Delaware River, and me shooting pool at the Village Pub after rotator-cuff surgery. I won!)

On the Road Again and Another Marriage

My ex-wife and I had a couple of issues, which led to, "If you don't like it, get out." I moved out and rented an apartment in Hastings-on-Hudson. I began meeting people, which was difficult at age seventy. I met a younger woman, Magdalena, a former model from Venezuela. We got married (too quickly). She had a daughter at the University of Arizona in Tucson, and asked if we could move there so she could be near her daughter. That was okay. I got us a house in Marana, a suburb of Tucson. (See photos: Marana home; with hot tub and miniature golf course)

We moved in a truckload of her stuff and another of mine. The next day, we drove into Tucson to surprise her freshman daughter. The lady in the registrar's office explained that by law, she could not give us any information. Magdalena became very agitated. I calmly, communicated a nonverbal message to the lady. She stepped away from her computer and motioned for me to look at the screen. As she turned her back and stepped away, I read the word *dismissed*. Yes, little Monica had been dismissed a few months earlier! We agreed that there was no sense staying in Marana (By the way, I was pissed big time). Magdalena said that she always wanted to live in Boca Raton, Florida. I sold the house, packed up, and shipped everything to Florida.

En route back east, we stopped in New York and found Monica. I phoned my former student, Father Mac, who was now the president of St. Thomas Aquinas College. He agreed to facilitate Monica's admission to the college. I gave Monica $300 or $400 to purchase books and other necessities and I paid for her first semester's tuition and room & board. Unfortunately, within months, she was dismissed for violating the college's drug policy.

We stayed in a renaissance hotel in Del Ray Beach, Florida for six weeks as we searched for a house. I bought a house in Boca Raton on a nice canal with an in-ground pool. We moved in. This was easier said than done.

Magdalena seemed to have a large extended family, most of whom were having financial problems. I found myself sending money to Venezuela, Costa Rica, and Colombia.

Soon I learned that I needed abdominal surgery. At Jackson Memorial Hospital in Miami, surgeons removed half of my pancreas as well as my spleen. At home, I was laid up, with a visiting nurse coming every day to drain the surgical site. It was clear that I would not be able to care for the property. I sold the house at a loss, and bought a condo in Miami Beach with great intracoastal waterfront activity.

Soon I stopped sending money to people who I had never met. I told Magdalena, "Enough of this charity stuff!" Two weeks later, Magdalena did not return home from her classes at the University of Miami, and my new car was gone. I went to the police station in Miami Beach. The desk officer asked me who owned the car. I did, but I had put the car in both of our names. The female officer said. "She took her car."

I had also stupidly put my condo in both of our names. Since my wife was homeless and unemployed, I was required to pay all of Magdalena's legal expenses, including two teams of divorce lawyers. She demanded fifty percent of our home. It turned out to be a very costly fourteen-month marriage.

Soon I met Erika, but I had also developed more abdominal pain. Erika drove me to Mt. Sinai Medical Center. CAT scans indicated I needed another operation. They removed more of my pancreas and some other stuff. I was out of it. Erika was with me every day at the hospital. Finally, I got fed up with all the tests and hours of CAT scans over a two-week hospital stay. I phoned Erika at 2 a.m. and told her to come get me. By the time she arrived, I had disconnected the tubes from my IV lines and nose. I had to cut the catheter tube off. Erika took me home.

(See photo: Not released by the hospital!)

I remember trying to eat a cup of yogurt, as I watched the Miami Heat in the playoffs, but didn't make it to the second half of the game. The yogurt wasn't going down, and the pain got bad. Apparently, one of the IVs must have been feeding me pain medicine!

I went back to Mt. Sinai. It was a nasty scene in the ER. Erika kept telling them, "He's been here for the past three weeks. You must have this information in your computer." Finally, they took me up to a room, hooked up the tubes, and removed and replaced the catheter (Ouch!). So began more CAT scans.

Finally, Dr. Bliss came into my room. He said that I needed more surgery. He had a team that would be ready to operate at two o'clock. I replied that I would like to think it over and let him know in the morning. He said, "You don't have that much time. Some of your organs are beginning to lose function."

"Okay, I get it," and signed permission to operate. They removed sections of intestines. (I believe that when they were putting my insides back during the previous surgery, they twisted some of the intestines?). In a week or so, a rehab therapist got me up and walking. Erika took me home and moved her cats in with me. She was really good at the recovery routine.

CHAPTER 12

The End of the Journey

Getting Married at Seventy-Six

Erika and I were married on September 4, 2014, at the justice of the peace's office in Miami Beach. Two of the office workers served as witnesses. It turned out that Erika had assumed that I would move into her home in Boca Raton, and I had assumed she would move into my home in Miami Beach. For me, Boca Raton had too much of an attitude—one of superiority. Erika would not be comfortable in my building, which was overwhelmingly populated with people from South America. Finally I said, "I'll sell my place, you sell your place, and we'll look for a place we both like."

Erika had lived in Europe for years and spoke German. I remembered that when I would visit my son who had been working at Enron headquarters in Houston, I had come across two towns where almost everyone spoke German. We checked them out, but decided it was too remote.

I was interested in a state that did not have an income tax. We came upon Tennessee, but were unable to find the right place. On September 9, 2014, I saw a listing that looked too good to be true. I suggested that it would probably be a waste of time, so I would just go there by myself to check it out. Erika agreed and gave me her cell phone to call her just in case it really is good. I flew to Charlotte, N.C. and rented a car for the drive to Kingsport. (Later, I would learn that I could have flown into Kingsport!)

A realtor took me to the house in Kingsport. The owner showed me the house, and Carol, the realtor and I walked the property. I whispered to her that I wanted to buy it. She had other clients that day, so we agreed to meet in her office at five o'clock. In the interim, I phoned Erika half a dozen times, but she did not answer the house phone in Miami Beach.

When I met the realtor at 5 p.m., she asked if I wanted to make an offer. I told her that I did. She started typing the contract. "How much do you want to offer?" she asked. I responded that the asking price was reasonable. She said that around there, buyers usually offered 15 to 20 percent less than the asking price. I had decided that I did not want anyone else to get this property. I waived inspections. There would be no mortgage. We would close in thirty days. Carol, the realtor, was a fast typist.

I went out for dinner and found an Asian restaurant in Virginia. I knew nothing about Kingsport, not even how close it was to the Virginia border. The next morning, the phone in my room at the Econo Lodge rang. It was Carol, "Congratulations, they accepted your offer."

When I got home to Miami Beach, Erika explained that she had been up in Boca visiting her friends. I described the house and property. She seemed surprised that this had all happened so quickly, and that it was a done deal. She listed her home with a broker in Boca Raton. I listed my condo with a Miami Beach realtor. We started packing.

I went up to Kingsport for the closing on October 6th. The listing broker was seated across the table from me. As office people were busy making copies of the documents, he said, "You would not have gotten this house without the offer you made." He explained that the owner was the general manager of the Meadowview Marriot and that he had been promoted to manage Marriot's New Orleans's facility.

An hour after the owner had signed my contract, his Marriot replacement had come into the listing broker's office to look at Mr. King's house. The listing broker told him that the house had just sold and that it was an ironclad contract. The new manager insisted on seeing the house anyway, so the listing broker showed it to him.

Discovering Kingsport

On October 26th, we drove down the steep horseshoe-shaped driveway with our suitcase and cats. Erika had never seen the property. We slept on the hardwood floor. After a hearty breakfast at Pop's, we went home to wait for the moving vans. One of the two trucks started down the driveway. His truck scraped the asphalt. The four moving guys managed to back the truck out. (I had previously described the difficult driveway to the owner of the moving company).

Our next-door neighbor came out to see what was going on. He sized up the situation and offered to use his smaller work truck to help out. Wally drove his truck into the darkness of night, with two van men off-loading our stuff from the vans up on Lakeside Drive, into Wally's truck which he drove down to the other two guys unloading below. Wally said they were 'flatlanders' and obviously had no experience with the challenge they were presented with. They finally left at about

10 p.m. Wally would not accept any money, saying, "That's what neighbors do here."

We moved there so quickly, I didn't realize that Patrick Henry Lake was eight miles long. We enjoy sitting on the back deck watching the various animals along the shoreline and boating activity on the lake. Our dog, Shep, and our three cats also have a great time. We are fortunate to have good neighbors: Wally on the left, and Sean on the right. Sean is a stand-up guy with two terrific sons, Grant and Gavin, who are both in college. Behind us are Richard and Jackie, who also have two wonderful sons, Nate and Gabe.

Others in the Kingsport community have welcomed us. Alex Looney is a Kingsport original. He also read the first draft of this book, and spared me some embarrassment. Alex is bright, trustworthy, and a gentleman. He has introduced us to at least a dozen folks who have enriched our lives. Alex also hosts a great St. Patrick's Day party at his home.

Colonel Patrick Shull gets us a good table at the annual Reagan Day Dinner and keeps us up-to-date on the political front. Pat is honest and direct—qualities which are rare among politicians. David G. takes care of us at Giuseppe's terrific restaurant. Alex and Edwina Anderson introduced us to several board members at the Barter Theater in Abington, Virginia. Erika and I enjoy ten shows each year at the Barter Theater. The actors are first-rate, and their performances add a special dimension to our lives. I've known several major league gastroenterologists in the past, but Dr. Doug Springer is at the top of my list. He retired a year ago, but his well-developed practice is in place.

Having lived in several small cities across the country, I've learned about the functioning of police departments. It is my studied judgment that the Kingsport Police Department under the leadership of Chief Quillin, is the best that I have observed in terms of professionalism and performance.

Erika joined the Christian Women's group, the Republican Women's Club, and the Kingsport Historical Society. She is also an associate member of the Daughters of the Confederacy in Johnson City, and was inducted into the Rotary Club of Kingsport. I obtained a Tennessee carry permit and joined the Cherokee Rod and Gun Club.

(See photos: Some target practice, Shep on the pontoon boat)

We built a Tennessee room, on the back of the house, with a huge glass window so that we could enjoy nature all year long. I replaced many of the property's old wooden steps with concrete ones, from the top down to the dock and connected the four sets of steps with concrete walkways. For me, working with concrete and mortar is like magic. I have always enjoyed building fieldstone walls. (See photos: Pouring concrete steps, and other walkways)

Building Fieldstone Walls and Other Projects

I built a fieldstone-walled driveway at my new home in 1965, another in Pearl River on the Pascack Brook, and one in front of my Prescott home. I built a circular brick terrace for my friend on Cape Cod.

(See photos: My first fieldstone wall. I do fancy brickwork)

My most famous fieldstone wall, however, I didn't build. I simply described the reconstruction of a deteriorated fieldstone wall that had graced the entrance to our fifty-five-acre campus at NHRHS. Two industrial arts teachers were beginning a summer landscaping class and asked me if I had any special projects. Pointing out my office window, I said something like,

"Every landscaper should know how to rebuild a fieldstone wall." As I gave them explicit instructions (two feet wide on top and four feet wide at the base), I drew a cross section of a trapezoid for them to get the picture.

After a few days, the two shop teachers came to my office and told me that the wall was done. I knew it could not possibly have been properly finished. I lost my temper, cursing at them with unpublishable language. After I calmed down, I told them to go out to the football stadium, to get one of the discarded wooden bleacher seats and a six-foot construction level from the shop, and to start over. They worked on it for two months.

At my retirement party in 1995 as a going away gift, the staff presented me with a framed picture of the fieldstone wall. Someone had taken photographs of the wall during each of the four seasons! My cursing at those shop teachers must have reverberated throughout the building.

(See photo: The Fieldstone wall in each season)

Kingsport, the Model City, has certainly exceeded my expectations. Soon we became familiar with Kingsport's rich history. During our first few months here, I bought several books on the history of Kingsport at estate sales. The town was named for Colonel James King who established a mill at the mouth of Reedy Creek in 1774, and who later used the port of Boat Yard extensively for the shipping of iron, bacon, salt, and other commodities to towns down the Holston River. In consequence of this activity, the port became known as 'King's Port', later contracted to Kingsport (See endnote #8).

Some historians, while agreeing that Kingsport was named for a Mr. King, are inclined to think this man was William King, of Abington, owner of the salt works north of that town, rather than Col. James King.....the Mr. King here referred to was probably William King, and it is possible that his activities at the little river port may have combined with those of Col. James King in giving Kingsport its name (See endnote #9).

In 1919, Kingsport was the first professionally planned and privately financed city in twentieth century America. It was also the first to adopt a city-manager form of government to professionalize the operation of city departments. It was nicknamed the Model City from this plan and developed its school system based on a model promoted by Columbia University. John B. Dennis and J. Fred Johnson cast about for the most eminent city planner available. As a result, John Nolen of Cambridge, Massachusetts, who had already achieved international fame in this line, was retained and was given full leeway in laying out what was to become a modern municipality (See endnote #5).

The Great Depression, the New Deal, and world war profoundly affected the Model City. The years of depression and war marked an extraordinary period of growth and maturation for Kingsport (see endnote#6).

George Eastman founded Eastman's manufacturing site in 1920, and its global headquarters remains a critical component of Kingsport. In 1942, Holston Ordnance Works (HOW) coupled with Tennessee Eastman employed almost half of the adult population of Kingsport. One can trace a direct line from HOW's RDX/Composition B to the Y–12 facility at Oak Ridge and the Manhattan Project. This research-production line led to the rapid destruction of numerous German U-boats and the Little Boy, which was dropped on Hiroshima.

Kingsport enjoys abundant natural resources. The mountains, streams, lakes, meadows, and wooded areas are a beautiful blessing. The people are well informed, socially and politically engaged, and the friendliest that I have ever met. Actually, these characterizations remind me very much of

Prescott, Arizona. The advantage of Kingsport, however, is its proximity to Washington, DC, Atlanta, and Charlotte, as well as the attractions and cultural richness of Virginia, Kentucky, and West Virginia.

Tennessee shares borders with eight other states: Kentucky and Virginia to the north; North Carolina to the east; Georgia, Alabama, and Mississippi to the south; Arkansas and Missouri on the Mississippi River to the west. No other state in the United States borders more states than Tennessee does! There is only one city in the United States named Kingsport. So I need not be concerned about any of my mail being delivered to someone in Hawaii or Utah. Moreover, in point of Google fact, there is only one other Kingsport in the entire world. Kingsport is a wonderful place to live.

Our Kingsport city government functions very well. A few months after Erika and I moved into our home, Mayor John Clark asked me, "What brought you to Kingsport?" As I began to respond, the mayor was summoned to the podium to make his presentation to the historical society. I'll send him *From Brooklyn to Kingsport* for the rest of my answer. It's been four years now, and Mayor Clark continues to demonstrate leadership. In fact, it would not surprise me to see him as our governor or very possibly, our senator representing our interests in Washington, DC.

My first read every morning is the *Kingsport Times*. I find the editorials timely, thoughtful, and put forth in a manner representing the interests of residents in the region. It beats *The Wall Street Journal* and the *New York Times* in giving the late night sports news to its readership in the morning.

Before the closing on our Kingsport property, Erika asked me, "Are you sure you'll be happy in Kingsport?" I replied that

Kingsport had excellent medical facilities and a couple of good restaurants. Beyond that, all I needed was one friend. It was difficult to make a new friend at my age, but Erika managed to solve that.

She bought a piano at a garage sale that weighed a ton. I noticed an ad in the *Kingsport Times* indicating that the Music Masters store had pianos for sale. We went to the store and asked the man at the counter, "How do you get a piano from your store to the buyer's home?" The man responded that Dan moved their pianos and gave us his phone number. Dan and his helper got Erika's piano into Dan's truck and into our home. The move cost more than the piano.

I mentioned to Dan that I wanted to do some renovating in the house. Dan introduced me to Jack, who did electrical, plumbing, and carpentry work. He was a Jack of many trades. Jack is my friend. Now I have two friends, Alex and Jack. I've got it all now. Jack built us a Tennessee Room.

Not counting my childhood homes, I have lived in twenty homes in half a dozen states. This is the end. I'll never move from this wonderful property, in this great small city of Kingsport. It has been a long and often bumpy road, but I've reached the end of my journey from Brooklyn to Kingsport.

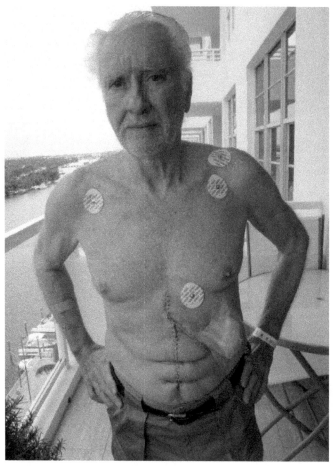

EPILOGUE

Mom lived a long life. Her last forty-seven years were very good compared to her first forty-seven years. I saw no indication that her early years had any impact on her thoughts, feelings, or happiness. However, it is likely that the money that she insisted Artie and I take at the end of every visit was unconsciously motivated by a sense of guilt.

While Loretta, Artie, and I enjoyed meaningful lives, each of us were scarred for life and have had to cope with the physical and psychological effects. The deprivation, physical abuse, and absence of parental love during our important developmental years had a formative impact throughout our lives.

Until his death, Artie was unable to spend money for pleasure. It appeared that his goal in life was to save money to secure his future. He did this to the extreme. Artie also became a world-class hoarder of food, way beyond keeping a well-stocked pantry and freezer. He had a fourteen-by-twenty-foot addition built onto his home, which he stocked with non-perishable food.

I had limited direct contact with Loretta over the years. We maintained a positive long-distance relationship. I did save the letters that she wrote to me, and it is possible to make inferences from the nature of the content. However, I'd rather stick to direct observations, even though they were limited. Unlike Artie and me, Loretta was comfortable spending money, both on herself and her children. She traveled and enjoyed dining in fine restaurants. Yet, the fact that she never saw Mom during her mother's last forty-seven years is indicative of the serious toll that the early years had on her. Loretta would not even discuss out childhood in Brooklyn.

Self-assessment is challenging. I have been mistrustful, fiercely independent, aggressive, and overly competitive. I have had too many marriages and have attended too many universities, likely I was unconsciously trying to eradicate the psychological impact of having failed first grade. Likewise, my other traits and endeavors are related to the experiences I had during my first fourteen years in Brooklyn. I made a good decision when I was fourteen years old. My years in Brooklyn prepared me to deal with the inevitable problems in life.

Suffice it to state that each of my marriages made sense at the time.

I was driven to secure my future through achievement and accumulating wealth.

Accumulating and saving money has always been pleasurable. Spending money has always been painful. Almost all of my clothing still comes from the Salvation Army and Goodwill Industries. The jacket that I'm wearing in the photograph at my grandfather's tombstone on a (-2°) degree day was bought at Kingsport's Goodwill Industries for $8! I still shop at Dollar Tree and frequent garage/estate sales. I am still mowing grass with the old lawnmower that I had bought at Traders Village for twenty-five dollars four years ago. This is a serious affliction, especially as I look at my financial statements and my age. But I'm working on it.

While I still have difficulty spending money, I am comfortable giving money away. Last year. I made significant contributions/gifts to good causes and good people. It gave me a good feeling.

In the first chapter, I alluded to my recurring nightmares which occurred three or four times a year. More recently, I am awakened once a month. Last night (9/23/18), it was a different variation of the 'lost in Brooklyn' nightmare which apparently reflect my searching for a home. Last night I was not lost, rather I was running for my life, following the same route that Loretta and I ran in 1952 which I traced in the map of Greenpoint.

With sixty-five years of drinking and smoking (1953–2018) that is more than I deserve. I'm ready. Writing this memoir has been a difficult, but therapeutic experience.

Note: In August 2018, after weeks of effort, my son, Mark, located my father's NYC death certificate, which led him to a gravesite. My father is buried in an unmarked grave….no headstone….no marker…no plaque…just grass. Mark is buying a headstone. I will not participate in a any manner.

NOTES

1. Frank McCourt, *Angela's Ashes* (New York: Charles Scribner, 1996) "Introduction."
2. Pete Hamill, *Once Upon A Barstool: A Drinking Life: A Memoir* (New York: Little Brown and Co., 1994) 265.
3. C. Stanley Ogilvy, The Larchmont Yacht Club: A History 1880-1990(Mamaroneck, New York: Bair Graphics, Inc., 1993) 354 pp.
4. David Garrahan, *Transition America* (Bloomington, Indiana: Xlibris Publishing Co., 2016) 178.
5. David Garrahan, *From Brooklyn to Kingsport* (Bloomington, Indiana: Xlibris Publishing Co., 2018) 328.
6. Howard Long, *Kingsport: A Romance of Industry* (Kingsport: The Sevier Press, 1928) 92.
7. Margaret Ripley Wolf, *Kingsport, Tennessee: A Planned American City* (Lexington: the University Press Of Kentucky, 1987) 116.
8. "Portrait of the Artist As an Unperson," *The Wall Street Journal*, May 17, 2018, 15.
9. Discover Kingsport.com/h-Kingsport-name.shtml
10. Thomas W. Preston, *Historical Sketches of the Holston Valley* (Kingsport, Tn: Kingsport Press, 1926) 186 pp.
11. Kingsport Times News, Tn. Vol.102, no. 133(Kingsport: Kingsport Publishing Co. May 13, 2018) 6.

APPENDIX

PUBLISHED MONTHLY BY THE BROWN BULLETIN PUBLISHING ASSOCIATION

Volume II   AUGUST, 1920   Number 2

FEDERAL CLUB ON A RAMPAGE

Saturday, July 10, at 2 p. m., were seen, leaving Green Square one auto (a Franklin) and two Buicks. By the looks of the suitcases and wardrobe trunks which encumbered the passengers, it was very evident that the party was leaving for a week-end and at quite a distance. Sure enough, they were the personnel of Mr. E. F. Bailey's office, who under his tutelage, together with wives, sweethearts, etc., were on their way to Indian Rock Camp, at Howard Lake, Hanover, Maine.

Sully, the last one to leave Berlin, arrived at the camp much ahead of the others. Elizabeth insisted on journeying to Grafton Notch but both Mr. Bailey and "Goldy" got sick of wandering around and finally decided to do without Elizabeth's direction and got to camp in time for supper, none the worse for their pilgrimage.

The first thing the girls insisted upon doing after our arrival, was to go in bathing, no doubt they needed it. "T," short in height but very ambitious, insisted on going out as far as the rest. The consequences were she lost her breath and proceeded to lose her head, when her faithful attendant did the heroic act and brought her ashore where, after being rubbed awhile, she recovered from her first ablutions in 1920.

Just about then the bell rang

for supper and it goes without saying that the water was soon deserted. After a good feed, for which the Indian Rock Camp is well known, we went boating till dark. Then we proceeded to Camp Contentment where dancing, games, etc., were enjoyed by *most* of the party.

Sunday was spent in bathing, boating, and mostly eating. Ask Sylvester where the boats were from nine until twelve.

At 4:30 the party departed for home. Stopped at Sunflower Inn where Mr. Bailey insisted that all have ice cream and cake.

Outside of a few serious cases of sunburn, every one was able to appear at work Monday morning.

Here's hoping that the Federal Club has many more outings in the future.

Sh-sh, she's asleep.

GOT A GOOD JOKE?

What's your best joke? The Bulletin wants it. Hundreds of funny things happen around the plant every day. If you're hep to any of them, send 'em in, names and all. But it isn't necessary to confine yourself to the plants a really good joke is always readable. But don't send in that joke that, when we first heard it, caused us to laugh until the tears rolled down over our pinafore. Doesn't have to be original, but if you clip it, give credit.

MY THREE OR FOUR VOYAGES TO SEA

While reading the Bulletin, when I turn over the leaves to Sulphite Mill Gas, I am surprised at the small quantity of gas there is in it. I don't know much about the manufacture of pulp, I will leave that for others who are better qualified to write on the subject, but for the benefit of the Bulletin and the amusement of my fellow workmen, I will write an article entitled "My Three or Four Voyages to Sea." In this article I will give my readers my views of the American Merchant Marines.

I was brought up in Liverpool on the Mersey River in England. There young boys are not men until they have made a voyage to sea, the longer the voyage the bigger the man when he comes back. Well, like all others I, at the ripe old age of fourteen, made my first voyage across the Atlantic Ocean on board the steamship Arizona of the Guion. At that time she was called the greyhound of the Atlantic, making the trip across in nine days.

We left the river Mersey and everything went well until we reached the banks of Newfoundland. There we met foggy weather and ice. We were going at a good rate of speed, but owing to the fog we could not see the bergs, so we struck one head on. The ship's bow went up and her stem went down and hundreds

The Brown Bulletin

Contributions of news items are requested from every employee. It is not absolutely necessary that you write an article. If you have any news to offer or an article to suggest, drop a note in the suggestion boxes placed in the different mills for that purpose.

Vol. II.	AUGUST, 1920.	No. 2

Editorial Staff:
Editor-in-Chief ....W. E. Taft
Associate Editors............ } Oscar P.Cole
                            { G. E. Richter
Business Manager......... ......J. H. Briggs

of tons of ice came down on the forecastle head or what was left of it. The engines went full steam astern and she slid off with forty feet of her bow stove in, and the forecastle filled with water. But the bulkhead stood the strain although she was well down by the head. She reached port safely and had a wood bow put in. She was then navigated back to Liverpool where a steel bow was put in. So my first trip came very near being my last.

I guess I got scared as I did not go out on the Arizona again, but I did make two voyages to Australia. But these voyages were too long for me, about 25,000 miles, so I gave that line up.

I then made four voyages to Bombay and Calcutta, calling at Colombo, in the island of Ceylon. This was a long voyage and very hot, passing through the Mediterranean and Red Seas, also the Indian Ocean and Bay of Bengal. This voyage I made on the Irranadi of the P. and O. line.

I quit this route and my next venture was on the Sesostris of the Moss line, up the Mediterranean for fruit. On one of these voyages I was on a steamship named the Dressong and had the good fortune to be on her when she brought Cleopatra's needle from Alexandria in Egypt to New York. The needle is in Central Park and is called the Obelisk. I deserted the Dressong in New York, but she sailed for a long time on the Savannah line between New York and Savannah.

I now made my first venture on American ships. I signed

articles on the British Empire of the Alexandre line running from New York to Havana, Vera Cruz and Tampico. I made three or four trips on this one, but could not stand the prosperity. I had too much money and had to get rid of it. I sure had to go home to England to spend my American money. Well, I could not get a job so I stowed away and that was breaking the law. We got across all right. This was on the Baltic of the White Star line. When the ship reached Liverpool I seemed to be very popular. The ship's officers ran a flag up to the mast head to notify H. R. H., Queen Victoria, that they had an American visitor on board. Her Majesty sent two of her officers on board and they escorted me ashore. I was invited to spend a month as a guest of Her Majesty in one of her castles that was not royal. Of course I could not refuse the invitation and I accepted, the castle being on the outskirts of Liverpool. Everything was very clean and nice, but Her Majesty's tables were set very poor. You can judge for yourself when I tell you I lost twenty-nine pounds in twenty-eight days. Well, most everything has an end, so had my visit and I left Walton without any regrets.

(To be Continued)

ANY SNAPS?

Now that you've dragged that camera out of winter quarters and begun a little snapshooting, let's suggest that you give your Bulletin friends a squint at your work. The Bulletin will take pleasure in publishing real good photographs taken by Brown employees especially those that show originality. Picturesque scenery, unusual events, unique situations - all these make good camera subjects, and when you get a good clear picture, why not share your pleasure with Bulletin readers?

Drop the picture or film in a Brown Bulletin box; if accompanied by name of owner, we will take care to return all films submitted.

VISITING NURSE SERVICE

At the same time that you secure your life insurance, you secure the privileges of the service of the Visiting Nurse. This means that if you are ill or injured, and live in a nursing district, you may have the service of a professional visiting nurse. This service costs you nothing, and no deduction will be made from the face value of your policy for it.

What to Do Now.

1. Read carefully the pamphlet "Your Friend, the Nurse."
2. Find out the name and address of the nurse in charge of the district in which you *live.*
3. Secure a mailing card and put it in a handy place. (Our Company has a supply of these.)
4. Put your insurance certificate in a safe place, so that you can show it to the nurse when she comes.

What to Do if You Are Ill.

Do at once one of these things:

1. Notify the Company that you are ill and want the nurse.
2. Post the mailing card which has been given you.
3. 'Phone or send someone for the nurse.
4. Notify the Metropolitan Life Insurance Company's office.

What the Nurse Will Do.

As soon as possible after you send for her, the nurse will call at your home and make you comfortable, carry out the instructions of the doctor, and give you general bedside care.

Although the nurse will not remain in your home, she will call as often as is necessary. The length of her visits varies from fifteen minutes to one hour, depending upon the care required by the patient.

The Company has arranged with our Insurance Company to furnish those of us who are covered by our Group Policy with this Visiting Nurse Service *with absolutely no cost to us.* It is part of our Group Insurance Plan.

ATOMIUM CLUB

A relatively new organization on campus, the Atomium Club serves to promote interest in chemistry and to supplement the regular classroom work. This club is open to all chemistry majors or minors and to those who wish to further their work in the chemistry field. Membership in the Atomium Club provides students with the opportunity to affiliate with the American Chemical Society.

SIGMA ZETA TAU

Sigma Zeta is a national honorary society which elects to its membersh those students who excel in science and mathematics. Tau chapter was founded East Stroudsburg in 1947. It has been the only chapter ever to receive the Four er's Cup twice at the National Convention. This award is presented for high tainment of the society's purpose which is "to promote exceptional achievem in the sciences through individual study and research."

The chapter offers its services to any student who desires scholastic ass ance in science or mathematics. This is an important activity of Sigma Zeta preparing its members to be experienced, capable teachers.

Row 1: Dr. Moore, S. Mick, H. Koch, J. Chick, L. Brewster, Mr. May. Row 2: H. Ph D. Garrahan, M. Reyda, S. Bright, M. Casciano, K. Stanat, I. Jurbala, J. Shafer, C. Watah J. Hoff. Row 3: D. Marvin, J. Frailey, R. Johnson.

Perhaps it is the house plants or silver lunch pail. Perhaps it is the man who has just offered you a seat. But the stark formality of what "Guidance Office" means is gone. Mr. David Garrahan has never forgotten how an unsure student feels. His warmth and casual manner eases the most troubled student. He makes human a system of subjects and tests and records, never talking a student into anything except his own dignity. No problem is ever too large or too small. Whether it be the anxiety of waiting for a college acceptance, a job after graduation, or a misunderstanding with a teacher or parent. All we can give in return for his faith in us is our faith in him. He has helped to teach us who we are, but knowing him has been the greater experience.

"THE UNEXAMINED LIFE IS NOT WORTH LIVING"

Socrates

Thank you for advising me of your views on President Nixon's actions and the current national situation.

When Congress reconvened October 23, I introduced a resolution calling for impeachment proceedings which, along with the other similar resolutions, have been referred to the Committee on the Judiciary.

The Committee is undertaking an exhaustive investigation to determine whether or not there are constitutional grounds for impeachment by the House of Representatives and ultimate trial by the Senate.

It is hoped and expected that the Committee will report its findings without delay. I and others will insist upon this.

I also have introduced a resolution establishing the office of special prosecutor entirely independent of the President to pursue the Watergate investigation and related matters.

With all best wishes, I am

Sincerely,

HENRY HELSTOSKI
Member of Congress

HH/isah

I appreciate the questions which prompted you to express your concern and I trust that you will understand that my decision in this matter has been guided by the desire to improve job training opportunities for our youth. Please be assured that I will continue rigorously to follow up on this objective.

With best wishes,

Sincerely,

Jacob K. Javits, U.S.S.

JKJ:hh

put out by the Office of Education which describes these opportunities. Let me assure you that I will do all I can to develop more assistance along these lines.

Again, thank you for taking the time to write to me. I hope I have stated my position on this matter clearly.

Sincerely,

Robert F. Kennedy

SENATOR BOB DOLE
MAJORITY LEADER
U.S. SENATE

March 29, 1995

Dr. David P. Garrahan
Superintendent
Northern Highlands
298 Hillside Ave.
Allendale, NJ 07401

Dear Dr. Garrahan,

After meeting with RNC Chairman Haley Barbour and his nominating committee, I am pleased to inform you that you have been recommended for membership on the Chairman's Advisory Board, one of the most effective and influential senior leadership councils within the national Republican Party.

The Chairman's Advisory Board offers a unique opportunity for you to participate personally in the development of Republican policy positions and campaign strategies at the highest levels of the Party.

DOLE KEMP

November 25, 1996

Mr. Dave Garrahan
423 Perry Street
Prescott, Arizona 86303

Dear Mr. Garrahan,

I wanted to thank you for your very kind letter and for the military buttonhook.

Though the results on November 5th were not what we had hoped, I know that there are far worse fates than to lose an election over things you believe in. It was the honor of my life to be the Republican nominee for President of the United States, and I am very proud of the issues we raised and the solutions we proposed for the challenges facing our country.

By far the highlight of this past year was the opportunity to meet so many Americans who, like you, love our country. There is no doubt that the American people are the most generous, compassionate, and caring on the face of the earth. While I do not know exactly what the future will hold, I do know that I will continue to work for an America that is worthy of her citizens.

Please keep in touch, and let me know if I can ever be of help. Elizabeth joins with me in sending our best wishes for a happy and healthy holiday season

President McGill did write me his response in great detail in which he thanked me for the courteous way in which I raised an extremely sensitive topic. He also called my attention to the Union's contract provisions as well as the budget constraints under which he was operating.

TG3502.   Community agencies and resources (2 or 3)
MRS. BYNUM: Autumn M 5:10–6:50.
Designed to familiarize students with community social service agencies functioning in the areas of family service, public assistance, mental health, recreational, protective and correctional care, gerontological service, employment, and vocational guidance. Field visits in small groups.

TI3502.   Human ecology (3)
PROFESSOR GRANNIS: Autumn Th 7:20–9 p.m.
Analysis of theory and research on the interaction of physical, social, and psychological factors in the settings of human behavior. Focus on the ecological problems of political, economic, educational, or health intervention in community and institutional settings.

TI3503.   Ecological observation for intervention (3)
PROFESSOR BROK: Spring Th 5:10–6:50.
Application of ecological observation techniques to community and institutional behavior settings for purposes of designing interventions. Training in behavior stream observation; behavior setting observation, and milieu description, with particular emphasis on the location of causality in the settings observed: classrooms, hospital wards, street corner gatherings, etc.

TG3510.   Field work in applied human development (2)
MRS. BYNUM (Sec 1), ITBA (Sec 2): Autumn HTBA.
Guided observation in selected human development settings such as schools, agencies, nursing homes, etc. Individual and group conferences with staff.

TG4011.   Multidisciplinary research in the service of human development (2)
PROFESSOR MORRIS: Autumn W 5:10–6:50.
Basic concepts and techniques for the conduct of simple research studies and the utilization of research findings from the literature which can be useful in improving practice and persuading others.

TG4110.   Implications of bio-social differences for guiding human development (2 or 3)
PROFESSOR GORDON: Spring Th 3–4:40.
Seminar on the nature and meaning of bio-social differences. Review of contemporary conceptions, issues and research concerning such aspects of human diversity as age, cognitive style, ethnicity, sex, and social context. Theoretical and practical implications for applied human development.

TG4111.   Educational and vocational implications of ethnic and social status differences (2 or 3)
PROFESSOR GARRAHAN: Spring M 5:10–6:50.
The relationship of economic, ethnic, and social status differences to educational and vocational opportunities and advancement. Implications for educational and career development.

TG5148.   Group process and human relations (3)
DR. POLLOCK (Sec 1), DR. FISCH (Sec 2): Spring Tu 10–12, DR. FULMER (Sec 3) HTBA.
Students will participate in a variety of experiences in group, organizational and community settings which will be designed to have them experience at first hand the life space of individuals from different backgrounds and sub-cultures.

TG5919.   Seminar in applied human development through leisure (3)
PROFESSOR BROK: Autumn M 3–4:40.
Developmental, personological and situational factors affecting the experience and use of time throughout the life cycle. Implications of various theoretical approaches for avocational and career counseling, social planning and educational practice. Critical issues in leisure and career development.

Unofficially Is It Official?
Did the NH Board Search
For New Superintendent?

The rumors have been circulating for a while.

putting on the pretense of a search committee.

Officially the Board prepared

N.J. official finds no flaw
in school appointment

By Robin Kamen
Staff Writer

State education for a school board search, as the board High School did

"The school district

Trustee appointment
stirs legal dispute

director of guidance for the ley High st year, which es, The ale and

ment of ege in each 1977. ool in

s said xperi he step

they're do now ld K.

D-10   THE RECORD, TUESDAY, MARCH 12, 1985   BERGEN

Affirmative-action issue
raised by appointment

'Troublemaker' Student

By JOHN HAMBROSE
Downvalley Bureau

Old Forge — A "troublemaker" while a student at the former Sibley School and Old Forge High School is now superintendent of an affluent New Jer-

for kids off the beaten path," said received certification from

THE SCRANTON TIMES, FRIDAY, MARCH 29, 1985 — 8

Now Heads School District

trict, of his school days in Old Forge. He said, "For the most part the teachers thought I was a smart aleck."

Garrahan said he moved to Old Forge to live with his aunt and uncle, Mr. and Mrs. John Buranick, 114 Hoover St., when he was in sixth or seventh grade. He graduated from Old Forge High School in 1957.

"When I graduated from Old Forge High School, I borrowed $5 and came to New York City and started thinking about the future," said Garrahan. From New York, Garrahan sent letters to East Stroudsburg Teachers' College, University of Scranton and Bloomsburg State College.

changes designed to open up guidance to the students," said Garrahan. He said his major introduction to the five-member guidance department was a calendar on which students could make appointments with their counselors months in advance.

"It gave the students the perception that they had control. It also made the counselors 100 percent accountable for their time," said Garrahan of the calendar. His innovations were successful.

"In one short year, his changes have turned the guidance department around," reads a sentence from an editorial recently published in The Highland Fling, the school's student

wide.

"What it does is keep guidance alive and vital, in perpetual motion," said Garrahan. He said the assessment is a questionnaire which gauges guidance needs of students, parents and teachers and then measures, how well these needs are being met.

"The bottom line is we get high priority areas," said Garrahan. He said the survey identifies areas not adequately provided by a school's guidance department. Under the survey, these areas become guidance department target areas, said Garrahan.

"You implement these changes and activities for one school year and you readminister the survey during the next school year," said Garrahan. At

289

Trustee Confirms Motion
To Name Dr. Garrahan
NHRHS Superintendent

Other Trustees Mum on Subject

selection process. Mr. Arnold is the best person to confirm or deny any statements." Mr. Hopkins, when asked who made up the membership of the Search Committee, said he thought it consisted of Mr. Arnold, Trustee Terry Bolles, Mrs. Aiuvalasit ...her person. ... he couldn't ... The Town ...en unable to ...ficially the ...f the search ... how Dr. ...me to be

Trustee appointment
stirs legal dispute

D-10   THE RECORD, TUESDAY, MARCH 12, 1985   BERGEN

Affirmative-action issu
raised by appointment

Unofficially Is It Official?
Did the NH Board Search
For New Superintendent?

The rum... ...culating for a   putting on the pretense of a search
while.
Unoffici
administra
name Dr. ...
tor of Pup...
Regional ...
Superinten...
Mr. Hopk...
Official ...
Marcie A...
the press
introduce
next mee...
Unoffic
vote will ...
Officia
either.
Unof...
Garraha...
...
Unof...

Vol. 11, No. 44   Entered as Second Class at Saddle River, N.J. 07458

It's Official:

Large Crowd
Opposes
Selection
Process

Dr. Ga
NH Su

Mary Service
Former ...
...sh Board of Education
Trustee Roy Hagen call...
the crowd larger than ...
he had seen in his 3 y...
on the Board. About 60 ...
people turned out to...
...rembers the Board'...
...ation about the propo...
appointment ...

Foreign trips banned indefinitel·

ly Jennifer Klein

In a memo issued to all foreign language teachers on March 11, superintendent Dr. David Garrahan "banned" all foreign trips originating at the school effective July , 1986. This action was prompted y "a combination of factors." According to Dr. Garrahan, "I have received governmental literature oma concerned parent who orks for an airline that suggests mitting foreign travel." Due to the recent terrorist activities in urope, the destination of the trips fected by this ban, and the "irrational nature" of Moummar Quadafi of Libya who has threatened to arget [our] children", Dr. Garrahan decided to place restrictions a all future trips. The decision, he ays "was not a Board decision - It as mine. It was intended to put e serious nature of these [terrort] incidents in perspective." The emo stressed the restriction of reign travel "as a group" and thus ot affect travel with AFS or study road programs. "I place those in different category as they usually don't involve large groups of students.", according to the Superintendent.

Dr. Garrahan also expressed concern due to rising insurance and liability rates, "Since last year, our insurance rates have gone up 182%." He cited a recent legal ruling in which a school was sued by parents of a student who was injured while on a trip originating at the school. "Although the school did not actually sponsor the trip, the students and teachers involved were from the school and promotional literature was posted in the school." Mrs. Rosemarie Mastropoalo had planned a trip to Italy and Greece for her Latin students, but due to the airport bombings in Rome and Athens, two of their principal destinations, 6 of the 10 participants withdrew. "We thought that it would be smart to go.", says Mrs. Mastropoalo.

Mr. Stephen Murray, though, did not cancel his students trip to Germany because of terrorist activity, but rather because it was "a question of finance." THe cost has become too high for many students to afford.

Dr. Garrhan's concern for this p... ·'·' .... —

On March 11, 1986, our Superintendent, Dr. David P. Garrahan, issued a memo to all the foreign language teachers, advising them to cancel their trips with students abroad (e.g. Mr. Gilli's trip to France, Mrs. Mastropoalo's trip to Italy and Greece) during the spring break. He issued this memo because of the"probability of danger as a result of terrorist activity" which was expressed in information that he received from certain government agencies. Dr. Garrahan also banned future student trips to foreign countries as of July 1, 1986. I asked Dr. Garrahan if this was his decision or the Board of Education's decision. It was his.

The ban states that the Northern Highlands School District will not sponser, support, or encourage in any manner foreign trips by students. It prohibits the distribution of literature relating to student tours in the building and states that no literature will be posted in the classrooms. The ban forbids the discussion of foreign trips with students on school property as well.

One fear that Dr. Garrahan has is the probable danger resulting from terrorist activity in foreign countries. In today's world, terrorist activity is possible, not probable, at anytime, anywhere. It is unpredictable. Terrorism can occur just as easily in New York City as it can in any other city in the world (it could even occur in Dr. Garrahan's secluded office). Does this mean that we should cancel our field trips to the Metropolitan Museum of Art? Or to the high school office? Does this mean that we should assume that terrorist activity will be a threat to us wherever we go?

Perhaps Dr. Garrahan is worried that the school will be held liable for any injuries that may occur to the students while on these trips. However, these tours are taken during the spring vacation; school is closed. The only connection these student tours have with the school is that both the students and the teachers go to the school. students and their parents sign a document with the companies that run these tours thar hold the parents responsible for any "accidents " over which the company has no control. On top of this, the companies carry insurance policies on each student and indemm/ty the schools.

The school is a meeting place. Most of the students and the faculty spent more than nine hours a day here. By placing a ban on student trips, Dr. Garrahan has made organizing a trip abroad extremely difficult, almost impossible. The Northern Highlands School District has never sponsored, supported, or encouraged these trips in the first place. The students and the teachers have cooperated to arrange all twenty of the past trips on their own time. Furthermore, what purpose could restricting even conversation about these trips possibly serve? Aside from being antieducational, this seems to violate our constitutional right to free

Leaching life blood from foreign travel

Back in the days of George Washington, in the uncivilized days of Colonial America, leeching was a common practice. This barbaric process was used to rid the body of harmful substances. But sometimes leeching was taken too far and the patient died from loss of blood. When used sparingly, leeching could be beneficial, but taken too extremes, the process did more harm than good.

In the same vein, the recent unqualified ban on student travel abroad is unjustified. The memo issued by Superintendent Dr. David Garrahan forbids all foreign travel priginating in the school, effective July 1, 1986. Granted, a certain amount of caution when abroad is no unwarranted, due to recent terrorist activity in Europe. But an absolute ban on student travel is not necessary. This measure does more harm than good to the students and foreign language department. This travel program is a valuable and an integral part of our language department. It should not be erradicated due to a few isolated incidents of terrorist activity. Yes, Quaddafi is quite "irrational" as Dr. Garrhan maintains, but the chances that a terrorist act will be committed at the exact time and place as the students from the school are present is highly improbable.

The ban by the school is an admirable protective parental gesture, but this concern for the welfare of the students has been taken to the extreme - possibly "leeching" the life out of an enjoyable, beneficial student experience. A simple "be careful" would have been welcomed. This radical action is not.

Union's demand quashes deal
NH board yanks 8-period day

Suzan Erein

NORTHERN HIGHLANDS — In negotiate the implementa... response to demands from the N...

Garrahan, Foerster and Ryan
Same questions, different answers

The following questions, formulated by The Town Journal, concerning the 8- because of scheduling conflicts. When surveyed, a significant portion of students

$20 Yearly, 45¢ Single Copy   Thursday, November 14, 1991

At NH meeting:
Talk but no action on 8-period day impasse

Dan Skelton, Jr.

NORTHERN HIGHLANDS — The board of education closed the high school Nov. 11 due to the walkout of Education Association members who were protest- said that he was in favor of the eight-period day, and that it is unfortunate that Highlands did not begin working on such a schedule in 1989 when the board and

Thursday, January 9, 1992   THE TOWN JOURNAL

David Valozzi, right, sophomore from Upper Saddle River at the NH sit-in last

Attention - Citizens
of Allendale & Upper Saddle River

There is a crisis at Northern Highlands Regional High School. The underlying reason for this crisis is that Superintendent David Garrahan, in partnership with the Board of Education, has failed to provide the school community with sound educational leadership. Therefore, a resolution has been passed by the Northern Highlands Education Association:

Whereas:

Superintendent Garrahan has neglected to organize a democratic coalition of students, parents, teachers and administrators to closely examine the current and future needs of the school, and to determine how the resources of the district can be used wisely and impartially for the greatest benefit of all students, and

Whereas:

Superintendent Garrahan has made contradictory statements regarding his own position on vital school matters thereby contributing to confusion and misunderstanding within the school community, and

Whereas:

Superintendent Garrahan has failed to encourage and maintain an atmosphere of mutual trust and respect once characteristic of Northern Highlands,

Therefore:

The members of the Northern Highlands Education Association have taken a vote of **No Confidence** in Superintendent Garrahan.

NORTHERN HIGHLANDS EDUCATION ASSOCIATION

by Northern Highlands Education Association, Pat Cline, president

293

Dr. Garrahan Aspires to Have NH In Top 10 Schools in the USA

Thursday, October 15, 1987   THE TOWN JOURNAL

Northern Highlands Honored in D.C.

A late morning ceremony at the White House highlighted activities honoring Northern Highlands Regional High School and 270 other outstanding schools named by the U.S. Department of Education in the 1986-87 Secondary School Recognition Program.

Principal John Mintzer and Superintendent David Garrahan were invited to Washington, D.C., to take part in the activities Oct. 4-5.

President Ronald Reagan praised representatives from the public and private schools in a Rose Garden ceremony. "You are here because your schools are part of what's right with American education," said the president. Secretary of Education William J. Bennett presided over the awards ceremony where he presented each school with a 4' x 6' flag that reads "Excellence in Education — 1986-87."

year come from 46 states, the District of Columbia and Puerto Rico.

Now celebrating its fifth year, the recognition program was initiated to focus attention on schools that work and to demonstrate that excellence in education can be achieved by communities that strive to attain it.

Dr. Garrahan's controversial policies praised Page 3

NH Among The Nation's Top Public High Schools

Northern Highlands Regional High School has been named one of the 1?? best public high schools in the nation i? the Secondary School Recognition Pr?? gram. Of 670 schools nominated throug?

Garrahan leads to excellence

By Bruce Namerow

Great change has come to this school since the arrival of Dr. David Garrahan four years ago... and plenty of controversy.

The opposition against Dr. Garrahan certainly has not been silent. From the words "Anarchy Now" scrolled across bathroom walls to the columns written in this paper comparing him to a jail warden possibly "sent by the devil", students seem to have forgotten all the good that has come from

School rated among top by government program

By Jen Klein

"It is the only rating program of its kind, so it's quite an achievement to be selected," says Dr. David P. Garrahan, superintendent, of the school's recent citation for excellence by the U.S. Department of Education. On May 27, the federal agency announced that 271 junior, middle, and high schools were chosen for the honor, out of 670 schools nominated nationwide.

Ridgewood High School and the Dwight Englewood School, a private day school in Englewood, were the other Bergen county schools selected by the national panel of 71 reviewers, two of who visited the school in

awards and scholarships in academic and vocational competitions; awards for outstanding school programs; and the school's civil rights record, according to Dr. Garrahan.

A separate panel of evaluators, many of them principals of school honored in the past, conducted on-site visits at schools selected by the national judges. The visits allow the evaluators to assess the school's climate, grounds, and physical plant. Schools which passed this stage of the competition were nominated to receive the Department of Education's citation of excellence certificate, according to Dr. Garrahan, "the nation's most prestigious academic dis-

Is it student piracy, or fair competition?

N. Highlands woos non-residents

By DEBORAH PRIVITERA
Staff Writer

When Northern Highlands Regional High School opened its doors nearly 30 years ago, 1,400 students roamed the hallways.

Now, the school has little more than

housing market in the area, Garrahan said.

Whatever the reason, the steady drop has prompted Garrahan to find ways to reverse the trend. One thing he has done is woo students from outside of the district, asking their parents to pay $8,000 a year in tuition. If families sent two chil-

---

Schools can set property value

Reading, 'riting, and reputation

By Olga Wickerhauser
Business Writer

I t is said that a good reputation is more valuable than money, and nowhere is that more true than for public school systems. The presence of a highly reputable public school can be the kiss of wealth for a community. Good schools can boost property values 25 percent or 30 percent.

The dry facts

There are books that list the dry facts used to evaluate schools — the percentage of students who go on to college, the pupil-to-teacher ratio, the average SAT scores. But real estate agents generally agree that the reputations of schools are made at cocktail parties and barbecues.

"In Morris County, we have a lot of corporate moves, and some of the corporate executives

"We have to do public relations, we have to go out and do marketing," says Garrahan.

The school district printed glossy, color booklets, the kind colleges send to applicants, describing the curriculum, campus, and special programs of Northern Highlands Regional High School.

Also, Garrahan has written about the school for the Northwest Board of Realtors' newsletter.

Vol. 18, No. 4   Entered as Second Class at Saddle River, NJ 07458 $20 Yearly 40¢ Single Copy   Thursday, May 23, 1991

NH 'offers better product at better price'

Dan Skelton, Jr.

NORTHERN HIGHLANDS — In response to the $314,000 cut to the $8.5 million Northern Highlands 1991-92 budget

Martin Luther King Observance:

NH Remains Open, Students Protest

Dr. King's day marked as he lived

Marches, expressions of belie

By Elizabeth Lu
Record Staff Writer

In a predawn candlelight vigil yesterday, about 25 students from Northern Highlands Regional High School

The Northern Highlan tion voted 6-0 last Febru on Jan. 18, the date re and state offices as a honor of the slain civil

No Holiday for Dr. King At Northern Highlands

A MESSAGE TO THE N.H ADMINISTRATION

WE SHALL OVERCOME

NH SPORTS
32

Board of Education

Missing from photo: Marcie Aiuvalasit

James Ryan, *President*
Margaret Capuano, *Vice President*

Marcie Aiuvalasit
John Butler
Patricia DeMilia
William Leonard

Helen Nicholas
Nora Oliver
Robert Wehner

John Kowalsky, *Board Secretary*
Dr. David P. Garrahan, *Superintendent*

Viewbook:
Bruce Emra and Jane
Garnes, *Editors*
Jane Garnes, *Photographer*

*For additional information
about Northern Highlands
Regional High School, see
School Profile and
Curriculum Guidelines. Call*
201-327-8700

23

298

High school ransacked by vandal

Vandal hits planetarium

FRO

Thursday, May 22, 1986   THE TOWN JOURNAL

Dr. Garrahan Says Thank You

(Continued from page 3)

Highlands picks up the pieces

Dr. Garrahan Thanks Those
Who Helped after Juvenile's Rampage

Mary Service

The morning after a juvenile wrecked the Northern Highlands planetarium and math and science classrooms, classes returned to schedule. Glaziers worked to replace corridor windows which had been smashed. Custodians put in extra hours to clear away glass shards, splintered wooden doors and hacked-off doorknobs. The most heavily damaged rooms were clear of debris and safe for students and teachers. Trophies, which had been thrown at the school before Dr. Garrahan himself;

- All the custodians, some who had just gone off the night shift, who put the building in safe condition;
- Blanche Hunt, secretary to Board Administrator John Kowalsky, who located custodial phone numers in the absence of Len Van Omen, buildings and grounds supervisor, who was in the hospital;
- Mr. Kowalsky, who returned from the first day of the Business Administra...

299

Referred to consultants' work as "legalized hit-and-run."

Jack Mintzer
NH principal

"The report calls for a redeployment of existing personnel."

Dr. David Garrahan
Supt. of NH

Despite gains in NH stature, staff and supt. divided

If it ain't broke, don't fix it:

NH staff angered by reorganiza

ALLENDALE — A standing-room only crowd jammed the Northern Highlands school library Feb. 13 and responded angrily to the summary of a management reorganization report.

Teachers and staff, the largest part of the audience, along with residents, criticized the recommendations, the rationale for doing such a study, and what they viewed as criticisms of a school that has earned state and national recognition.

Recommendations

Board president James Ryan, introducing Dr. Robert Savitt, president of Guidelines, Inc., Huntington, N.Y., whose company did the study, explained that the board wanted to examine supervisory and management functions, while maintaining the excellence of the school. At an earlier meeting, trustees called this study a response to criticisms made last spring that the district is top-heavy with administrators.

Dr. Savitt recommended hiring a director of educational services to coordinate curriculum; establish long and short range goals; and improve communications

---

Northern Highlands (Continued from page 8)

of the administrators and teachers that were so highly recognized nationally...Is this a 'vendetta' or a diversion to justify a $94,000 superintendent of schools for a one-school district..."

Dr. Garrahan confirmed that his son at an out-of-state college had received a letter suggesting that his father would not have a job next year. (Dr. Garrahan's position as superintendent is tenured.)

Asked to comment, teacher and union president Cathy Mahoney responded, "I hate to think someone in the school would be so stupid" as to do something like that.

Family

"We are a family," insisted Ms. Mahoney and teacher Ann Ahnemann several times, referring to the unity among teachers, many of whom have spent the largest part of their careers teaching at

Asked about the role of the superintendent, Ms. Mahoney and Mrs. Ahnemann said that while he is a "good administrator," he is not a "people person." According to Mrs. Ahnemann, "He doesn't feel the beat of the place."

Their comments are reflected in the results of the staff survey, in which the teachers who took part said they were very satisfied with their professional relationships and employee/principal relationships. They were most dissatisfied with board of education decisions, the superintendent's performance and policy changes. Several sources who would not be identified said the discontent may be related to removing three teachers from

the science department over the past few years.

Principal's position

Jack Mintzer, Highlands principal since 1966, sees no reason to change a system that has operated so well. His opinion of consultants is not high — he referred to their work as "legalized hit and run." "All curriculum changes are a joint effort among teachers, supervisors and administrators," he told The Town Journal. "Teachers are always encouraged to review curriculum. The strength of the school is in the teachers...That's all you need for a good school — good teachers and good kids."

"In department offices," he continued.

Teachers rebut financial summary

300

Referred to consultants' work as "legalized hit-and-run."

Jack Mintzer
NH principal

"*The report calls for a redeployment of existing personnel.*"

Dr. David Garrahan
Supt. of NH

Despite gains in NH stature, staff and supt. divided

Faculty critical of Savitt report

Mary Service

NORTHERN HIGHLANDS — When the board of education commissioned a study of the administrative structure of the high school last fall, it undoubtedly did not expect Al Vinci, the recently retired vice principal, to declare, "You're going to tear down the school and ruin morale." But that was one of many negative comments when the Savitt report was discussed in the school library Feb. 13 at the board of education meeting.

That evening Dr. Robert Savitt, president of Guidelines, Inc., which prepared

(Continued on page 8)

Resignation causes controversy

By Stacey Mellides

Several people stood behind the podium at the January 13 board of education meeting to speak about the eight-period day issue. However, when Mr. Robert Manzo, music teacher, stepped up, letter of resignation effective at the end of the 1991-92 school year. "Mr. Manzo came to me, I didn't ask him He asked if the board would consider letting him teach one more year, I urged them to accept his request," commented Dr. Garrahan.

Mr. Manzo explains that he was Garrahan, the confusion resulted because "Mr. Manzo has a long history of miscommunicating."

At the December 1991 board of education meeting, Dr. Garrahan stated his intent to recommend that the board continue the instrumental program

According to Dr. Garrahan, any reinstatement of the instrumental/band teaching position is contingent upon class enrollment and the budget vote. It is not yet known if there will be any position, a part-time position or full time position, or

'I was forced to retire," Manzo claims

Resignation controversy ends in "no" vote

y Stacey Mellides

The controversy concerning music teacher Mr. Robert Manzo's position resulted in a 6-0 vote of refusal to accept his letter of resignation at the purported that even if the act is determined to be legal, the superintendent's actions were inhumane and not understandable.

Mr. John Biondi, representative of the New Jersey Education Association, through a letter read at the meeting, and and music." When the budget cuts were being decided, according to Dr. Garrahan, two people approached him— Mr. Ben Grant and Mr. Manzo.

Mr. Grant proposed an "artist in residence" in order to keep Ms. Karen Rossen instructing art at this school. Determined to institute this program—in could not accept this letter.

When Dr. Garrahan suggested at the meeting that Mr. Manzo had approached him with another "deal" involving a monetary "sweetener," Mr. Manzo blurted out that Dr. Garrahan was "out of order" and that he was "making it up as he [went] along".

Allendale

Highlands board will not rescind Manzo resignation

by Susanna White

The Northern Highlands Board of Education voted unanimously against rescinding the resignation of music teacher Robert Manzo. Manzo's resignation was submitted and approved by the board on May 28, 1991 and will become effective this June.

teachers want to know why the board condones such unethical behavior."

One resident commented that at the time of the budget cuts, "Manzo sought guidance to save the music program and his job. Events show that he resigned unwillingly. I and we want the board to reinstate him and right the wrong."

Garrahan added that, last May, Manzo came to him asking if the board would give him an additional year so he could qualify for pension benefits.

"I said I would take this request to the board and support it," the superintendent said. "The deal we shook on was that the board would hold the position for a year," Garrahan commented "I did not force him

Light is cast on resignation of principal

N. Highlands crowd riveted

By CHARLES SAYDAH
Staff Writer

ALLENDALE — During an emotional Northern Highlands Board of Education meeting Monday night, the silence surrounding the resignation of the school's popular principal started dissolving.

Former board President James Ryan of Allendale cast some of the strongest light on the resignation of Geoffrey Gordon, the 46-year-old principal whom students and parents had credited with restoring spirit in the 685-student school.

His brief statement riveted more than 50 people still left in the school library two hours after the discussion about Gordon's resignation began. Ryan hinted at some aspects of the affair that had never been considered.

"The board knows very well that they did not have to accept Dr. Gordon's resignation," Ryan said. "But the fact is that nine out of nine accepted it."

don's action, and on the board for acquiescing. The board said it would set up a committee to hire a search firm, which would select five candidates to be considered by the board.

Despite the light Ryan shed on the inner workings of the board, spectators who left the meeting a half-hour earlier had few concrete answers to explain why Gordon will leave on June 30.

As for Gordon's departure, board attorney Jamie Plosia said a gag order signed by both Gordon and the board prohibits any discussion. No school official or board member will say anything concerning Gordon's job performance. Gordon will not say whether it was a personality conflict with Garrahan that caused him to resign.

In addition, Garrahan and board members will say nothing derogatory or negative about Gordon; Gordon will say nothing derogatory or negative about Garrahan or the Northern Highlands Regional School District. In ex-

Code of silence in principal's ouster

By PAUL DAVIDSON

ALLENDALE — A former official of Northern Highlands Regional High School believes the school district's controversial recommendation not to retain the school's well-liked principal was not sparked by a glaring wrongdoing or personality clash.

The official, who requested anonymity, said there is an erroneous public perception that Principal Geoffrey Gordon may have committed a malfeasance or locked horns with Schools Superintendent David Garrahan.

Rather, the source thinks the decision was based on an evaluation of Geoffrey Gordon's "behind-the-scenes" administrative performance at the school, which serves 685 students from Allendale and Upper Saddle River. The source would not elaborate.

Citing an agreement binding all parties to vows of silence, Gordon, Garrahan and board of education members have refused to discuss the reasons for the resignation, fueling public speculation and rumors.

Since taking the job last July, the 46-year-old Gordon has been praised by parents for his dealings with students and for restoring school spirit after a long teacher contract dispute.

"What they don't see is what goes on behind the scenes," the former school official said.

(See PRINCIPAL, page 4)

"So take your anger out on me," he said, referring to the strong support expressed for Gordon by parents and students. Much of it came as virulent denunciations of Garrahan, who was portrayed as the villain in a melodrama fabricated by rumor and inference as well as hard facts.

That task involved designing the process to find Gordon's successor, the item that started the audience of 110 on its dual attack — on Garrahan for forcing Gor-

Garrahan had tried to end the public discussion at about 11 p.m. "This is precisely what Dr. Gordon and I did not want to happen tonight," he said, characterizing some of the remarks made about him as offensive and libelous.

But Ryan had the last word.

"Dr. Garrahan has served the board well, and in my opinion the board has served the people well," he said, his voice shaky. "All the board members are like the people you know."

By CHARLES SAYDAH
Staff Writer

ALLENDALE — On the morning after their popular principal resigned, more than 200 students at Northern Highlands Regional High School spent their first period in the cafeteria protesting the series of events that lead to Jeffrey Gordon's sudden decision to leave.

"At first, the Student Council president [Brian Knispel] stepped in and said there was nothing they could do about it," said Michael Dombeck, next year's Student Council president. "Then the vice principal, Mr. [Vincent] Herold, came in and said if you 'sit-in' today, you're going to have to make up the day at the end of the year. It started fizzling after that."

But Tuesday's show of support for Gordon, whose contract was up for renewal on Monday, brought students no closer to understanding the reasons for his stunning announcement.

"People are waiting to hear from Dr. Gordon," Dombeck said. That statement hasn't come, although it had been expected on Wednesday and Thursday. After Monday night's school board meeting, Gordon said he would not discuss his decision.

David Garrahan, superintendent of the 685-student district that serves Allendale and Upper Saddle River, said terms of Gordon's resignation constrained him from discussing the matter. He said he could not speak to the rumors circulating among students and parents, many of whom signed petitions urging the board to renew Gordon's contract.

Parents speculate the dispute centers on personal and professional tensions between Gordon and the superintendent, who hired him last year. Parents discounted allegations of improper behavior,

Principal's departure shocks Highlands

by Hollis K. Osher

In an unexpected turn of events, Dr. Geoffrey Gordon, principal of Northern Highlands Regional High School, resigned from his position last week. His decision was apparently a surprise to the approximately 60 people who attended the meeting, expecting to see Dr. Gordon's contract renewed for the coming year.

Exercising his legal right to confidentiality, Dr. Gordon refused to give much comment about his unexpected decision. However, while Dr. Gordon chose to not voice any specific reasons for his resignation, he indicated that his decision was not made lightly, and that his reasons were of a nature personal to himself and his family.

Though he only held his position for less than one year, Dr. Gordon will be missed by the parents and students of Northern Highlands, observers said. He will most likely finish out the school year, and remain in his post through June. This will give him a chance to finish up any last minute business he might have, and give students and parents an opportunity to say good-bye.

At present, the Northern Highlands Board of Education has not made definite public plans regarding who will fill the principal's position. Though there are some contenders, it may be some time before anyone is chosen as a permanent replacement, officials said.

The next board of education meeting is scheduled for Monday, May 24, at 8 p.m.

Presented to

DR. DAVID P. GARRAHAN

SUPERINTENDENT
NORTHERN HIGHLANDS
REGIONAL HIGH SCHOOL

In Recognition Of Your
Significant Contribution
To The Borough Of Allendale

**ALLENDALE
POLICE DEPARTMENT**

Chief Robert L. Herndon
-- MAY 4, 1995 --

Northern Highlands Regional High School District
Special Board of Education Resolution
May 22, 1995

WHEREAS,   DR. DAVID CARRAHAN is retiring from his position as District Superintendent of the Northern Highlands Regional High School District, and

WHEREAS,   He served with distinction as Director of Pupil Personnel Services and District Superintendent since 1984, and

WHEREAS,   Dr. Carrahan executed the duties and responsibilities of his leadership position in a consistently forthright and courageous manner, and

WHEREAS,   His exceptional organizational skills, high energy level, and task orientation resulted in the school's national recognition as an Exemplary High School, and

WHEREAS,   Dr. Carrahan's Herculean efforts to eradicate and prevent substance abuse by students led to the District's national recognition as a Drug-Free School, and

WHEREAS,   As a result of these efforts and initiatives he was twice honored at White House ceremonies, and

WHEREAS,   His scholarly publications brought state and national renown to the Northern Highlands District, now therefore, be it

RESOLVED   That the Northern Highlands Board of Education express its deep appreciation to him for his many years of dedicated and devoted service to the school-community, and be it further

RESOLVED   That the Board of Education express its best wishes to him for a retirement which is relaxing, satisfying, healthy, and happy

State of New Jersey
DEPARTMENT OF EDUCATION
BERGEN COUNTY OFFICE OF EDUCATION
327 E. RIDGEWOOD AVENUE
PARAMUS, NEW JERSEY 07652
(201) 599-6256
(201) 599-6255 FAX

M. RAY KELLY
COUNTY SUPERINTENDENT

JOHN ELLIS
COMMISSIONER

R E S O L U T I O N

WHEREAS, Dr. David P. Garrahan has had a distinguished career in education; and

WHEREAS, he has consistently exemplified the characteristics of an outstanding educational leader; and

WHEREAS, his leadership has extended throughout the Northern Highlands Regional High School District by serving as Superintendent of Schools; and

WHEREAS, Dr. David P. Garrahan has demonstrated superior professional skills, and a strong commitment to the well-being of students, teachers, staff members, colleagues, and parents:

N O W ,   T H E R E F O R E

BE IT HEREBY RESOLVED, that Dr. David P. Garrahan be recognized as a "Distinguished Educator" by the Bergen County Superintendent of Schools on this date, June 28, 1991.

BERGEN COUNTY SUPERINTENDENT OF SCHOOLS

Future Farmers of America

The National Organization of Boys

Studying Vocational Agriculture, Founded 1928

This certifies that _David Harrahan_ of

Bangor was awarded the

Degree of Honorary Chapter Farmer

of the _Belvedere_ Chapter Future Farmers of

America and is entitled to this testimonial.

Given this _Fourteenth_ day of _December_ 19 _61_.

John W. Wyckoff
Chapter President

Harry Schneider
Chapter Advisor

308

The University of the State of New York

Education **[seal]** Department

Private School Teacher's License

Be it known that .... DAVID P. GARRAHAN ....,

having satisfied the minimum requirements prescribed by the State Education Department, is hereby granted
this license which is valid for service as a teacher of...MEDICAL ASSISTANT (APPLIED PSYCHOLOGY, ENGLISH AND
BUSINESS COMMUNICATIONS)..........................

at .... EASTERN TECHNICAL SCHOOL ....

In witness whereof, the State Education Department grants this
license number ....3901.......... at Albany, New York,
this ...22nd... day of ......September...... 1981...

Gerald L. Freedman
Assistant Commissioner for Occupational and Continuing Education

Gordon M. Ambach
Commissioner of Education

309

GARRAHAN'S PUBLISHED ARTICLES

REPORT
OF THE STUDY OF
COLLEGIATE
COMPENSATORY
PROGRAMS FOR
DISADVANTAGED
YOUTH

AN ANALYSIS OF THE RELATIONSHIP BETWEEN FEELINGS OF POWERLESSNESS AND THE
SUCCESS OF SOCIALLY DISADVANTAGED STUDENTS IN HIGHER EDUCATION

GARRAHAN
1972

THE RIVER REPORTER

online

VOLUME XXXII No. 28   Narrowsburg, NY   July 13 - July 19, 2006

Sections

...
...
Opinion
...
Arts & Leisure
Outdoors
Sports
Obituaries
...
...
Classifieds

Directories
...
...
...

TRR
...
...
Archives
Advertise
Photo Reprints
...
Back Issues
Contact Us

Submission
...
...
Classifieds

Amphibian
Amphibian
...

editorialcomment

The meaning of community

My home on Delaware Drive was among the many flooded out on the flats. I applaud Tusten's rapid response in providing several large dumpsters, where we could quickly discard our damaged furniture and appliances. Carol Wingert came by twice in a dump truck and took all of our wooden debris.

By 5:00 p.m. on Saturday, my son, his girlfriend and I concluded that it was imperative to remove all of our carpeting next. My son said if we just concentrate on the carpeting we could get it out before dark. We decided to call a man named Falk who had helped Mark earlier in carrying out a sofabed. Reluctantly, I phoned him. A Mrs. Falk answered and told me that all of the Falks were helping out at Tom's house, "you know, the Narrowsburg Inn owner." Much more reluctantly, I tiptoed onto Tom's backyard, and privately asked him if I might be able to hire one of his workers. Tom turned to his group, and shouted out my request. I saw two heads nod affirmatively; another hand went up, and yet another guy said, "hell, let's all go down and just do it".

I had barely gotten back when the pickups arrived. My son was on the muddy floor asking me for big scissors, as his razor blade gadget wasn't cutting it. I believe these men saw a much uglier scene than they had imagined. They quickly eyeballed it and agreed on an attack plan. Using their own utility knives, and later picks and crowbars, they began deconstructing the flood-damaged carpeting, walls, molding, etc. In one room, Tenbus had fastened two-by-fours into the concrete floor, placed insulation between the floor studs, then covered the entire floor with plywood and put carpeting on top. The guys decided they had to do it right, i.e. rip up everything and carry all into their trucks. They did everything that Dave Sparling directed me to have done and more, going well above the high-water line when they judged it necessary.

My guess is that this took more than two hours—my mini-family team would not have finished before dark (what dreamers we were.)

I did a quick ATM run, only to learn that none of the men would accept payment. I think their names were Barry, Dennis, Gary, Eric and son, and at least one more guy who hopped into his now un-white pickup and rode away—I think he may have been the Lone Ranger!

There were numerous other community members who came by with coffee, donuts, garbage bags... and lots of advice. Thanks to all. This is a " community" in the finest sense of the term. Thanks.

Dave Garrahan

Narrowsburg, NY

RESUME

David P. Garrahan
160 West End Ave. #140
New York, N.Y.
10023

East Stroudsburg State College	1961	B.S. (Mathematics, Science)
Lehigh University	1963	M.Ed.(Guidance,Counseling)
Columbia University	1972	Ed.D. (Applied Human Devlpmt.)
Rutgers - The State University	1963	Guidance & Counseling Institute
Cornell University, New York Univ., Univ. of Scranton	1961-67	Additional Graduate Study
Institute for Advanced Study of Rational Psychotherapy	1974	Certificate (Clinical Supervision by Albert Ellis)
Transactional Analysis	1984	Certificate
School Executive Academy	1985	Program Certificate
Harvard University	1990	Current Issues in School Law Institute
NJ Assn. of School Administrators	1994	Diplomate in Educational Administration

PROFESSIONAL EXPERIENCE

1985-1995	Northern Highlands Regional High School District	District Superintendent
1984-1985	Northern Highlands Regional High School District	Director of Pupil Personnel Services
1982-1984	Teaneck High School (NJ)	Director of Guidance
1978-1982	Pascack Valley H.S. (NJ)	Guidance Counselor

1977-1978	Frostburg State College (MD)	Associate Professor of Psychology and Director of Graduate Programs in Counseling, Psychology, and Guidance
1975-1977	Teachers College Columbia University	Assistant Professor of Education and Coordinator of Masters and Doctoral Guidance Programs and Clinical Associate Psychological Consultation Ctr.
1974-1975	Teachers College Columbia University	Deputy Chairman - Dept. of Human Development (Gerontology, Guidance, and Leisure Education)
1972-1974	Teachers College Columbia University	Assistant Professor of Education and Coordinator of Elementary and Secondary Guidance Programs
1969-1972	Teachers College Columbia University	Instructor and Research Associate
1963-1969	Washingtonville High School (NY)	Guidance Counselor
1961-1963	Belvidere High School (NJ)	Teacher (Mathematics and Science)

PROFESSIONAL CONSULTING

Bridgewater-Raritan Regional School District (NJ)	1988	In-service: Back to the Future - A View from the Top
Watchung Hills Regional High School (NJ)	1986	Responding to Community Expectations
Bloomfield Public Schools (NJ)	1985	Needs Assessment Program Evaluation

3.

Airco Corporation - Computer Learning Center Division	1984	Staff Development and Training
New York City Board of Education	1980-82	Grant Proposal Writer
New York City Board of Education	1979	Operation FAR CRY: Training Consultant
New York City Board of Education	1979	Administrator of School Security Officer Program
Vaslock Corporation (NYC)	1978-82	Management Consultant: Market Research; Personnel Training; Publications
Eastern Technical School, Inc. (NYC)	1978-82	Consulting Director of Educational Services
New York City Board of Education	1978	Staff Development - Auxiliary Services for High School
New York City Board of Education	1978	Consultant to the President of the Board of Education
Eastern School for Physicians Aides, Inc. (NYC)	1977-78	Liaison to State Education Services Department and Accrediting Agencies
Institute of Gerontology College of Misericordia (PA)	1977	Nursing Home Administrator - Training Workshops
Ridgefield Park High School (NJ)	1977	School-Community Needs Assessment
Metuchen High School (NJ)	1977	Elementary Guidance: Behavior Modification Techniques for Teachers
Delehanty Institute, Inc. (NYC)	1976-78	Grant Proposal Writer and Federal Projects Coordinator
Watchung Hills Regional High School (NJ)	1976	Series of In-service Staff Development Seminars

4.

Hastings-on-Hudson School District (NY)	1976	Pupil Personnel Services (K-12) Five-Year Reorganization Plan
Institute for Human Development, Resource Development Associates, Inc. (NJ)	1975-76	Fund-raising; Grants; Seminars
Greenburgh Central School (NY)	1975	Evaluation of Professional Personnel
Teaneck School District (NJ)	1974	Evaluation of District Guidance Services
Great Neck Public Schools (NY)	1974	Reorganizing Guidance Services
New York City Bd. of Ed.	1971-74	Member - Board of Examiners
Norwalk Public Schools (CT)	1973	Third Party Evaluation - U.S.O.E. Career Education
Leonia High School (NJ)	1973	Guidance Program: Evaluation
Hackensack High School (NJ)	1972	Career Education: In-service Training
New York State Education Department	1972	Guidance Study Kit: Research and Development
Glen Rock High School (NJ)	1971	Reconceptualizing Guidance: In-service Workshop

PUBLICATIONS AND RESEARCH REPORTS

Garrahan, D. The Application of a Systems Approach to Substance Use Prevention: Linking Interventions to the Infrastructure. Journal of Alcohol and Drug Education, Vol. 40, No. 3, pp. 74-83, Spring 1995.

Garrahan, D. and Plosia, J. Time's Up for Teacher Tenure. New Jersey Reporter, Vol. 25, No. 1, pp. 8-9, May/June 1995.

Garrahan, D. and Plosia, J. Time's Up for Tenure: A Plan for a Better System (reprint). The Press (Atlantic City) , p. A-11, June 28, 1995.

David Garrahan, Transition America (Bloomington, Indiana: Xlibris Publishing Co., 2016) 178.

David Garrahan, From Brooklyn to Kingsport (Bloomington, Indiana: Xlibris Publishing Co., 2018) 328.

Garrahan, D. A Bold New Reform for the Year 2000. The Record, Vol. 101, No. 14, p. 10, June 20, 1995.

Garrahan, D. Healing a "Sick" System: Disjointed Education Reform Efforts Need the Salve of Unity to Succeed. School Leader, Vol. 24, No. 5, pp. 32-34, 50, March/April 1995.

Garrahan, D. Spotlighting: Northern Highlands Regional High School. The Northwest News, Vol. 3, No. 11, p. 11, November 1994.

Garrahan, D. Military Tradition: African-Americans in Military Service. Barr's News, Vol. 20, pp. 1 and 68, October 3, 1994.

Garrahan, D. Education's Most Sacred Cow. School Leader, Vol. 24, No. 1, pp. 27-29, 42-43, July/August 1994.

Garrahan, D. Buttonhooks in America: A Reflection of Social Class (Reprint). The American Collector, Vol. 24, No. 1, pp. 10-11, March 1994.

Garrahan, D. Cancelled Cards Document Racism in American Social History. Postcard Collector, Vol. 11, No. 8, pp. 51-53, August 1993.

Garrahan, D. School Board Reform: The Case for Redefining the Role of Lay Governance in Public Education. Perspective, Vol. 10, No. 1, pp. 4-10, Spring 1993.

Garrahan, D. Regionalization - Sensible Strategy or Quick Fix? Point-Counterpoint article. School Leader, Vol. 21, No. 5, pp. 38-39 and 46-47, March/April, 1992.

Garrahan, D. Regionalization and the Organizational Transformation of Education. Perspective, Vol. 8, No. 4, pp. 27-31, Winter, 1992.

Garrahan, D. School Regionalization Makes Sense. Commentary, New Jersey Reporter, Vol. 21, No. 3, pp. 39 and 45, September/October, 1991.

Garrahan, D. Superintendent Opposed to Tenure. The Town Journal, Vol. 18, No. 3, p. 3, May 16, 1991.

Garrahan, D. Monitoring and School Deregulation. School Leader, Vol. 19, No. 6, pp. 26-29, 43, May/June, 1990.

Garrahan, D. Implementing a School Security Program. Perspective, Vol. VI, No. 1, pp. 13-14, Spring 1989.

6.

Garrahan, D. and Simeonidis, M. Partners in Education: Tots, Teens, and Parents. School Leader, Vol. 17, No. 7, pp. 36-48, September/October 1988.

Garrahan, D. Buttonhooks in America: A Reflection of Social Class. The Antique Trader, pp. 102-103, October 1986.

Garrahan, D. Gerontological Counseling: A Developmental Life Stage Approach. N. J. Journal of Professional Counseling, Vol. 49, No. 1, pp. 4-6, Spring, 1986.

Garrahan, D. Administering a Needs Assessment Evaluation of Student Services. Perspective, Vol. 3, No. 4, pp. 12-13, 35-36, Fall/Winter, 1985.

Garrahan, D. Guidance Evaluation. Bloomfield, NJ, Public Schools, 115 pages, June, 1985.

Garrahan, D. College Admissions Experience Profile: Development and Implementation (Cassette tape). Instant Replay Services, Inc., Arlington, VA, October, 1984.

Garrahan, D. Cargo Security: Moving Out of the Dark Ages. Enroute, Vol.12, No. 5, pp. 18-19, May 30, 1982.

Garrahan, D. Vaslock Training Manual. Vollmer Auto Security Corporation, New York, 57 pages, May, 1981.

Garrahan, D. Guidance and Counseling Internship Guide. Frostburg State College, Maryland, 27 pages, 1978.

Garrahan, D. and Stewart, K. Counseling Psychology Internship Guide. Frostburg State College, Maryland, 12 pages, 1977.

Garrahan, D. Employment, Economic Conditions, and Adaptability. Delehanty Digest, Vol. 1, No. 4, November, 1977.

Garrahan, D. Evaluative Self-Study. Teaneck, NJ, 36 pages, June, 1974.

Garrahan, D. The Relationship Between Social Activism and Feelings of Powerlessness Among Low Socioeconomic College Students. Journal of College Student Personnel, Vol. 15, No. 2, pp. 120-124, March, 1974.

Garrahan, D. Guidance Services Study. Leonia, NJ, 61 pages, July, 1973.

7.

Morris, C. and Garrahan, D. Guidance Study Kit. Bureau of Guidance (N.Y.S. Education Department) and Institute of Field Studies (Teachers College, Columbia University), 1972.

Garrahan, D. An Analysis of the Relationship Between Feelings of Powerlessness and the Success of Socially Disadvantaged Students in Higher Education. Copyrighted Doctoral Dissertation, Teachers College, Columbia University, 1972.

Gordon, E., Garrahan, D., Bynum, E., and Lewis, A. Report on the Study of Collegiate Compensatory Programs for Disadvantaged Youth. Ford Foundation and the College Entrance Examination Board, 575 pages, 1972.

Garrahan, D. Friends of the East Harlem Block Schools. Concern, Vol. 10, No. 5, pp. 4-5, February, 1971.

Garrahan, D. In Support of Recruiting NEGROES. The Pocono Record (Stroudsburg, PA) Editorial Page, April, 1970.

Garrahan, D. Empathy and the Counseling Process: Historical Overview. Journal of the New York School Counselor Association, Vol. 2, No. 1, pp. 4-7, Spring, 1968.

Garrahan, D. How to Help the Forgotten Students in the School. N. J. Association of High School Councils, Yearbook, pp. 94-96, June, 1962.

PROFESSIONAL PRESENTATIONS

1995 National Conference of Christians and Jews (Youth Conference, Ramapo College of NJ, May 15, 1995) Plenary Session Moderator.

1991 National Conference of Christians and Jews (Spring Conference, Ramapo College of NJ, May 17, 1991) Program Coordinator and Workshop Leader (Control Orientation).

1986 N. J. Professional Counselors Association (Annual Spring Conference, Princeton, NJ, May 1, 1986) Invitational Address - "Pursuing Excellence: An Administrative Perspective."

1984 National Association of College Admissions Counselors (40th National Conference, Boston, MA, October, 1984) Presenter: "College Admissions Experience Profile: Development and Implementation." Conference Program #145, p. 26.

1983 Teaneck Board of Education (In-service Workshop - 15 sessions)
Workshop Leader: "Human Relations in Education - Teachers as
Helpers," October 1983 - January 1984.

1981 Economic Development Council of N.Y.C. Participating Speaker Award,
June 11, 1981.

1980 Eastern School for Physicians' Aides. Commencement Address, September
27, 1980.

1978 Institute of Gerontology (College of Misericordia, PA, Feb. 16-17, 1978)
Seminar Leader: "Psychological Intervention with the Aged."

1978 American Personnel and Guidance Association (National Convention:
Washington, D.C., March 1978). Presenter:
"Sex Equality in Educational and Vocational Guidance," Convention
Program #494, p. 70; Abstracts p. 198.

1978 American Personnel and Guidance Association (National Convention:
Washington, D. C., March, 1978) Presenter: "Designing Socially and
Psychologically Supportive Environments for the Aged," Convention
Program #166, p. 44; Abstracts p. 50.

1977 Denmark's International Educational Forum (Teachers College,
Columbia University, June 29, 1977). Speech: "Counseling in
American Schools."

1977 Title IX Conference (Lake George Central School District and
BOCES Regional Planning Center, April 13, 1977). Title IX Consulting
Speaker: "Equity in Educational Guidance and Career Development."

1977 Title IX Conference (New York State Central Western Region,
Rochester, NY, March 9, 1977). Title IX Consulting Speaker:
"Affirmative Action Compliance: Sex-Role Stereotyping in Schools."

1977 Institute of Gerontology (College of Misericordia, PA, Feb. 8-9,
1977) Workshop Leader: "Counseling the Aged" and "Designing
Ecologically Supportive Environments for the Aged."

1975 Association of Counselor Education and Supervision (National
Convention: New York, NY, March, 1975) National Program
Chairman.

9.

1975 <u>Old Forge High School</u> (PA). Commencement Address, June 16, 1975.

1974 <u>Educational Testing Service</u> (Urban Education Conference:
        Princeton, NJ, June, 1975) Speech: "Locus of Control - Guidelines
        for Future Research."

1973 <u>Florida Personnel and Guidance Association</u> (State Convention:
        Miami, FL, November, 1973) Invitational Address: "Evaluating
        Guidance Services: Consumer Perceptions - Needs Assessment
        Approach," Convention Program #062, p. 19.

1973 <u>Glen Rock Educational Symposium</u> (Glen Rock, NJ, January, 1973)
        Speaker: "Evaluation - Making Public Schools More Responsive to the
        Changing Needs of Youth."

1972 <u>College Entrance Examination Board</u> (Regional Conference: New
        York, NY, February, 1972) Presenter: "Report on the Status of
        Minority Programs in Higher Education."

1970 <u>College Entrance Examination Board</u> (National Emergency
        Conference: Yellow Springs, OH, September, 1970) Presenter:
        "Higher Education for Poor and Minority Youth - the State of Affairs."

1965 <u>New York Congress of Parents and Teachers</u> (State Convention:
        Ithaca, NY, April, 1965) Workshop Leader: "P.T.A. - An Action
        Image."

1962 <u>World Order Day</u> (Belvidere Methodist Church, NJ) "The Importance
        of World Law."

1961 <u>New Jersey Association of High School Councils</u> (State
        Convention: New Brunswick, NJ, November 15, 1961) Seminar
        Speaker: "How the Student Council Can Help the Forgotten Students
        in the School."

SPONSORED RESEARCH

As a member of the graduate faculty of Teachers College, Columbia
University, between 1972 and 1978, I sponsored fourteen successful
doctoral dissertations; co-sponsored an additional twenty doctoral dissertations;
and served as an oral examiner for numerous dissertations prepared by doctoral

candidates in school administration, curriculum and supervision, and psychology. Following are several of the doctoral dissertations which I sponsored to successful completion:

1978 An Exploratory Study of the Nature of the Academic High Risk Students' Perceived Frequency of Selected Study Skills.

1977 The Development of an Inventory of Career Concerns for Non-College Bound Students and an Analysis of These Concerns as Perceived by Students, School Career Counselors, and Business People in the Community.

1977 An Assessment of the Need for Pupil Personnel Services as Part of the Secondary School System of Liberia.

1977 An Examination of the Relationship Between Locus of Control, Socioeconomic Choice, Individual Performance and Group Effectiveness in Human Relations Training.

1977 Secondary School Education and Employment in Nigeria: Implications for Career Guidance.

1977 College Selection and Its Relationship to College Satisfaction.

1977 An Analysis of Occupational Preferences of Secondary School Students in Guyana with Particular Reference to the Manpower Needs of the Country.

1976 Originality Training: A Method for Locus of Control Change.

1975 Auxiliary Services for High School: A Model for Change.

1975 An Investigation of Play Group Counseling.

HONORS AND RECOGNITION (post 1985)

1994 Northern Highlands honored at the White House reception as a Drug-Free School.

1991   Acknowledged as a contributor to The Report of the Quality Education Commission entitled, <u>All our Children: A Vision for N.J. Schools in the 21st Century</u>, 1991. p. 51 Appendix of Contributors.

1991   Distinguished Educator Award: State Education Department. June 28, 1991.

1991   N.J. Council of Education: Inducted March 8, 1991.

1986-91   Northern Highlands Regional High School District cited in over a dozen regional, State, and national publications.

1989   Northern Highlands' Child Development Program included in National Resource Guide to School-based Family Support and Education Programs by Harvard University.

1989-90   D. Garrahan included in <u>Who's Who in American Education.</u>

1989   Northern Highlands' School Security Program featured in <u>Perspective</u> - N.J.A.S.A.

1987-88   D. Garrahan included in <u>Who's Who in Educational Administration.</u>

1988   Northern Highlands' Nursery School-Child Development Program featured in <u>School Leader</u> - N.J.S.B.A.

1988   Northern Highlands ranked among the Ten Best Public High Schools in <u>New Jersey Monthly.</u>

1988   Northern Highlands honored at White House Reception as an Outstanding Secondary School.

1987   Northern Highlands recognized by the U.S. Department of Education as one of 123 exemplary public high schools in the United States.

1986   Northern Highlands' Basic Skills Program included in a Compendium of Model Programs by the N.J. Department of Education.

CPSIA information can be obtained
at www.ICGtesting.com
Printed in the USA
LVHW031101221218
601107LV00001B/2/P